THE SACRAMENT OF EASTER

THE
SACRAMENT
OF
EASTER

Revised Edition

Jeremy Haselock

and

Roger Greenacre

GRACEWING

First published in England in 1989
by
Gracewing
2 Southern Avenue
Leominster
Herefordshire HR6 0QF
United Kingdom
www.gracewing.co.uk

Second Revised Edition 1991
New Edition with Wm B Eerdmans Publishing Co. 1995
Fourth Edition, further revised and updated, 2024

ISBN 978 085244 674 4

Typeset by Word and Page, Chester, UK

Cover design by Bernardita Peña Hurtado

Front cover image: The Anastasis. Fresco, 1315–21, apse of the
Parekklesion, Mone Chora, Constantinople. Photo: Till Niermann.

Back cover image: Image of a deacon reading the Exsultet roll
in church, with the top of the roll draped over the ambo,
beside the Paschal candle: Monte Cassino Exultet Roll,
British Library Add. MS 30337, membrane 11.

CONTENTS

INTRODUCTION & ACKNOWLEDGEMENTS

The Sacrament of Easter by Roger Greenacre was first published in 1965 by the Faith Press as no. IV in the series Studies in Christian Worship. This study of the liturgy of Lent, Holy Week and Eastertide grew out of a series of Lent addresses given by Fr Greenacre in 1963 at the church of the Annunciation, Marble Arch, and at St Mary's, Bourne Street, in London. Behind these talks lay Roger's considerable knowledge of continental liturgical scholarship and pastoral practice as well as his familiarity with Anglican liturgy and worship. The addresses were worked up into book form at the insistence of Dr Eric Mascall, OGS, who was Professor of Historical Theology at King's College, London, at the time, with the encouragement of Dr Ronald Jasper, Chairman of the Church of England Liturgical Commission and Publishing Director of the Faith Press.

That first version of the book was warmly welcomed and when it went out of print there were many requests for a new edition. It soon became clear that any such edition would need to be a very substantial revision because of the liturgical changes in both the Roman Catholic and Anglican Churches since 1965 and the huge growth in the body of scholarly literature generated in part by those changes.

In 1986, the Church of England published *Lent, Holy Week, Easter. Services and Prayers*, the first of two major collections of commended liturgical material designed to supplement the somewhat meagre seasonal provision in the *Alternative Service Book 1980*. This volume brought into more regular and general use services which had long been valued by parishes where worship and teaching were in the Catholic tradition of the Church of England. With the spirit of liturgical co-operation which was a mark of ecumenical relations at the time, the shape of these rites — if not all the texts — owes much to the reformed Holy Week liturgies of the Roman Catholic Church and to the work of the Joint Liturgical Group. These new circumstances prompted the by now Canon Roger Greenacre to take up his pen once again and begin a thorough revision of his original work.

It was at this point that I became involved in the project, initially merely as one less easily defeated by modern word-processing technology than Roger, but soon, at his generous suggestion, as a full co-author. My view was that we should broaden the scope of the work to include rather fuller reference to the Holy Week rites of the Roman Catholic Church as promulgated in the new *Roman Missal* of 1969. This would mean our study could be of interest and usefulness to English-speaking Roman Catholics.

With the help and advice of a large number of people, the new version of the book was finished in 1988 and published the following year by Fowler Wright Books in their Gracewing imprint. It was followed by a second, slightly revised, edition in 1991 and then published again in 1995 in a co-edition by Gracewing and Eerdmans Publishing Company in the United States.

Since then a great deal more has happened in the world of liturgy and worship: the Methodist Church in Britain published its new *Worship Book* in 1999, making available much new seasonal material, including services for Holy Week and Easter; the Church of England began publishing its comprehensive *Common Worship* series of volumes beginning on 2000 and including, in 2006, the *Times and Seasons* volume which contained a much expanded and revised version of the Lent, Holy Week and Easter provision of ten years earlier; and most recently the Roman Catholic Church, sadly abandoning the spirit of ecumenical co-operation which had previously shaped the English-language version of the *Roman Missal*, and the common texts in the Church of England's *Common Worship* series, produced in 2010 a new translation which claims to reflect more precisely the Latin text of the amended third *editio typica* of 2008. Of more positive ecumenical significance was the erection in 2011 of the Personal Ordinariate of Our Lady of Walsingham in England in accordance with the apostolic constitution *Anglicanorum coetibus* of Pope Benedict XVI, followed in 2012 by similar organisations in the United States and Australia. This provision included permission for the preparation of liturgical books that draw upon the liturgical and spiritual patrimony of Anglicanism. Accordingly, in 2015 *Divine Worship: The Missal*, for these Ordinariates, was published with material for the celebration of Lent and the Paschal mystery in what the Church of England would describe as traditional language and including prayers familiar from *The Book of Common Prayer* of 1662 and 1928. This was followed in 2021 by *Divine Worship: Daily Office*, even more closely dependent upon *The Book of Common Prayer*.

A further significant change in what might be styled liturgical ethos has become evident since 2007, when, in a *motu proprio, Summorum pontificium,* Benedict XVI authorised the more widespread use of the 1962 edition of the Tridentine Missal, described in the *motu proprio* as an 'extraordinary form' of the Roman rite, alongside the 'ordinary form' represented by Paul VI's rite of 1969. Like many of his generation, Roger Greenacre was not an enthusiast for the Tridentine rite and its Anglican counterpart, the English Missal. In his own ministry he set his face firmly against using it and his own liturgical style was unmistakably that which he found in France in the 1970s, when he was chaplain to the congregation at St George's, Paris. Accordingly, there is very little reference to the pre-conciliar Holy Week rites in the early editions of *The Sacrament of Easter,* a lacuna which certainly needs remedying, given the enthusiasm with which a younger generation of clergy, both Anglican and Roman, have welcomed the apparently permissive reintroduction of these rites and ceremonies. How far this revival of the pre-Conciliar rites will prove to be a flash in the liturgical pan after the douche of cold water administered in the heavy-handed papal *motu proprio, Traditionis custodes,* of July 2021 remains to be seen, but some discussion of these beautiful—if sometimes obscure—services has been added to this book.

Well before *Summorum pontificium* and *Anglicanorum coetibus* it had become clear that if *The Sacrament of Easter* was to retain any degree of usefulness to contemporary Anglican and Roman Catholic readers—not to mention extending its interest to Methodists—it would require a further revision. A considerable amount of new material, both scholarly and devotional, has appeared since 1995 and cannot be ignored. There have also been new studies of the Liturgical Movement and the work of the liturgists who reinvented the Roman Holy Week rites after the Council. Roger and I discussed this project many times before and after his retirement in 2000, and while we compiled several files of articles and references to useful new material we never embarked upon the work with any seriousness of purpose.

Roger died, alas, in 2011, and so the revision has had to be my work alone. I could not have brought this to a satisfactory conclusion without the advice and helpful criticism of many of our mutual friends, several of whom assisted with the first revisions. One of the questions raised by these kind critics concerns how far a revision of this study should continue to reflect the liturgical theology and scholarship of the group of twentieth-century French liturgists whose work had particularly influenced and inspired Roger. I gave this question much serious consideration and concluded that this material remains useful and of interest. It is, as it were, a time capsule of theological reflection, looking back to the work of the pioneers of the Liturgical Movement and forward to the Holy Week reforms which inspired the radical reform of the Roman Missal and liturgical reform in the Anglican Communion. Where possible I have supplemented this cache of historic material with some of the recent research of more archaeologically minded scholars. In this respect I am particularly grateful to Professor Paul Bradshaw for his help and great encouragement and to Canon Christopher Irvine for also drawing my attention to new material. Fr Peter Anthony, Fr John Alexander, Fr Andrew Archie, Dr Charlotte Gauthier, Fr Nathan Humphrey, Fr William McKeachie, Dr Colin Podmore and Fr Steve Rice have all read or heard some chapters of the book at various stages of revision and made helpful suggestions for improvement. I am very grateful to Dr Clive Tolley for expert editorial assistance and many helpful suggestions for improving the text. Thanks to the generous sponsorship of Fr Charleston Wilson, rector, and the vestry and people of the church of the Redeemer, Sarasota, Florida, this edition is able to boast an index.

On the back cover of the 1965 edition, the publishers printed this brief description, which I still believe to be applicable to the present work:

> This book is neither a theological study of our Redemption nor a devotional commentary of the Cross and Resurrection, but rather an introduction to the liturgical celebration of Holy Week and Easter. It is written in the double conviction that the depth of meaning of the Paschal Mystery is seriously weakened if it is not given its full liturgical and sacramental expression, and that the Holy Week liturgy demands from all who participate in it a more profound awareness of its biblical background and of its central place in the Church's life.

London, 2024
Jeremy M. Haselock

PART ONE

THE SACRAMENT OF EASTER

The Pilgrimage of Lent

'The rhythm of the Christian year,' writes Rowan Williams, 'is not just a matter of ecclesiastical convenience but a map of the soul's seasons.'[1] The season of Lent, perhaps more than any of the others, is a well-mapped journey with a definite destination. 'Above all,' writes Alexander Schmemann, 'Lent is a spiritual journey and its destination is Easter, the Feast of Feasts.'[2] Unfortunately, many English-speaking Christians undertake to follow Lent without realising it is a journey, a pilgrimage, let alone that it has a clear destination.

> Forty days and forty nights
> Thou wast fasting in the wild;
> Forty days and forty nights
> Tempted and yet undefiled.[3]

This Victorian poem by George Hunt Smyttan is among the most popular and widely used Lent hymns, certainly among Anglicans, who, for better or for worse, unconsciously learn much of their theology from the hymns they sing. The first verse of this hymn, embroidered in large letters, was even used to adorn a set of Lenten Array eucharistic vestments for use in an English cathedral. The regular singing of this hymn has probably reinforced the widespread but inaccurate notion that whatever its origins might have been, Lent is observed by Christians today primarily as a conscious

[1] Rowan Williams, foreword to Alan Luff, ed., *Strengthen for Service: 100 Years of the English Hymnal, 1906–2006* (Canterbury Press, Norwich 2005), p. viii.

[2] Alexander Schmemann, *Great Lent* (St Vladimir's Seminary Press, New York 1974), p. 11. Schmemann was an influential Russian Orthodox theologian and liturgist who, at his death in 1983, was Dean of St Vladimir's Orthodox Theological Seminary in Yonkers, New York.

[3] *New English Hymnal*, no. 67, words by G. H. Smyttan in 1856 and used by F. Pott in 1861 in his *Hymns fitted to the Order of Common Prayer*.

imitation of our Lord's forty days in the wilderness before the beginning of his public ministry.

Although hard evidence remains difficult to find, most scholars today believe that the origin of Lent lies in an annual forty-day season of fasting unrelated to Easter observed by Christians in Egypt, perhaps, indeed, in imitation of our Lord's fast in the wilderness. However, after the Council of Nicaea in 325, this was adopted by the other churches, but now combined with a final period of baptismal preparation that was already located immediately before Easter in those places—particularly Rome and North Africa—where baptism at Easter was already the norm.[4] For more solid evidence, it is necessary to look to the Festal Letters of St Athanasius issued on the Epiphany each year to inform the faithful of the date of Easter and the beginning of the Paschal Fast. The second of these letters, issued in 330, announces the beginning of a forty-day fast before Easter, incorporating within it an older six-day fast comprising the period we would know as Holy Week.[5] From some of Athanasius's later letters it appears that that the forty-day fast was something of an innovation, resisted in some conservative communities, but rapidly becoming universal. His letters frequently make reference to scriptural precedents for forty-day fasts—Moses, for example, spent forty days on Mount Sinai, talking with God (Exodus 24:18), Elijah walked for forty days and nights on his way to Mount Horeb (1 Kings 19:8) and the timetable for Nineveh's repentance (Jonah 3:4)—but interestingly never make mention of the fast of Jesus in this context. Rather, St Athanasius presents Lent as an extended period of ascetical preparation for Easter.[6] In his sixth letter, for the year 334, he writes:

> Just as Israel, advancing toward Jerusalem, was purified and instructed in the desert, so that they would forget the customs of Egypt, so it is right during the holy Lent, which we have taken

[4] *The Pilgrimage of Egeria. A New Translation of the Itinerarium Egeriae*, trans. A. McGowan and P. F. Bradshaw, Alcuin Club Collections 93 (Liturgical Press, Collegeville, Minnesota, 2018), p. 89. See further P. F. Bradshaw and M. E. Johnson, *The Origins of Feasts, Fasts and Seasons in Early Christianity*, Alcuin Club Collections 86 (Liturgical Press, Collegeville, Minnesota, 2011), pp. 75–86.

[5] *The Festal Letters of St Athanasius* (Parker, Oxford, 1854), p. 21.

[6] Thomas J. Talley, *The Origins of the Liturgical Year* (Pueblo Publishing, New York, 1986), p. 169.

upon ourselves, we should give our attention to our cleansing
and purification, so that setting forth from here and mindful of
fasting we can ascend to the upper room with the Lord and dine
with him and share the joy in heaven. For otherwise, without
keeping Lent, it would not be allowed us either to go up to
Jerusalem or to eat the Pascha.[7]

Even when adopted universally, the length of the fast varied. In
Rome what is now the fifth Sunday in Lent was curiously named
Domenica in mediana, suggesting that this Sunday once fell in the
middle of a three-week Lent which was only later extended to its
current length.[8] Lenten length varies still for two reasons. The first
was uncertainty as to whether forty days of actual fasting were
to be counted (and the Eastern Rites forbid fasting on Saturdays
as well as Sundays), or merely a season totalling forty days; the
second was a difference in reckoning when exactly Lent ended.
So, the Roman, and hence the Anglican, tradition begins Lent on
Ash Wednesday; the Ambrosian Rite of Milan, faithful to a more
ancient tradition, on the following Sunday (the sixth before Easter);[9] and the Byzantine Rite (according to which Lent ends on the
Friday evening before Palm Sunday and is therefore quite distinct
from Holy Week) at Vespers on the seventh Sunday before Easter.

The Book of Common Prayer still bears witness to some lingering
doubts about the length of the Lenten fast in the character of the
three Sundays leading up to Ash Wednesday—Septuagesima, Sexagesima and Quinquagesima. These Sundays, which foreshadow
the character of Lent, were taken directly from the provisions of
the Sarum Rite, including the readings and two of the collects (the
collect for Quinquagesima was a new composition in 1549). They
were suppressed in the revised *Roman Missal* of 1970 but, together
with their traditional observances, remain in the revised Tridentine
rite authorised in 2007 as the 'extraordinary form' of the Mass,
and in *Divine Worship*, the missal of the Anglican Ordinariates,
where the collects are those of *The Book of Common Prayer*. The word
'Septuagesima', which is found for the first time in the eighth-century Gelasian Sacramentary, comes from the Latin for seventieth,

[7] R. Cantalamessa, *Easter in the Early Church* (The Liturgical Press, Collegeville,
Minnesota, 1993), p. 71.
[8] *Ibid.*, p. 167.
[9] This was the case in Rome until the seventh century; see G. G. Willis, *A History
of Early Roman Liturgy* (Henry Bradshaw Society, London, 1994), pp. 62–3.

and similarly 'Sexagesima' means sixtieth, and 'Quinquagesima' fiftieth. While there is a lack of scholarly consensus on the origin of these Sundays, it has been suggested that their names arose by analogy with Quadragesima, the first Sunday in Lent, known as the 'fortieth day' before Easter, which in the Roman rite gives its name to the whole season of Lent. Quinquagesima is exactly fifty days before Easter, but Sexagesima and Septuagesima are only approximations.

To discover the real meaning and significance of Lent it is necessary to examine its liturgy, and this study will concentrate primarily on the Roman and Anglican liturgies. Since 1980 the Church of England has authorised the use of the weekday eucharistic lectionary of the modern Roman Rite (The *Ordo Lectionum Missae* of 1969) and since 2000 has authorised, in the *Revised Common Lectionary*, a three-year Sunday cycle of readings derived from the same source. An examination of the Lenten lectionary material reveals the dominance of three distinct but related themes. These are *Penitence and Self-Denial*; *Christian Baptism*; and *The Passion of the Lord*. The readings appointed for the weekday Lenten masses illustrate these themes in order. From Ash Wednesday until the end of the second week of Lent the first theme clearly predominates; it is illustrated by Old Testament readings such as the repentance of Nineveh at the preaching of Jonah (Jonah 3:1–10) on Wednesday of the first week, and Daniel's confession of the sins of Israel (Daniel 9:4–10) on Monday of the second week, and by Gospel readings such as the parable of the sheep and the goats (Matthew 25:31–46) on Monday of the first week; Christ's call for us to be reconciled to our brother (Matthew 5:20–6) on Saturday of the first week, and the parable of the prodigal son (Luke 15) on Saturday of the second week. The theme of baptism emerges strongly in the third week; it is illustrated by Old Testament readings such as the healing of Naaman in the waters of the Jordan (2 Kings 5:1–15) on Monday of the third week, and the stream of water issuing from the Temple (Ezekiel 47) on Tuesday of the fourth week, and by Gospel readings such as the three classic passages from John used from the earliest times for the instruction of candidates for baptism: the Samaritan woman (John 4) in the third week, the healing of the man born blind (John 9) in the fourth week, and the raising of Lazarus (John 11) in the fifth week. From then on it is the theme of the Lord's Passion that predominates; it is illustrated by Old Testament readings such as the fiery serpent (Numbers 21) on Tuesday of the fifth week and by Gospel readings from the 8th, 10th and 11th chapters of John.

That which links these three themes, which underlies their progress, is the Feast of Easter, the liturgical celebration of the Paschal Mystery. Whatever its origins, Lent does not exist for its own sake in any sense: it is nothing if it is not a thorough preparation for Easter, a kind of corporate retreat for the whole Church militant to prepare it for an informed and engaged participation in the paschal solemnities. As Laurence Stookey has observed, the 'season engages us in the process of confronting who we are by nature, who we are by God's purpose and redeeming action, and what we can become by divine grace'.[10] This understanding is clearly expressed in the presidential introduction provided in the Church of England's *Common Worship* liturgy of Ash Wednesday:

> Brothers and sisters in Christ, since early days Christians have observed with great devotion the time of our Lord's passion and resurrection and prepared for this by a season of penitence and fasting. By carefully keeping these days, Christians take to heart the call to repentance and the assurance of forgiveness proclaimed in the Gospel, and so grow in faith and devotion to our Lord. I invite you, therefore, the name of the Church, to the observance of a holy Lent, by self-examination and repentance, by prayer, fasting and self-denial; and by reading and meditating on God's holy word.[11]

Perhaps with slightly less clarity, this understanding of Lent is similarly set forth in Preface I of Lent in the *Roman Missal*:

> For by your gracious gift each year your faithful await the sacred paschal feasts with joy of minds made pure, so that, more eagerly intent on prayer and on the works of charity and participating in the mysteries by which we have been reborn, they may be led to the fullness of grace that you bestow on your sons and daughters.[12]

The liturgical year of the Christian Church up to the time of the Council of Nicaea and the 'Christianisation' of the Roman Empire by the Emperor Constantine was extremely simple. Practically its

[10] L. H. Stookey, *Calendar: Christ's Time for the Church* (Abingdon Press, Nashville, 1996), p. 88.

[11] *Common Worship: Times and Seasons* (Church House Publishing, London, 2006), p. 223.

[12] *The Roman Missal* (Catholic Truth Society, London, 2011), p. 580.

only features were the weekly Lord's Day and an annual *Pascha* or Passover. The content of both was the whole mystery of our redemption and, in particular, the Passion, Resurrection and Ascension of Christ, the Descent of the Holy Spirit and the Second Coming of the Lord. Every first day of the week, every Sunday, was from New Testament times the weekly celebration of the Christian mystery, when the People of God assembled together to proclaim in the Eucharist the Lord's death on the day of his Resurrection. It was not primarily a memorial of the Resurrection but a 'key weekly expression of the constant eschatological readiness for the Parousia which was intended to permeate the whole of a Christian's daily prayer and life'.[13] Sunday was not only a commemoration of the past and its actualisation in the present — 'an inbreaking of the eternal order of God',[14] but also an anticipation of the End, for it was the 'eighth day', the ushering in of the new and definitive creation.

The calendar and lectionary reforms of the last century in both Roman and Anglican rites have restored the primacy of Sunday as a Feast of our Lord and only a few major Saints' Days may now be observed on Sunday. This principle was clearly set out in *Sacrosanctum Concilium*, the Constitution on the Sacred Liturgy of 1963:

> By a tradition handed down from the apostles, which took its origin from the very day of the Lord's resurrection, the Church celebrates the paschal mystery every seventh day, which day is appropriately called the Lord's Day or Sunday. For on this day Christ's faithful are bound to come together into one place. They should listen to the word of God and take part in the Eucharist, thus calling to mind the passion, resurrection, and the glory of the Lord Jesus, and giving thanks to God who 'has begotten them again, through the resurrection of Christ from the dead, unto a living hope' (1 Peter 1–3). The Lord's Day is the original feast day, and it should be proposed to the faithful and taught to them so that it may become in fact a day of joy and of freedom from work. Other celebrations, unless they be truly of greatest importance, shall not have precedence over Sunday, which is the foundation and kernel of the whole liturgical year.[15]

---

[13] Bradshaw and Johnson, *Origins*, p. 13.

[14] Richard F. Buxton in *The New SCM Dictionary of Liturgy and Worship*, ed. P. F. Bradshaw (SCM-Canterbury Press, London, 2002), p. 452.

[15] Austin Flannery, OP, ed., *Vatican Council II, The Conciliar and Post-Conciliar Documents* (Fowler Wright Books, Leominster, 1975), pp. 29–30, para. 106.

Alongside this weekly celebration of the whole mystery of redemption there was an annual celebration, the Christian Passover, the *Pascha* or *Festum Festorum*. Essentially this consisted of a vigil beginning before sunset and culminating with the Eucharist at or just after midnight. It is not known exactly how far back this goes, though some scholars have claimed to find evidence of the observance in some of the New Testament writings notably 1 Peter;[16] the clear reference to Christ as 'our Passover' in 1 Corinthians 5:7 cannot be taken to imply a Christian adaptation of the Passover festival by St Paul himself, but it would have served as a powerful encouragement to those who were to take that step. It is possible that many early Gentile Christian communities did not observe the *Pascha* at all—especially those who contested the authority of the Old Testament and were strongly anti-Judaistic, and those who were held back by St Paul's own criticism of the observance of 'special days, and months, and seasons and years' (Galatians 4:10). But if, as Thomas Talley has written,

> the promulgation of annual festivals had little place in the agenda of the Gentile mission ... there would have been less diffidence (towards continuity with Passover) in the primitive community of Jerusalem, and there, we can believe, the observance of Passover continued, its ancient theme of redemption transformed by the triumph of the Paschal Lamb of the Covenant renewed.[17]

It is known that there was controversy over the date of the Christian *Pascha* during the second century. Sources suggest that in Asia Minor Christian communities kept the *Pascha* on a fixed day of the Jewish lunar month (14th Nisan), the day on which the Jews immolated the paschal lamb. Those who followed this custom were know by other Christians as Quartodecimans because of this insistence upon the fourteenth day of Nisan whereas they had come to observe *Pascha* invariably on a Sunday. Hitherto the scholarly consensus has been that the Sunday observance was the older of the two and the other merely a local aberration. However, others have suggested that Quartodeciman practice was an early

[16] Cf. F. L. Cross, *1-Peter, A Paschal Liturgy* (Mowbray, London, 1954), and M. H. Shepherd: *The Paschal Liturgy and the Apocalypse* (Lutterworth, London, 1960).
[17] Talley, *Origins of the Liturgical Year*, p. 5.

Jewish-Christian adaptation of the Passover and gone on to suggest that other Christian communities had no annual Easter observance until sometime in the early second century, when they innovated with a Sunday celebration.[18] In about the year 155 St Polycarp, Bishop of Smyrna, tried in vain during a visit to Rome to persuade Pope Anicetus to adopt the Quartodecimans' usage; despite their continued disagreement there was no breach of communion. Some forty years later however, Pope Victor attempted to stamp out Quartodeciman practice. When the recalcitrant Polycrates, Bishop of Ephesus, refused to conform, arguing that the Asian Churches were doing no more than faithfully continuing the tradition that they had received from the Evangelist John himself, Victor excommunicated him. This action provoked a strong protest from St Irenaeus, himself a native of Asia Minor who had become Bishop of Lyon, and who made a plea for tolerance and a respect for diversity. The argument Polycrates employed against Pope Victor might be evidence for the priority of the Quartodeciman usage.

In the years after the council of Nicaea the *Pascha*, the vigil between Saturday and Sunday, had its prolongation (the great fifty days of the Pascha-Pentecost celebration) and its preparation, at first the one or two days preceding the Vigil, kept as days of strict fasting, and by now, the forty days of Lent. As yet, however, there was not a Palm Sunday, a Maundy Thursday, or a Good Friday, for the Vigil was the inclusive celebration of the one mystery of our redemption, which, though it had its two key moments in the death and resurrection of the Lord, constituted an unbreakable unity. It was only later in the fourth century that a historical sequence began to work itself into the paschal celebration; working forwards to the institution of Ascension Day and the transformation of Pentecost into a specific commemoration of the descent of the Spirit and backwards into the chronological observance of the events of the passion in Holy Week. This change in the character of Holy Week began in Jerusalem and this will be examined more closely in Chapter vIII. It is important, however, to grasp from the outset that this almost revolutionary new rememorative approach did not altogether obliterate the older unitive celebration of the whole

---

[18] See Paul Bradshaw and Lawrence Hoffman, ed., *Passover and Easter: Origin and History to Modern Times* (University of Notre Dame Press, Notre Dame, 1999).

mystery: the Easter Vigil retained its former character and even the liturgical texts for the new observance of Good Friday and Easter Day (the Day of the Resurrection) bore witness to the theological conviction that the Cross and the Resurrection form an indivisible unity and a single mystery. In the medieval West, however, this unity was obscured, and Cross and Resurrection became separated in theology, in devotion and in art with consequences that were to weigh heavily at the time of the Reformation. One of the most conspicuous manifestations of this divorce for Anglicans is the Prayer of Consecration in the Communion Service in *The Book of Common Prayer*, which concentrates exclusively on Christ's Passion and omits all references to his Resurrection.

From early times the Paschal Vigil was associated with the rites of Christian initiation: although it has been argued that 1 Peter represents a paschal baptismal liturgy,[19] the earliest clear reference to this practice comes from Tertullian in North Africa in his *De Baptismo*[20] at the beginning of the third century. 'The Pascha affords a more (than usually) solemn day for baptism, since the passion of the Lord in which we are baptised was accomplished (then).'[21] By the time of Nicaea, at any rate, the Vigil had become *the* occasion for the reception of new members into the Church by the three distinct sacramental acts of Baptism, Confirmation and First Communion. The drawing together of the mystery of Christ's death and resurrection and of the believer's identification with that mystery in baptism goes back at least to Romans 6:3–11 which now forms the liturgical epistle of the Easter Vigil in both Roman and Anglican rites:

> Do you not know that all of us who have been baptised into Christ Jesus were baptised into his death? Therefore we have been buried with him by baptism into death, so that, just as Christ was raised from the dead by the glory of the Father, so we too might walk in newness of life.
>
> For if we have been united with him in a death like his, we will certainly be united with him in a resurrection like his. We know that our old self was crucified with him so that the body of sin might be destroyed, and we might no longer be enslaved to sin. For whoever has died is freed from sin. But if we have

[19] Cross, *1-Peter*.
[20] *Tertullian's Homily on Baptism*, ed. and trans. Ernest Evans (SPCK, London, 1964).
[21] Cantalamessa, *Easter*, p. 91.

died with Christ, we believe that we will also live with him. We
know that Christ, being raised from the dead, will never die
again; death no longer has dominion over him. The death he
died, he died to sin, once for all; but the life he lives, he lives
to God. So you also must consider yourselves dead to sin and
alive to God in Christ Jesus.

If Easter was the chosen and privileged occasion for the conferring of baptism, so the time before Easter was given over to the
immediate preparation of the catechumens for their participation
in the Easter mystery. A rigorous preparation was demanded of
them, and it was often long. A second stage of their preparation
followed upon an examination of their conduct during the time
of their catechumenate; those who satisfied this examination were
now called the *electi*; and they had to undergo a season of more
intense preparation for their baptism, a time of instruction, prayer,
fasting and exorcism. The solemn enrolment of the *electi* by the
bishop took place at the time we would now call the beginning
of Lent, and the season of Lent in its present form developed out
of this time of discipline and final preparation of the catechumens for their initiation into the Christian mystery at Easter. This
understanding of Lent and the appropriate use of the season has
today become familiar to those Christian communities which have
revived the adult catechumenate. The extended Roman *Rite of
Christian Initiation of Adults* provides liturgical material marking
the stages in a lengthy catechumenate culminating in initiation
ideally at Easter.[22] The Church of England now provides a series
of *Rites on the Way* which present materials for parishes and other
nurturing communities wishing to offer a similar staged process
of support and encouragement leading to the baptism of young
people and adults. One of the recommended patterns sees those
fully instructed and ready for initiation called together in church on
the First Sunday of Lent, presented liturgically with one of the four
key texts representing the key elements of the 'Christian knapsack'
on each of the Second to Fifth Sundays, and then baptised (and
confirmed if the bishop is present) at the Vigil or on Easter Day.[23]

[22] *Rite of Christian Initiation of Adults* (Continuum, London, 2004).
[23] *Common Worship: Christian Initiation* (Church House Publishing, London,
2006), pp 16–56.

It is easy to understand how those who were already Christians came to feel that they could not be passive and indifferent spectators during the catechumens' time of final preparation but needed to manifest their solidarity with the candidates. Especially was this so since the celebration of the Paschal Vigil involved them no less that the catechumens, and it was already recognised that it needed to be prepared for by a time of fasting. As early as the fourth century the evidence makes it clear that 'the church member was expected to approach the *Pascha* each year in the way he had done when he himself was solemnly preparing for his baptism'.[24]

It is important to understand the development of Lent in order to appreciate that it exists not only or primarily as a season of self-denial but also and more significantly as a time for the intensification of the whole Christian life, a time of preparation leading to a climax. Like the monk in *The Rule of St Benedict*, every Christian is called upon to keep Lent in such a way that he or she may look forward to the holy *Pascha* with the joy of spiritual longing ('cum spiritalis desiderii gaudio sanctum Pascha exspectet').[25] The catechumens were fasting, but they were also learning, as were the members of the community which sponsored them. At the end of the fourth century, the pilgrim nun Egeria describes the 'open' classes given in Jerusalem by the bishop during Lent for those to be baptised at the *Pascha*; 'all those of the people who wish to listen—but only the faithful—come in and sit'.[26] So for every Christian, Lent is a time for penetrating more deeply into the mysteries of the Faith; it is a time for learning.

The Vigil from early times has had a strong baptismal reference and, very properly, this is inescapable today. In one of the most brilliant and profoundly pastoral of all modern liturgical innovations—or renovations, the solemn renewal of baptismal promises, made whether there are candidates to be baptised or not, was introduced into the Roman liturgy as far back as 1951 and made obligatory in the reform of Pius XII in 1955. With this now a significant element in the Easter liturgy for Anglicans also, it is more than ever helpful to see Lent as a corporate retreat for the whole

[24] A. A. McArthur, *The Evolution of the Christian Year* (SCM, London, 1953), p. 129.
[25] *Rule of St Benedict* 49.7, translated in Dom David Parry, OSB, *Households of God* (DLT, London, 1980), ch. 49, p. 134.
[26] Egeria, trans. McGowan and Bradshaw, p. 189.

Church, a refresher course on our baptismal vows of renunciation, faith, and obedience. Those who have been present at the Easter Vigil when baptism has been administered need little convincing that all the traditional rites and ceremonies that are distinctive to the *Pascha* become clear, transparent and far more comprehensible with this essential component reinstated.[27] In this perspective participation in the Easter Vigil—the centre, the climax, the highlight of the whole Christian year—ought to be regarded as little short of an imperative by the committed and instructed Christian.

The sense of Lent having a momentum leading to a joyfully awaited climax accounts for the paradoxical note of joy which is clearly expressed by St Benedict. Witness is borne to this in more than one Christian tradition. In the Orthodox Church Lent is a season of 'bright sadness', a 'Lenten Spring' whose arrival is to be greeted with Joy, 'a time of gladness'.[28] As mentioned earlier, the first Preface of Lent in the *Roman Missal* thanks God that 'each year your faithful await the sacred paschal feasts with joy of minds made pure'. This is echoed in the current Church of England provision which blesses God 'as we prepare to celebrate the Easter feast with joyful hearts and minds'.[29] In this Anglican tradition the seventeenth-century parson-poet George Herbert provides the cheerful paradox of Lenten fasting called a feast as he exclaims, 'Welcome, deare Feast of Lent'.[30]

There is another feature of the ancient Lent that is important for an understanding of its meaning today, particularly for an understanding of the theme of penitence. A good starting point from an Anglican perspective is the now rarely used Commination Service, provided for use on Ash Wednesday is the 1662 *Book of Common Prayer*. At the beginning of the rite the priest is ordered to read the following exhortation to the people:

27 Jeremy Haselock in David Kennedy, *Using Common Worship: Times and Seasons—Lent to Embertide* (Church House Publishing, London, 2008), pp. 17–19.
28 Schmemann, *Great Lent*, pp. 31 and 43. See also Thomas Hopko, *The Lenten Spring* (St Vladimir's Seminary Press, New York, 1983).
29 *Common Worship: Services and Prayers for the Church of England*, Core Volume (Church House Publishing, London, 2000), p. 309.
30 John Drury, *Music at Midnight, The Life and Poetry of George Herbert* (Allen Lane, London, 2013), p. 266. See also the volume on George Herbert in *The Classics of Western Spirituality* (SPCK, London, 1981), pp. 204–6.

> Brethren, in the primitive Church there was a godly discipline, that, at the beginning of Lent, such persons as stood convicted of notorious sin were put to open penance, and punished in this world, that their souls might be saved in the day of the Lord, and that others, admonished by their example, might be more afraid to offend.
>
> Instead whereof, until the said discipline may be restored again (which is much to be wished) it is thought good that at this time (in the presence of you all) should be read the general sentences of God's cursing against impenitent sinners . . .

Lent was for a long time the period in which public penitents had to carry out the penances imposed upon them by the bishop. At the beginning of the season they were enrolled in the order of penitents so that on Maundy Thursday (not normally of the same year, for the time of penance tended to be lengthy) they could be formally reconciled by the bishop and so share more fully in the Easter Eucharist. In seventh-century Rome, Ash Wednesday was appointed for the opening of public penance and a dramatic rite devised for that purpose. Though it had long fallen into disuse, it was printed—along with such archaic rites as those for the blessing and imposition of the Crusader's cross; the handing over of degraded clerics to the tender care of the secular arm; the processional reception of the Holy Roman Emperor, and the reconciliation of penitents on Maundy Thursday—in editions of the *Pontificale Romanum* published up until the time of the Second Vatican Council. According to this rite the penitents are to prostrate themselves *cum lacrymis* (with tears) on the pavement of the church, and the bishop puts ashes on their foreheads saying, 'Remember, man, you are dust and to dust you will return. Do penance and you will have eternal life.' They are then clothed with sackcloth and then prostrate themselves once more while the whole assembly recites the seven penitential psalms and the litanies. The bishop is then to preach on the expulsion of Adam from Paradise before leading the penitents to the doors of the church and ejecting them *cum lacrymis*. As they kneel outside the bishop exhorts them 'not to despair of the Lord's mercy but to devote themselves to fasting, to prayers, to pilgrimages, to almsgiving and to other good works, so that the Lord may lead them to the worthy fruit of true repentance'. The doors are then solemnly closed, and the bishop returns to the sanctuary to begin the Mass. Thus is enacted a liturgical drama—

the expulsion from Paradise and the first steps on the long journey towards reconciliation with God.[31]

This would have been a deeply impressive ceremony and would have had considerable impact on the whole congregation and not only the unfortunate penitents. All were to recite together the penitential psalms and it seems clear how—as in the case of the catechumens—the whole Christian people developed a strong sense of solidarity with the public penitents. Indeed, though it is impossible after baptism to become a catechumen again, it is possible to become a penitent and must remain so. With the development of Christian spirituality, penitence came to be seen not just as a necessary activity after lapses into grave sin but as a positive and permanent Christian virtue. It was natural as the discipline of public penance fell into disuse between the eighth and tenth centuries that the Ash Wednesday rite should be transformed, and the whole congregation with the celebrant and ministers receive the ashes of penitence. 'Remember that you are dust, and to dust you shall return. Turn away from sin and be faithful to Christ.' This transformation was already widespread in 1091 when Pope Urban II added the full weight of his authority in extending this practice to the whole of Western Christendom:

> *Now is the healing time decreed*
> *For sins of heart and word and deed,*
> *When we in humble fear record*
> *The wrong that we have done the Lord.*[32]

The Constitution on the Sacred Liturgy summed up all this concisely:

> The two elements which are especially characteristic of Lent—the recalling of baptism or the preparation for it, and penance—should be given greater emphasis in the liturgy and in liturgical catechesis. It is by means of them that the Church prepares the faithful for the celebration of Easter, while they hear God's word more frequently and devote more time to prayer ...
>
> During Lent, penance should be not only internal and individual but also external and social. The practice of penance

---

[31] See P. Regan, *Advent to Pentecost: Comparing the Seasons in the Ordinary and Extraordinary Forms of the Roman Rite* (Liturgical Press, Collegeville, 2012), pp. 80–1.

[32] Latin office hymn *Ecce tempus idoneum*, from before the twelfth century. *New English Hymnal*, no. 59

should be encouraged in ways suited to the present day, to different regions and to individual circumstances.[33]

These defining characteristics of Lent have long been implicit in Anglican liturgical spirituality. For example, in a sermon preached by Thomas Ken at the King's Chapel in Whitehall in 1685, when Bishop of Bath and Wells, he describes Lent as a 'penitential martyrdom', and continues, 'A devout soul, that is able duly to observe it, fastens himself to the cross on Ash Wednesday, and hangs crucified by contrition all the Lent long [so that] he may by his own crucifixion be better disposed to be crucified with Christ on Good Friday'.[34] They were given explicit recognition in the Church of England in1986 with the publication of *Lent, Holy Week, Easter — Services and Prayers*.[35] This collection contained an Order for the Beginning of Lent to be used at the Eucharist on Ash Wednesday or optionally on the First Sunday of Lent which suggested the imposition of ashes officially for the first time since the Reformation. The image of Lent as journey or pilgrimage was clearly present from the outset as the authors claim the rite was designed 'not only to mark a special day but to start the local Christian congregation off on a path that can be seen, even at this early stage, to be leading to the Good Friday and Easter celebrations'.[36] The 'two-fold character' of Lent is also clearly expressed in the words of introduction used by the celebrant at the outset of the rite:

> At first this season of Lent was observed by those who were preparing for Baptism at Easter and by those who were to be restored to the Church's fellowship from which they had been separated through sin. In course of time the Church came to recognise that, by a careful keeping of these days, all Christians might take to heart the call to repentance and the assurance of forgiveness proclaimed in the Gospel, and so to grow in faith and devotion to our Lord.[37]

The Ash Wednesday rite in *Common Worship: Times and Seasons*, which supplanted that in *Lent, Holy Week, Easter* in 2006, takes

---

[33] Flannery, *Vatican Council II*, pp. 30–1, paragraphs 109 and 110.

[34] *The Prose Works of the Right Reverend Thomas Ken, D.D.*, ed. W. Benham, Ancient and Modern Library of Theological Literature (Griffith, Farran, Okeden & Welsh, London, 1889), p. 85.

[35] *Lent, Holy Week, Easter — Services and Prayers* (SPCK and others, London, 1986).

[36] *Ibid.*, p. 12.

[37] *Ibid.*, pp. 14–15.

this piece of history for granted and omits it from the presidential introduction but the direction of liturgical travel is the same and the rite itself is derived from its predecessor.

Recognising the feeling of solidarity with individual sinners felt by Christian people and wishing to stress even more strongly the ecclesial dimension of penance—the fact that sin has effects felt by the whole community and that the community has an important part to play in the reconciliation of sinners in its midst—the Roman Catholic Church introduces in its *Ordo Penitentiae* of 1973 the idea of a public liturgy of penance. This service includes the reading of scripture and a homily, both of which are intended to prompt an examination of conscience; prayer; a general confession and in some circumstances absolution; the reconciliation of individual penitents in private, and a final thanksgiving. Obviously, such services are particularly appropriate in Lent as the whole community prepares itself for full participation in the paschal mystery. For Anglicans in England *Common Worship: Christian Initiation* provides a Corporate Service of Penitence, similarly structured, with a rich resource of seasonal material including that for Lent.[38] In the preliminary notes to this service it is observed that, 'Where appropriate, an explicit link may be made between corporate penitence and the reconciliation of individual penitents. In some communities, provision for individual confession and absolution will be the natural pastoral outworking of such corporate services.'[39] With the virtual disappearance of the Commination, with its fierce denunciations and the sort of anathematising which is unsympathetic to modern ears, this form of service ought to reintroduce into Anglican Lenten worship a dimension which has been sadly lacking.

This chapter began with the 'forty days and forty nights' of the Gospel for the First Sunday of Lent. The introduction of this narrative is not an irrelevant addition to the basic themes of Lent, nor a distraction from its real meaning and purpose. Rather, at the beginning of the old Lent (for at one time Lent began on this day), it sets before the worshipper the Lord's renunciation of the Devil and of the temptations of the world and the flesh which the Devil was seeking to exploit. Formerly this would have reminded the catechumens of the triple renunciation they had to prepare themselves

---

[38] *Common Worship: Christian Initiation*, pp. 227–308.
[39] *Ibid.*, p. 229

to make at their Easter baptism: today it serves as a reminder to all Christians that the profession of faith in Christ and the promise of obedience to God's will, need constantly to be reaffirmed, and that this is done in a particularly solemn and corporate fashion at the end of the Lenten journey in the Paschal Vigil.

The custom of self-denial still commended to the faithful as a part of Lenten discipline should not be trivialised. For Anglicans in England, Canon B 6.3 makes clear that:

> the days of Fasting and Abstinence and the vigils which are to be observed in the Church of England are set out in *The Book of Common Prayer*, whereof the 40 days of Lent, particularly Ash Wednesday, and the Monday to Saturday before Easter, ought specially to be observed.

This element of renunciation, mortification and self-denial is an inescapable element in the Christian life and must always be seen in the context of the baptismal covenant and of the paschal mystery. Christians must never practise self-denial in order to assert the dominance of their wills over their bodies, for that in itself cannot bring us nearer to God; indeed, it may only increase the potentiality for evil. Alexander Schmemann has written, 'Christian asceticism is a fight, not *against* the body but *for* the body', and again, 'In this world everything—even "spirituality"—can be demonic'.[40] For Christians need to be very much on their guard against the heresy of the Manichees, which identifies evil with the material creation and seeks to release the spirit from the prison of the body: our Lord, on the other hand, identifies the *heart* of man as the source of the evils that defile him (Matthew 15:18). Charles Williams, a great Anglican layman, poet, novelist, and theologian—one of the 'Inklings' group around J. R. R. Tolkein—who died in 1945, put this point very cogently when he wrote:

> The body was holily created, is holily redeemed, and is to be holily raised from the dead. It is, in fact, for all our difficulties with it, less fallen, merely in itself, than the soul in which the quality of the will is held to reside; for it was a sin of the will which degraded us.[41]

[40] Schmemann, *Great Lent*, pp. 38 and 84.
[41] Charles Williams, 'The Index of the Body', *The Dublin Review* 211 (July 1942), reprinted in The Image of the City of God and Other Essays (Oxford University Press, London, 1958), pp. 80–7.

No form of self-denial (so-called) is of any value whatever—it can often be the reverse—if it is not directed to the love and service of God and neighbour. The model here must be Christ the Servant, laying aside his garments to wash the feet of his disciples. Lenten discipline must, of course, include a certain laying aside; we strip off our garments not because they are sinful but because they would hinder or limit our possibilities of service.

It is a true instinct that has led to the recovery today of the ancient link between fasting and sharing one's food and resources with the hungry and underprivileged. This link is clearly affirmed in the Old Testament and particularly in the passage from Isaiah 58, which is appointed in the eucharistic lectionary for the Friday and Saturday after Ash Wednesday. In the second century CE the following passage occurs in *The Shepherd of Hermas*:

> in that day on which you fast you shall taste nothing except bread and water, and you shall reckon the price of the expense for that day which you are going to keep, of the foods which you would have eaten, and you shall give it to a widow or an orphan or to someone destitute.[42]

The Divine Office of the Roman Rite provides part of a sermon by St Peter Chrysologus—a fifth-century bishop of Ravenna—in the Office of Readings for Thursday in the third week of Lent:

> The fasting man should realise what fasting is. If anyone wants God to perceive that he is hungry, he should himself take notice of the hungry. If he desires fatherly kindness, he should display it first.[43]

So, the *no* to self is said only in order to be able to say *yes* to God and to neighbour; to say *yes* more meaningfully and more authentically by attacking at the roots all the obstacles to full self-surrender. In baptism candidates are called upon to say *no* to the Devil so that they might say *yes* to God: they are made to die with Christ to the old Adam so that they might rise with him to the glory of the new humanity.

The whole observance of Lent must help the whole Christian community to be conformed more closely to the death and resurrec-

---

[42] *The Apostolic Fathers*, vol. 2, trans. Kirsopp Lake for the Loeb Classical Library (Heinemann, London, 1913), p. 161.
[43] *The Divine Office*, vol. 2 (William Collins, London, 1974), p. 155.

tion of Christ in the Easter mystery. Lent should not be observed as if the Church was awaiting redemption, but rather, believers, having the sign of the Cross on their foreheads, should spend the season in attempting to make themselves better conformed to Christ's death, in order that the Resurrection might always be experienced in the clearest manner possible. The austerity of the Lenten liturgy itself and the way in which it is offered is designed to help with this. Traditionally, the music of the liturgy is simpler than at other times in the year, with the organ used only to support the singing. The Gloria in Excelsis is not sung at the Eucharist and the acclamation 'alleluia' is banished so that both may ring out more gloriously at Easter. Liturgical dress is marked by a measure of austerity also: where vestments are worn, and altar frontals employed, they are violet in colour or fashioned of unbleached linen of the type known as Lenten Array. Altar flowers are eschewed, and images may be veiled. Only on the Fourth Sunday of Lent, *Laetare* or Refreshment Sunday, is there some respite and Rose-coloured vestments are permitted as a sign of the relaxation of Lenten rigour allowed on this day. From the very beginning of Lent all these elements—textual, ritual and ceremonial as well as self-denial and austerity of life—combine to set before the worshipping community the truth expressed so clearly by Louis Bouyer:

> The Pasch is not a mere commemoration: it is the cross and the empty tomb rendered actual. But it is no longer the Head who must stretch himself on the cross in order to rise from the tomb: it is his Body the Church, and of this Body we are members.[44]

---

[44] Louis Bouyer, *The Paschal Mystery*, English translation of the second edition of 1947 of *Le Mystère paschal* (Allen & Unwin, London, 1951), p. xiv. More recent French editions have been revised in the light of the liturgical revisions of 1951 and 1955.

II

The Passover of the Jews

It is a pity that the English language has only a poor word like *Easter* to describe the centre and climax of the Christian year. It is an Anglo-Saxon word of debated origin, but it appears to be related to ancient words, either for 'dawn' or for 'spring'; according to the Venerable Bede it is derived from *Eostre*, a goddess whose festival was celebrated at the vernal equinox.[1] Similarly, the word *Lent*, which is also of Anglo-Saxon origin—*lencten*, simply means spring, the time when the days begin to lengthen. The French language has *Carême*, deriving ultimately from the Latin *Quadragesima* describing the forty days of the season. For Easter, most European languages have words derived from the Latin and Greek *Pascha*, a version of the Hebrew *Pesach* translated in our Old Testament as *Passover*—a word coined by William Tyndale for his English translation of the New Testament published in 1526—so French uses *Pâques* and Italian *Pasqua*. The adjective *paschal* is familiar to most churchgoers from such phrases as 'the paschal candle', 'the paschal vigil', and 'the paschal mystery' but the English are not accustomed to talk of Easter as the *Pasch*. Inevitably two words have to be used—*Passover* and *Easter*—and something significant is lost in having this double terminology. It would be less disadvantageous to have only one, the better to indicate that Easter is the Christian Passover.

The Old Testament narrative of the Exodus from Egypt features very prominently in the Lent and Holy Week liturgy. This background is provided in its most extended form in the Divine Office. The Office of Readings in the Roman Rite begins the reading of Exodus on the Thursday after Ash Wednesday and then continues from the Fourth Sunday of Lent with passages from Leviticus and

---

[1] Bede, *De Temporum Ratione*, xv (Patrologia Latina 90).

Numbers. Then on the Fifth Sunday and until Easter readings are taken from the Letter to the Hebrews. The Church of England's *Common Worship* provides a two-year lectionary for use at Morning and Evening Prayer which begins its continuous reading of Exodus on the Friday after the Third Sunday of Lent and concludes it on the Saturday before the Fifth Sunday of Easter. In the first year these lessons are read at Morning Prayer, in the second year at Evening Prayer.

It is not, however, only in the Divine Office that the Exodus story makes its appearance. Two key passages for the understanding of the Jewish Passover are Exodus 12, in which the God gives Moses and Aaron detailed instructions concerning the Passover meal, and Exodus 14, which describes how the people of Israel passed through the Red Sea on dry ground. The first of these two passages is now the first reading at the evening liturgy on Maundy Thursday in both the Roman and Anglican rites; the second is the one Old Testament reading which must never be omitted at the Easter Vigil.

Above all it is in the Easter Vigil that the reference to the Exodus story is at its strongest; not only or even primarily in the course of the Old Testament readings but even more vividly in the triumphal chant of the *Exsultet*, the *Praeconium Paschale* or Paschal Proclamation.

> *This is the Passover feast,*
> *when Christ, the true Lamb of God, is slain*
> *whose blood consecrates the homes of all the faithful.*
> *This is the night when you first saved our ancestors,*
> *freeing Israel from her slavery*
> *and leading her safely through the sea.*
> *[This is the night when the pillar of fire*
> *destroyed the darkness of sin!]*[2]
> *This is the night when Jesus Christ vanquished hell,*
> *broke the chains of death*
> *and rose triumphant from the grave.*
> *This is the night when all who believe in him are freed from sin,*
> *restored to grace and holiness,*
> *and share the victory of Christ.*[3]

[2]   This line is sadly missing from the version printed in *Common Worship: Times and Seasons.*

[3]   *Common Worship: Times and Seasons,* pp. 410–11.

This magnificent lyrical hymn of praise first appears in three Gallican Sacramentaries: the seventh-century Bobbio Missal, the eighth-century Missale Gothicum and the Missale Gallicanum Vetus, but the text may be earlier. There is an unsubstantiated tradition that it was written by St Ambrose (d. 397) based on a feeling that its spirit is very much that of his acknowledged poetical work but also because of a reference to bees and their work, inspired by Virgil and alluded to by Ambrose, which was evidently in the proclamation from a very early date. In his *Epistola XXVIII, Ad Praesidium, de Cereo paschali*,[4] St Jerome declines the deacon Praesidius's request to write a blessing for the Paschal Candle, because of a lack of reference to wax in the scriptures. He is also scornful of the praise of bees in an existing prayer, finding such material entirely out of place in the Easter liturgy. The text used today may be different from the earliest versions, but Jerome's letter would have been written before 420, confirming that at least the bees were in the text by then. More importantly, the linking together of the Old Testament Passover story and the death and resurrection of Jesus was already part of the tradition and seems to have been normative in these prayers of blessing from the outset.

Described by F. L. Cross as 'the most important addition to Patristic literature in the present century', the *Peri Pascha* of Melito, the Quartodeciman Bishop of Sardis, was brought to light by Campbell Bonner in 1936 and presented to scholars as a paschal homily and haggadah-style prayer dating from between 16 and 170 CE.[5] Whatever its original purpose might have been—and it may come from the same genre that developed into the *Exsultet*—the text proves conclusively that a reading of the twelfth chapter of Exodus was already a key element in the Christian paschal celebrations in second-century Asia Minor. It begins thus:

> The scripture from the Hebrew Exodus has been read
> and the words of the mystery have been plainly stated,
>   how the sheep is sacrificed
>   and how the people is saved
>   and how Pharaoh is scourged through the mystery.

4   J. N. D. Kelly, *Jerome: His Life, Writings and Controversies* (Harper & Row, New York, 1975), p. 111 and note.
5   Melito of Sardis, 'The Homily on the Passion by Melito, Bishop of Sardis', in *Mélanges Franz Cumont*, ed. Campbell Bonner, Annuaire de l'Institut de philologie et d'histoire orientales et slaves 4 (1936), pp. 107–19.

Understand, therefore, beloved,
  how it is new and old,
  eternal and temporary,
  perishable and imperishable,
    mortal and immortal, this mystery of the Pascha:
old as regards the Law, but new as regards the Word;
temporary as regards the model, eternal because of the grace;
perishable because of the slaughter of the sheep,
  imperishable because of the life of the Lord;
mortal because of the burial in the earth,
  immortal because of the rising from the dead.
Old is the Law, but new the Word;
temporal the model, but eternal the grace;
perishable the sheep, imperishable the Lord;
not broken as the lamb, but resurrected as God.[6]

Almost the only remaining vestige of this tradition to be preserved in *The Book of Common Prayer*, apart from the Easter Anthems, is the Proper Preface for Easter in which thanksgiving is made for the glorious Resurrection of Jesus Christ our Lord: 'for his is the very Paschal Lamb, which was offered for us, and hath taken away the sin of the world; who by his death hath destroyed death, and by his rising to life again hath restored us to everlasting life'. This was taken over directly from the Sarum Missal in 1549 and is still preserved as the short Preface of Easter in *Common Worship* and the first Preface of Easter in the current Roman rite.

Further strictly 'paschal' material to remedy the comparative paucity of the Prayer Book was provided for Anglicans in the nineteenth century by the translations of ancient Greek and Latin hymns by J. M. Neale and others. A typical example is the Eastertide evening Office Hymn, *Ad cenam Agni providi*:

Ad cenam Agni providi,   The Lamb's high banquet we await
stolis salutis candidi,   In snow-white robes of royal state,
post transitum maris Rubri   And now, the Red Sea's channel past,
Christo canamus principi.   To Christ, our Prince, we sing at last.

Cuius corpus sanctissimum   Upon the altar of the Cross
in ara crucis torridum,   His Body has redeemed our loss;
sed et cruorem roseum   And tasting of his precious Blood
gustando, Deo vivimus.   Our life is hid with Christ in God.

[6]   Melito of Sardis, *On Pascha*, ed. S. G. Hall (Oxford University Press, Oxford, 1979), p. 3.

Protecti paschae vespero	That Paschal eve God's arm was bared,
a devastante angelo,	*The devastating Angel spared;*
de Pharaonis aspero	*By strength of hand our hosts went free*
sumus erepti imperio.	*From Pharaoh's ruthless tyranny.*
Iam pascha nostrum Christus est,	*Now Christ our Passover is slain,*
agnus occisus innocens;	*The Lamb of God that know no stain;*
sinceritatis azyma	*And he, the true unleavened Bread,*
qui carnem suam obtulit.	*Is truly our oblation made.*
Esto perenne mentibus	*Maker of all, to thee we pray,*
paschale, Iesu, gaudium	*Fulfil in us thy joy today;*
et nos renatos gratiae	*When death assails, grant, Lord, that we*
tuis triumphis aggrega.	*May share thy Paschal victory.*[7]

From an analysis of this rich profusion of liturgical material a triple pattern emerges. First, the Passover of the Old Testament is treated in these liturgical texts as a *type*, meaning a model, figure or prophetic image, of a fulness of redemption yet to come. Secondly, the Passion and Resurrection of Christ are seen in terms of a passage — *transitus* — and of a paschal sacrifice. Thirdly, our Christian life is also seen as a passage through death to life, or rather as a participation in the unique passing-over of Christ himself; in particular the passage through the Red Sea is seen as a type of Christian baptism. These are not so much three themes as three variations on a single theme; a single theme that is fundamental to an understanding of the meaning of Holy Week and the key which alone can unlock the complexities of the Holy Week liturgy.

The introduction of this theme into the Paschal Liturgy is due to two developments. The first was the association of baptism with the Easter Vigil. This association is not made by Melito of Sardis but is clearly stated for the first time by Tertullian at the end of the second century. The second was the influence of the third-century Alexandrian biblical scholar and theologian, Origen. He challenged the faulty etymology of the Quartodecimans of Asia Minor, who had derived *Pascha* from the Greek word *paschein* (the present infinitive of *pascho*, to suffer),[8] and convincingly argued that its true meaning was *Transitus*, 'passage'. It was Origen too who applied this understanding of *Pascha* to Christ's passage into his eternal

---

[7]   *New English Hymnal*, no. 101.

[8]   Cf. Melito, *On Pascha*, p. 46: 'What is the Pascha? It gets its name from its characteristic: from suffer (*pathein*) comes suffering (*paschein*).'

kingdom.[9] But these developments, far from deforming a primitive celebration of the 'event' of Christ's death and resurrection into a somewhat Platonic feast of an 'idea', in fact succeeded in giving explicit expression to a truth that is implicit both in the theology of St Paul and that of the Fourth Gospel. Paul not only referred to Christ as 'our Passover' (1 Corinthians 5:7) but also spoke of baptism in terms of identification with the death, burial and resurrection of Christ (Romans 6:3). The Fourth Gospel's account of the Last Supper begins with the words, 'Before the festival of the Passover, Jesus, knowing that his hour had come *to pass from this world to the Father,* having loved those who were in the world, loved them to the end' (John 13:1).

The threefold Passover has known some variation in its historical development—Origen, for example, distinguishes between the Old Testament Passover, the Church's Passover and the Eternal Passover—but the triple pattern always begins with the Old Testament. Before looking at this material, a note of caution needs to be struck. One aspect of the pre-critical approach to scripture—the idea of the 'type' as a straightforward prediction or foreshadowing of a future event or person—is alien to most modern readers but basic to the understanding and interpretation of the Old Testament from Patristic times right up until the Reformation and beyond. Simplified and codified in such late-medieval publications as the *Biblia Pauperum* and the *Speculum Humanae Salvationis*, types and antitypes were key to the study of the relationship between the scriptures of the Old and New Covenants and the source of much Christian art and iconography. Modern critical study of the New Testament has clarified how an author like St Matthew felt free to shape his narrative around a retrospective reinterpretation of Old Testament prophetic material. Today's familiarity with the literary and theological impulses which shaped the scriptures, gained through studying them from a literary-critical standpoint, in no way invalidates the powerful way in which the liturgy still reads back Old Testament words and events in the light of the New Testament.

It is important to have a grasp of the main elements in the Old Testament Passover story in order to understand the role this narrative has in the Paschal liturgy. At the beginning Israel is not yet

---

9   Origen, *De Pascha*, cf. Talley, *Origins of the Liturgical Year*, p. 26.

a people or a nation but an enslaved, dispirited and unorganised group of immigrants with no real sense of their identity. They are in a condition of abject and helpless servitude under the iron fist of a ruthless and idol-worshipping Egypt. Moses, a fugitive from justice, receives a divine call and commission and to him is revealed the sacred name of the God of his fathers, *Yahweh*, who says to him: 'I will send you to Pharaoh to bring my people, the Israelites, out of Egypt' (Exodus 3:10). Things go from bad to worse: Moses is reluctant and timid, Pharaoh reacts with contemptuous anger, 'Who is the Lord, that I should heed him and let Israel go? I do not know the Lord, and I will not let Israel go' (Exodus 5:2). He imposes an even heavier burden on the Hebrews, who turn in bitter resentment upon Moses and his brother Aaron. There now follows a series of crippling plagues which bring disaster upon the Egyptians but leave the Hebrews untouched (Exodus 7, 8, 9 and 10). These plagues reach their climax in the death of all the firstborn of the Egyptians—the Israelites being spared through observing a sequence of new rites which involve the slaying of a sacrificial lamb 'without blemish' (Exodus 12.5). They mark the doorposts and lintel of their houses with the blood of the lamb and then, packed and ready for a hasty departure, eat its flesh roasted. The panic-stricken Egyptians capitulate to the demands of the Hebrews and drive them out of the land (Exodus 12:33). Not for the first time, however, Pharaoh changes his mind and pursues the Hebrews with the full might of his army so that it seems their darkest hour has come when they find themselves trapped between their pursuers and the waters of the Red Sea. At the last possible moment, the waters are parted and the Hebrews escape, but as the Egyptian chariots and horsemen follow them the waters return and overwhelm them (Exodus 14:5–31).

In the desert, the Hebrews are found to be fickle and faithless but Yahweh travels with them, making his presence known to them in a pillar of cloud by day and a pillar of fire by night (Exodus 13:21). When they complain about lack of food, God feeds them with mysterious manna and quenches their thirst from a fountain of water struck from the rock (Exodus 16 and 17). Led by Moses, they journey through the wilderness towards the land which God has promised them, a land flowing with milk and honey. Reaching at length the foot of Mount Sinai, Israel—a people now and no longer a rabble—accept the Law of God and enter into a covenant with the

Lord who has redeemed them (Exodus 19, 20 and 24). God says, 'Now therefore, if you obey my voice and keep my covenant, you shall be my treasured possession out of all the peoples. Indeed, the whole earth is mine, but you shall be for me a priestly kingdom and a holy nation' (Exodus 19:5–6). This covenant is solemnly celebrated at the foot of Mount Sinai; sacrifices are offered, and half the blood is thrown against the altar; then Moses reads the book of the covenant to the assembled people. They give their assent—'All that the Lord has spoken we will do, and we will be obedient' (Exodus 24:7). Moses then takes the rest of the blood and throws is jupon the people, crying out, 'See the blood of the covenant that the Lord has made with you in accordance with all these words' (Exodus 24:8). Yet the Israelites continue to rebel against God and to give shocking evidence of their faithlessness so that their entry into the promised land is delayed a whole generation. Moses dies within sight of their goal and it is Joshua, his lieutenant and successor, who leads the people across the River Jordan (Deuteronomy 34, Joshua 3), in a way which is clearly intended to recall the earlier crossing of the Red Sea.

Reflection on the magnificent sweep of this story in the context of the development of the Easter liturgy leads inevitably to a number of conclusions. First comes a confrontation with the characteristic mode in which Scripture conveys to the reader the things concerning God and his relations with his people. Here is not doctrinal statement but *narrative*—story, from which first the Jews and then the Church, the believing community, has had to distil the truths it seems to require. As will become clear, it is pre-eminently through worship, through the liturgy, that the Church responds to this narrative, by participating in the story, inhabiting it, as it were, and by re-enacting it.[10] Neither the New Testament itself nor the Church's tradition of doctrine and worship can be fully understood without the recognition that they are set against the background of this particular story. This is most clearly true of everything that relates to the passion, death and resurrection of Christ and to the initiation of new members into the Body of Christ and the sacra-

[10] See Anthony Harvey, 'Attending to Scripture', in *Believing in the Church*, Report by the Doctrine Commission of the Church of England (SPCK, London, 1981), pp. 30–1. Also, John Barton and John Halliburton, 'Story and Liturgy', pp. 79–107 of the same collection.

mental life of the Church. Only in the light of the Exodus narrative do liturgical references to the paschal lamb and the blood of the lamb make sense. The same applies to the 'sealing' of initiates with the sign of the cross just as the doorposts and lintels of the Hebrew's houses were sealed with the blood of the Passover lamb. The same narrative undergirds the idea of baptism as a kind of passage through the Red Sea and makes sense of the words of St Paul in his First Letter to the Corinthians (10:1–4).

> I do not want you to be unaware, brothers and sisters, that our ancestors were all under the cloud, and all passed through the sea, and all were baptised into Moses in the cloud and in the sea, and all ate the same spiritual food, and all drank the same spiritual drink. For they drank from the spiritual rock that followed them, and the rock was Christ.

The Exodus theme develops the idea of 'Covenant' — first offered to Noah (Genesis 9:9–17), to Abraham (Genesis 15:18), and then to Moses (Exodus 31:18) but given its most profound development by Jeremiah and Ezekiel — and makes sense of the Lord's reference at the Last Supper to the 'cup that is poured out for you' being 'the new covenant in my blood' (Luke 22:20). Yet at this point it could appear that here is nothing more than a rather fanciful allegorisation of the Old Testament, an arbitrary and artificial selection of random details and images.

The second conclusion is that it is the Exodus story *as a whole* which points to the mystery of redemption *as a whole*, because it shows forth the way God deals with his people. The human predicament is one of servitude in the spiritual Egypt of sin, a servitude that leaves humankind weak and divided and incapable of initiative, for — as one of the old Lenten collects puts it — 'we have no power of ourselves to help ourselves'.[11] Redemption can only come from the direct initiative and intervention of God himself, which is worked out in and through the history of a people. The lamb without blemish that is to be offered as a paschal sacrifice and consumed as a paschal meal, whose blood is shed to spare the firstborn of God's people from death, points to an awareness of the need for a pure and spotless victim who will offer himself

---

[11] Collect for the second Sunday in Lent in the old *Roman Missal* and the *Book of Common Prayer*. Now the Post-Communion prayer for the same Sunday in *Common Worship*.

as a vicarious sacrifice for the sins of his people and give them life through his death. The effect, moreover, of God's saving intervention is always to bring the redeemed into a close unity as the people of God and to establish a covenant relationship with them, not on the basis of human merit or as a bargain struck between equal partners, but on the basis of God's choice and calling, of his grace and love.

In 1 Corinthians 10, St Paul makes it clear that 'these things happened to them (that is the Israelites) to serve as an example, and they were written down to instruct us, on whom the ends of the ages have come' (1 Corinthians 10:11). One strain in early Christian tradition tended to assert that the original Exodus was nothing but a type of what was to come, with no intrinsic value of its own. So Melito of Sardis in his paschal homily could argue in a blatantly supercessionist way:

> The people then was a model by way of preliminary sketch, and the law was the writing of a parable: the gospel is the recounting and fulfilment of the law, and the Church is the repository of the reality. The model then was precious before the reality, and the parable was marvellous before the interpretation; that is, the people was precious before the Church arose, and the law was marvellous before the gospel was elucidated. But when the Church arose and the gospel took precedence the model was made void, conceding its power to the gospel, and the law was fulfilled, conceding its power to the gospel. In the same way as the model is made void, conceding the image to the truly real, and the parable is fulfilled, being elucidated by the interpretation, just so also the law was fulfilled when the gospel was elucidated, and the people was made void when the Church arose; and the model was abolished when the Lord was revealed, and today, things once precious have become worthless, since the really precious things have been revealed.[12]

If, however, even granting the supercessionist view, it is true that the most important thing about the Exodus story is that it is a 'model' or 'preliminary sketch' of the true redemption, yet it is also true, as St Paul affirms, that 'God has not rejected his people whom he foreknew' and that 'the gifts and the calling of God are irrevocable' (Romans 11:2 and 29). It follows that it must also be affirmed that the Exodus event was a true and valid experience

---

[12] Melito of Sardis, *On Pascha*, pp. 21–3.

of God's redeeming power for the people of Israel. It must be recognised that it was a real act of God and an integral part of his plan of redemption, and furthermore that both those who lived through it historically and those who have relived it liturgically in the annual Passover festival can in some sense be said to have eaten and drunk a supernatural sustenance, drinking from the rock that was Christ.

For the Jews the Exodus event constituted the central crisis of their history and their religion; it was a foundational experience, the event that gave them identity both as a nation and as the holy people of God. It is because the Christian Church is in direct continuity with this nation and people as 'a chosen race, a royal priesthood, a holy nation, God's own people, in order that you may proclaim the mighty acts of him who called you' (1 Peter 2:9) that it can sing in the *Exsultet* of the people of Israel as 'our fathers' and celebrate the Exodus event as part of its own history and corporate experience of salvation. Christians can identify themselves with the act of praise in the *Haggadah*[13] (the second- or third-century-CE compilation which contains the liturgy of the *Seder* or Jewish Passover meal) when all raise their glasses and say:

> *Therefore, let us rejoice*
> *At the wonder of our deliverance*
> *From bondage to freedom,*
> *From agony to joy,*
> *From mourning to festivity,*
> *From darkness to light,*
> *From servitude to redemption.*
> *Before God let us ever sing a new song.*[14]

If for the Christian this *Haggadah* finds its true fulfilment only in the *Exsultet* of the Easter liturgy this is not to empty the Jewish Passover of all meaning but rather to give it a richer and heightened and universal significance.

---

[13] The Hebrew word means 'narrative'. See Barton and Halliburton, 'Story and Liturgy', p. 106, note 2.

[14] *A Passover Haggadah*, prepared by the Central Conference of American Rabbis, ed. Herbert Bronstein (Penguin Books, London,1978), p. 57. This passage leads immediately into the recitation of the first one or two of the *Hallel* psalms (Psalms 113–18); see also *The Passover, the Last Supper and the Eucharist* (The Study Group for Christian Jewish Relations, London, 1975), and Chaim Raphael, *A Feast of History* (Weidenfeld & Nicolson, London, 1972).

Because the Exodus was so crucial to the Jews, the original core of history has been heavily overlaid with 'myth' due to some extent to the annual re-enactment of the historical events in the dramatic and liturgical celebrations of the Passover festival.[15] The Exodus narrative is *Heilsgeschichte*—'salvation history'—in which historical events, their theological interpretation and their liturgical commemoration are bound inextricably together. Even the origins of the Passover are not free from obscurity; though it seems clear that two original distinct festivals, probably earlier in date that the Exodus event itself—a feast of the Paschal Lamb with a pastoral origin and a feast of Unleavened Bread with an agricultural origin—were at some time fused together as a single feast of the spring equinox. Again, at some time these Bedouin sacrificial customs were radically transformed, historicised and given their continuing legitimation by being related to the events of the Exodus narrative.[16] Furthermore, it is not clear what the original meaning of the Hebrew word *Pesach* really was, for the later Jewish tradition differed over its interpretation. Josephus took it to mean the passage of the angel of the Lord over the dwellings of the Israelites at the slaughter of the Egyptian firstborn, while Philo took it to mean the passing-over of the Red Sea: 'after the new moon comes ... the Crossing-Feast, which the Hebrews in their native tongue call Pascha'.[17] The Old Vulgate translation of Exodus accepted what is common to these two interpretations in its gloss on 12:11—'Est enim Phase (id est transitus) Domini'—'It is the Passover (i.e. the Passage) of the Lord.'

What is important is the increasingly significant place the Passover came to fill in the life of the Jewish people. It was first of all 'eucharistic'; a great thanksgiving for deliverance and redemption, which came to include a commemoration of the mighty deeds of the God of the Exodus in their history, some of which, like the deliverance from exile in Babylon, had already been seen by many of the prophets to fit into the same pattern. For example, in Isaiah 48:20–1, and in Jeremiah 23:7–8, the promise of return from exile is clearly and explicitly modelled on the Exodus narrative.

---

[15] For a clear account of exactly what seems to be 'history' and what seems to be 'myth', see Siegfried Herrman, *Israel in Egypt*, Studies in Biblical Theology, Second Series, 27 (SCM, London, 1973).

[16] *Ibid.*, pp. 54–6.

[17] Trans. Cantalamessa, *Easter*, p. 28.

Go out from Babylon, flee from Chaldea, declare this with a shout of joy, proclaim it, send it forth to the end of the earth; say, 'The Lord has redeemed his servant Jacob!' They did not thirst when he led them through the deserts; he made water flow for them from the rock; he split open the rock and the water gushed out.

The days are surely coming, says the Lord, when it shall no longer be said, 'As the Lord lives who brought the people of Israel up out of the land of Egypt', but 'As the Lord lives who brought out and led the offspring of the house of Israel out of the land of the north and out of all the lands where he had driven them.' Then they shall live in their own land.

The process is still operative today when, for example in the modern State of Israel, the 'holocaust', the return to Israel and the other events of recent history might also be recalled at the Passover meal. It was, secondly, a memorial of so intense and vivid a kind as to bring back the past in some sense right into the present.[18] So in the *Haggadah* the leader says at a certain point:

In every generation, each person should feel as though he himself had gone forth from Egypt, as it is written; 'And you shall explain to your child on that day, it is because of what the Lord did for me when I, *myself*, went forth from Egypt ...' Not only our ancestors alone did the Holy One redeem but *us* as well, along with them, as it is written: 'And he freed *us* from Egypt so as to take us and give us the land which he had sworn to our fathers.'[19]

These first two characteristics of the Passover were admirably summarised by Rabbi Albert Friedlander in an article in *The Times*:

Ritual is frozen theology which only comes to life when actual devotion and personal commitment by the worshipper turn the text and ceremony into a personal experience. 'I was brought out of Egypt', says the Jew on the first day; and many of us who came out of the much darker Egypt that was Nazi Germany

---

[18] So in the 1971 Windsor Agreement on the Eucharist of the Anglo-Roman Catholic International Commission it could be said: 'The notion of *memorial* as understood in the Passover celebration at the time of Christ—i.e. the making effective in the present of an event in the past—has opened the way to a clearer understanding of the relationship between Christ's sacrifice and the Eucharist.' Anglican-Roman Catholic International Commission, *The Final Report* (CTS, SPCK, London, 1982), p. 14.

[19] *A Passover Haggadah*, pp. 56 and 57, quoting Exodus 13:8 and Deuteronomy 6:23

say this with the deepest conviction and the most profound gratitude.[20]

For this reason, the introduction to the Prayer over the Gifts in the Maundy Thursday evening Eucharist in the Church of England's *Common Worship: Times and Seasons* deliberately echoes the Haggadah:[21]

> *At the eucharist we are with our crucified and risen Lord.*
> *We know that it was not only our ancestors,*
> *but we who were redeemed*
> *and brought forth from bondage to freedom,*
> *from mourning to feasting.*
> *We know that as he was with them in the upper room*
> *so our Lord is here with us now.*
> *Until the kingdom of God comes*
> *let us celebrate this feast.*

The Exodus was, thirdly, intensely eschatological, since the Jews could not give thanks as they looked backward into their history without looking forward in prayerful longing and strong hope to a greater, more perfect and final act of liberation and redemption. Certainly, in the time of Jesus there was always considerable excitement and unrest among the Jews at this season, so strong was the expectation of the Messiah's coming on Passover night. The Roman Procurator had to take special security precautions and make a point of always being in Jerusalem for the Feast. In the *Haggadah* today, the eschatological note is strong, particularly as the meal draws to a close. The Cup of Elijah, which is set in the middle of the table, is filled with wine; the door is opened and the whole company rises, for, according to tradition, Elijah will come to announce and usher in the presence of the Messiah on Passover night. Shortly after comes the closing proclamation, which brings the formal part of the meal to its conclusion.

> LEADER: *The Seder Service now concludes:*
> *Its rites observed in full,*
> *Its purposes revealed.*
> GROUP: *This privilege we share will ever be renewed*
> *Until God's plan is known in full,*
> *His highest blessing sealed.*

---

[20] Albert Friedlander, 'Expressions of Joy and Gratitude', *The Times* (9 April 1980), p. 10.
[21] *Common Worship: Times and Seasons*, p. 300.

LEADER: *Peace!*
GROUP: *Peace for us! For everyone!*
LEADER: *For all people, this is our hope:*
GROUP: *Next year in Jerusalem!*
                Next year, may all be free![22]

It is easy to understand how even those Jews who have renounced or ceased to practise their religion can still be profoundly influenced by the Passover. So an agnostic Zionist can write:

> What admirable teaching value there is in this recital of the enslavement of our people in Egypt and in their deliverance. I know of no other remembrance of the past which I so entirely turned toward the future as this memorial of the exodus from Egypt. How profound is the instinct of liberty in the heart of a people, if it has been able since its springtime to create this work of genius and transmit it from generation to generation ... This creation (the Passover Liturgy) has played a role it is impossible to neglect in the destiny of all the fighters and martyrs for liberty who have been raised up from the people of Israel.[23]

In reading this testimony, it is difficult not to think of the role of the liturgy of Easter night in the Orthodox Church in the darkest days of Soviet Russia and of its power to sustain faith and renew hope in the most difficult circumstances.

The Christian Church must affirm with the greatest realism in its teaching and liturgy the positive value of all that led up to our redemption by Christ in the fullness of time. This involves giving full weight to the privileged witness of the Old Testament, for 'we worship what we know, for salvation is from the Jews' (John 4:22), but without ignoring the work of God in the rest of humanity. Maria Boulding, OSB, explained this wider perspective, which perhaps may reconcile the English to the pagan word 'Easter':

> Christ died and rose in the spring, fulfilling the hope of the Jewish Passover feast which directly and primarily commemorates the exodus from Egypt. But behind the Passover stood ancient spring rituals, the sacrifice of spring lambs to ensure the fertility of the flock and the offering of the first sheaf of corn. Outside the chosen people the myths of death and rebirth were very powerful: the memories of the king who had to be sacrificed for

---

[22]   *A Passover Haggadah*, p. 93.
[23]   Bert Katzenelson, quoted in 'Pâque juive et chrétienne aujourd'hui', *Verité* 25–6 (Paris, 1970), p. 5.

the people, and the resurrection of the spring god as vegetation and crops were reborn after the death of winter. They were all vindicated in Christ's Passover, those worshippers of Tamuz and Adonis and Osiris, the initiates of the mysteries that promised immortality, the Indo-Aryans who had rejoiced as Agni, their fire-god, sprang from the soft wood, and all those who through the ages had projected their hopes 'into gods of unbearable beauty that broke the hearts of men'. They are with us still, hiding in the shadows as we celebrate Easter night with the new fire and the water, the bread and the wine, because no fragment of truth, no gleam of beauty, no act of heroism or kindness or prayer can finally be lost.[24]

---

[24] Maria Boulding, *Marked for Life: Prayer in the Easter Christ* (SPCK, London, 1979), pp. 72–3. She quotes G. K. Chesterton, *The Ballad of the White Horse*, book 2.

III

The Passover of Christ

The basic theme of the Passover is dynamic, it is that of a 'movement from degradation to glory'.[1] It is a journey towards God, towards his Kingdom and the fulness of union with him; a movement that involves a pattern of deliverance from slavery through the shedding of blood; a movement that seems to end prematurely in the deep waters of destruction and death but which in God's mercy continues on through these waters to the Promised Land. This was understood by Philo, writing for the Jewish community in first-century Alexandria: 'This is the real meaning of the Pascha of the soul: the crossing over from every passion and all the realm of sense ... to the realm of mind and of God.'[2] The Mosaic Exodus was both a real act of deliverance by God of his own chosen people and also a type, figure and prophecy of the central event in the history of salvation. This typological aspect is that which is taken up in the New Testament and in the liturgy to explain how the death and resurrection of Jesus Christ can be seen as his 'Passage' (*transitus*) to the Father and the fulfilment of the Old Testament Passover. 'The sacrificial death of Christ was seen as the realisation of all the expectations and foreshadowings contained in the ancient *Pesach*.'[3]

To understand this, it is essential to look carefully at the Gospels, beginning with the sayings attributed by their writers to the Lord himself. Most of the relevant passages are concentrated in the last days of Holy Week and more particularly in the sayings at the Last Supper, but there are a few sayings of an earlier period that relate directly to the *transitus* theme. In the predictions of his coming

---

[1]   *A Passover Haggadah*, p. 6, from the Preface by Rabbi Herbert Bronstein.
[2]   Trans. Cantalamessa, *Easter*, p. 28.
[3]   *Ibid.*, p. 6.

passion, death and resurrection Christ, on at least one occasion, makes special refence to Jerusalem (Luke 18:31–3):

> See, we are going up to Jerusalem, and everything that is written about the Son of Man by the prophets will be accomplished. For he will be handed over to the Gentiles; and he will be mocked and insulted and spat upon. After they have flogged him, they will kill him, and on the third day he will rise again.

The explicit mention of Jerusalem is particularly significant in Luke, for whom the city plays a crucial role as the *locus* of God's action. It is found also in the parallel passage in Matthew (20:18–19) and in one of the Markan references (10.33), but it is Luke alone who records a further saying (13:33):

> Yet today, tomorrow, and the next day I must be on my way, because it is impossible for a prophet to be killed away from Jerusalem.

Jesus was making this journey to a particular place for a particular occasion—to celebrate the Passover in the holy city to which every devout Jew (until the destruction of the Temple and the termination of the Temple sacrifices in 70 CE) was expected to come for this festival.

Another important saying is found in Mark immediately after the prediction of death a resurrection in Jerusalem: James and John, the sons of Zebedee, ask to sit at the right hand and the left hand of Jesus in his glory, and he replies (10:35–40):

> You do not know what you are asking. Are you able to drink the cup that I drink, or be baptised with the baptism that I am baptised with?' They replied, 'We are able.' Then Jesus said to them, 'The cup that I drink you will drink; and with the baptism with which I am baptised, you will be baptised.

This needs to be understood alongside another saying recorded by Luke (12:49–50):

> I came to bring fire to the earth, and how I wish it were already kindled! I have a baptism with which to be baptised, and what stress I am under until it is completed!

When Christ speaks of his baptism in these texts, he is evidently not referring to his baptism by John the Baptist in the Jordan, for that is already behind him; he is speaking of his passion and death—and also of his resurrection. If the passage of the Red Sea can be seen as a type of Christian baptism (see above, p. 27); it might also be seen here as a type of our Lord's death and resurrection, a passage through the waters of death to the right hand of the Father.

According to Hebrew cosmology in the biblical period, humans lived in a 'three-decker universe' consisting of heaven, earth, and the parts 'under the earth', and this last level was equated with the element of water. The sea was regarded as God's primordial enemy (Job 7:12), which it was his triumph to contain, and the deep waters are seen as the dwelling place of monsters, Leviathan (Isaiah 27:1) and Rahab (Isaiah 51:9). Considered also as the abode of Satan and of Sheol, water is often used as a synonym of death or Sheol. This sign of water, however, is ambivalent; it can be both life-giving and death-dealing; it can bring salvation and destruction. The Old Testament is full of the imagery of the waters of death and of death by drowning, and this is particularly true of the Psalms (42:7, 69:1 and 124:4):

> Deep calls to deep at the thunder of your cataracts; all your waves and your billows have gone over me.

> Save me, O God, for the waters have come up to my neck.

> Then the flood would have swept us away, the torrent would have gone over us; then over us would have gone the raging waters.

It is also strikingly true of the Song of Jonah, a mosaic of Psalm-texts, which he prayed to the Lord his God from the belly of the great fish (Jonah 2:2–6):

> *I called to the Lord out of my distress,*
> *   and he answered me;*
> *out of the belly of Sheol I cried,*
> *   and you heard my voice.*
> *You cast me into the deep,*
> *   into the heart of the seas,*
> *   and the flood surrounded me;*
> *all your waves and your billows*
> *   passed over me.*
> *Then I said, 'I am driven away*
> *   from your sight;*
> *how shall I look again*
> *   upon your holy temple?'*
> *The waters closed in over me;*
> *   the deep surrounded me;*

weeds were wrapped around my head
at the roots of the mountains.
I went down to the land
whose bars closed upon me for ever;
yet you brought up my life from the Pit,
O Lord my God.

Matthew and Luke both record that Jesus rebuked his generation as an evil generation seeking for a sign, but 'the only sign it will be given is the sign of the prophet Jonah' (Matthew 12:39 and Luke 11:29). They differ, however in the interpretation of this sign which they attribute to Jesus himself. For Matthew (12:40) it is the claim that:

> For just as Jonah was for three days and three nights in the belly of the sea monster, so for three days and three nights the Son of Man will be in the heart of the earth.

but for Luke (11:30) it is the preaching of repentance:

> For just as Jonah became a sign to the people of Nineveh, so the Son of Man will be to this generation.

However, if in this instance, Luke chooses an interpretation of the sign of Jonah that does not connect it with the paschal mystery of Christ's death and resurrection, it cannot be said that he is insensible to the importance of the Passover theme. In his account of the Transfiguration, he records that Moses and Elijah 'appeared in glory and were speaking of his departure, which he was about to accomplish at Jerusalem' (Luke 9.31). The Greek word translated *departure* is in fact *exodos* and it is clear that Luke has used this word deliberately. Thus, one of the Bible's great recurrent images reaches its culmination and final transformation in the experience of Jesus. Abraham led an Exodus from Ur of the Chaldees, Moses led the Exodus of Israel from Egypt, there was the Exodus of the remnant from Babylon after the exile and Isaiah writes of the Exodus of the Suffering Servant by way of death from Israel's dream of national restoration. From the Transfiguration on Mount Tabor onwards, the Gospel narrative gains momentum and the final Exodus begins. Jesus, his face set towards Jerusalem, leads an uncomprehending and reluctant company of followers who are to be the new Israel carried with him through the waters of death, baptised with his baptism. So too when the risen Christ, talking to the two disciples on the road to Emmaus, exclaims (Luke 24:25–7):

'Oh, how foolish you are, and how slow of heart to believe all
that the prophets have declared! Was it not necessary that the
Messiah should suffer these things and then enter into his glory?'
Then beginning with Moses and all the prophets, he interpreted
to them the things about himself in all the scriptures.

The Passover theme may not be the only one referred to here, but
it is clearly one theme among them and one of the most prominent.

The next set of relevant texts cluster around the Last Supper narratives where all three of the Synoptists refer to it as the Passover
meal. That this was in fact the case has been argued persuasively
and with an impressive accumulation of evidence by Joachim Jeremias.[4] But Jeremias has not silenced all doubters.[5] Thomas Talley,
for instance, points out that

> while it has been easy at times past to dismiss this Johannine
> chronology (i.e. that the crucifixion occurred on 14 Nisan at
> the time of the slaying of the lambs for the Passover feast) as
> conscious theologising of little historical merit, more recent
> exegetical opinion has been less inclined to reject the historicity
> of the Johannine chronology.[6]

There is much to be said on either side of this argument:[7] suffice it to
say that the Latin Church, in using unleavened bread for the Eucharist, sided with the Synoptic chronology while the Greek Church,
in using leavened bread, sided with the Johannine. This would
seem to indicate that the argument has little or no importance in
interpreting the Last Supper and the Eucharist which developed
from it. In fact, as Louis Bouyer has explained, the paschal context
of the cross and Eucharist are not dependent upon the paschal
character which may or may not be attributed to the Supper.

> In the first place, the Passover setting is no less relevant to the
> Last Supper whether it preceded Passover (the immolation of
> the lambs coinciding in time with the death of the Saviour in
> this case) or was actually the Passover meal. But—and this is of

---

4 J. Jeremias, SJ, *The Eucharistic Words of Jesus*, trans. Norman Perrin (SCM,
   London, 1966).
5 Cf. C. H. Dodd, *Historical Tradition in the Fourth Gospel* (Cambridge University
   Press, Cambridge, 1963) and A. M. Hunter, *According to John* (SCM, London,
   1968).
6 Talley, *Origins of the Liturgical Year*, pp. 3 and 4.
7 See B. Pitre, *Jesus and the Last Supper* (Eerdmans, Grand Rapids, 2015), ch. 4
   and p. 373.

special importance — the paschal references were present not only in the prayers of this one night but in all meal prayers. And in fact, whether the Supper was this special meal or another, there is no doubt that Jesus did not connect the eucharistic institution of the new covenant to any of the details that are proper to the Passover meal alone. The connection is solely with what the Passover meal had in common with every other meal: that is, the breaking of bread in the beginning and the rite of thanksgiving over the cup of wine mixed with water at the end. And, we may add, this is what made it possible for the Christian eucharist to be celebrated without any problem as often as one might wish and not only once a year.[8]

So, there is firm ground to be found in asserting the paschal character of the Last Supper, whether or not it was actually the paschal meal, and of giving a paschal reference to the Words of Institution. The bread is designated by Christ as his body and it is the body of one who offers himself for his people, of one who is himself the paschal lamb. The Lamb is slain: the blood is already separated from the body and the cup is designated by Christ as his blood 'poured out for many' (Mark 14:24). Moreover, there is reference to the covenant in the words over the cup recorded by St Paul and the Synoptists. This reference is also undoubtedly sacrificial, but its allusion is to a later episode in the Exodus narrative, to the sacrifice which ratified the covenant between God and Israel at the foot of Mount Sinai (Exodus 24:3–8). Then there is the command, recorded only by St Paul but in what is in fact the earliest of the New Testament texts on the Last Supper, 'Do this in remembrance of me' (1 Corinthians 11:25). If the Last Supper was the Passover meal, then clearly the word 'remembrance' has precisely the meaning it had for Passover: 'This day must be commemorated by you, and you must keep it as a feast in Yahweh's honour. You must keep it as a feast-day for all generations; this is a decree for all time.' But the character of the Eucharist as the Christian paschal memorial does not depend upon the Synoptic dating; it is not clear in any case that St Paul adopted it.[9] The word 'remembrance' (in Hebrew, *zikkaron*; in Greek, *anamnesis*) — sometimes rendered 'memorial' — is a strong, active word here, meaning the making real in the present of a saving event

8   L. Bouyer, *Eucharist (Theology and Spirituality of the Eucharistic Prayer)*, trans. C. H. Quinn (University of Notre Dame Press, Indiana, 1968), p. 99.
9   Cf. Talley, *Origins of the Liturgical Year*, p. 4.

in the past. The word has this same strong sense in other Jewish rabbinical and liturgical texts. As Louis Bouyer has argued, 'it in no way means a subjective, human psychological act of returning to the past, but an objective reality destined to make some thing or some one perpetually present before God and for God himself'.[10]

In the Synoptic Gospels there is a further reference by Jesus to the Passover in the narratives of the Last Supper (Luke 22:14–18):

> When the hour came, he took his place at the table, and the apostles with him. He said to them, 'I have eagerly desired to eat this Passover with you before I suffer; for I tell you, I will not eat it until it is fulfilled in the kingdom of God.' Then he took a cup, and after giving thanks he said, 'Take this and divide it among yourselves; for I tell you that from now on I will not drink of the fruit of the vine until the kingdom of God comes.'

According to Matthew and Mark this saying came at the end of the meal, and in a slightly different form (Mark 14:25):

> Truly I tell you, I will never again drink of the fruit of the vine until that day when I drink it new in the kingdom of God.

According to the Lucan version—the most complex and difficult of the Synoptic narratives of the Last Supper—Jesus spoke explicitly about the fulfilment of the Passover in the coming of the kingdom. Moreover, in all three accounts the coming of the kingdom is seen in joyful terms of the messianic banquet—eating and drinking in joyful communion with the Lord and his Anointed. But whereas in Mark and Matthew the coming of the kingdom seems to be set in a distant eschatological future, Luke gives a rather different interpretation. It is his Gospel which emphasises the meals which the risen Christ took with his disciples and which gives to them a eucharistic significance (Luke 24:28–32, 41–3; Acts 1:4, 10:41); his purpose seems to be to present the death and resurrection of Christ as in fact inaugurating the kingdom and fulfilling the Passover, and the Eucharist as the sign of the presence of the kingdom within the Church.

---

10 Bouyer, *Eucharist*, pp. 103–4. Bouyer's interpretation of anamnesis in this context represents an impressive consensus of scholars from very different traditions and is reflected in a number of recent ecumenical texts. It is, however, contested by some scholars in the Evangelical tradition, for example by R. T. Beckwith in *The Study of Liturgy*, ed. C. Jones, G. Wainwright and E. Yarnold (SPCK, London, 1992), p. 49.

In the Fourth Gospel—in striking contradiction to the other three—the chronology of the passion narrative is different. As noted already, according to John the Last Supper was held on the night before the Passover and Jesus died at the very hour when the paschal lambs were being ritually slaughtered for that Feast. Significantly, John notes at this point that, 'these things occurred so that the scripture might be fulfilled, 'None of his bones shall be broken' (John 19:36). The quotation comes from the regulations for the serving and eating of the paschal lamb in Exodus 12:46 and Numbers 9:12. If John's dating is correct, this is a rare and significant instance of his narrative presenting historical facts more accurately than the Synoptic authors. If, however, the chronology established by St Mark is correct then John is here allowing his theological purposes to dictate the timing of events and emphasise that Jesus died as the true Passover lamb. Moreover, it is in the Fourth Gospel that we are given sayings of Christ about his death and resurrection that express most clearly the idea of a passage (*transitus*) to the Father. Time and time again he links together the Passion and Resurrection in one 'Hour' of his destiny: 'For this reason the Father loves me, because I lay down my life in order to take it up again' (John 10:17). Later at the Last Supper, 'Jesus knew that his hour had come to depart from this world and go to the Father. Having loved his own who were in the world, he loved them to the end' (John 13:1). He repeatedly warned his disciples, 'I am going to the Father ... I am leaving the world and am going to the Father' (John 14:28; 16:28); and that in the final high-priestly prayer before setting out for Gethsemane he prayed, 'Father, the hour has come; glorify your Son so that the Son may glorify you ... now I am coming to you' (John 17:1; 13). Clearly, for John, Jesus was not so much going *to* his death as *by way* of it to his Father.

Some scholars have detected a subtle paschal background to the whole of John's Gospel and observed that it unfolds against the backcloth of the Exodus, that exemplar of the paschal mystery:

> The Word has set up his tabernacle among us (1:14) just as God encamped among the Jews; Christ must be lifted up like the serpent (3:14); he has come down from heaven like manna and will become our food (6:48ff); his followers will be refreshed by him as by the rock in the desert (7:37); they will follow him as the Israelites followed the pillar of fire (8:12). Christ is the paschal lamb (19:36). If this mention of the Exodus is to remind

us of a very definite plan, then clearly St John saw the paschal mystery of the Exodus as being repeated and perfected in the Word made flesh. He signposts his account by indicating the paschs that occurred during our Lord's public life (2:13,23; 6:4; 11:55; 12:1; 13:1). He does this so often that it imparts to the story a definite sense of direction.[11]

In fact, the whole narrative of the Fourth Gospel can be seen as inserted between two proclamations of Christ as the Lamb of God and thereby defined—in virtue of the principle of 'semitic inclusion'—as a 'Paschal Gospel'. At the very beginning of the narrative John the Baptist introduces Jesus to his audience and to the reader with the words, 'here is the Lamb of God who takes away the sin of the world!' (John 1:29); and at the climax of the account of Christ's 'exaltation' we find a clear reference to the Paschal Lamb: 'none of his bones shall be broken' (John 19:36). Here, in one term—'Lamb of God', the Evangelist gathers together significant allusions from a diversity of backgrounds but clearly focusing on the eucharistic practice of the Christian community for which he wrote.[12]

Putting aside the Gospels, the rest of the New Testament has a number of references to the image of the lamb, many of them not necessarily strictly paschal in character but drawn from the whole wealth of Old Testament ovine material. A passage like 1 Peter 1:18–19, for example: 'You know that you were ransomed from the futile ways inherited from your ancestors, not with perishable things like silver or gold, but with the precious blood of Christ, like that of a lamb without defect or blemish' or the many references to the Lamb in the revelation to John (in chapters, 5, 6, 7, 12, 13, 14, 15, 19, 21 and 22) can be read as paschal but this is but one element among many. There is however one passage from St Paul's letters where the reference is explicit and unambiguous. 'Your boasting is not a good thing. Do you not know that a little yeast leavens the whole batch of dough? Clean out the old yeast so that you may be a new batch, as you really are unleavened. For our paschal lamb, Christ, has been sacrificed. Therefore, let us celebrate the festival, not with the old yeast, the yeast of malice and evil, but

[11] F.-X. Durrwell, CSsR, *The Resurrection* (Sheed and Ward, London, 1960), pp. 17–18.
[12] J. Marsh, *The Gospel of St John*, Pelican New Testament Commentaries (Penguin, London, 1968), pp. 123–4. C. K. Barrett, *The Gospel according to John* (SPCK, London, 2nd edn, 1978), p. 176.

with the unleavened bread of sincerity and truth' (1 Corinthians 5:6–8). Christ both fulfils the whole Passover story, transforming its meaning and significance for the Christian, and is also in his own person the paschal lamb.

> A close examination of the words of institution reveals that Jesus not only saw his imminent death as a redemptive sacrifice, but by means of the words of institution, he revealed himself as the eschatological Passover lamb of the eschatological exodus. Moreover, by means of his command to repeat his actions, he deliberately instituted a new Passover sacrifice and thus a new cultic act.[13]

So, in the *Exsultet* in the Easter Vigil liturgy, the deacon can proclaim, 'For this is the Passover feast, when Christ, the true Lamb of God, is slain whose blood consecrates the homes of all the faithful'.[14]

The Easter liturgy, in which the *Exsultet* finds its context, is described fully in Chapter XIII but one of its most powerful symbols, the Paschal Candle, is relevant here as it bears eloquent witness to the Passover of Christ. It is, of course, a symbol of Christ himself, crucified and risen. Lighted from a new fire which is traditionally kindled from striking a flint, this great candle is borne by the deacon into the empty and darkened church, its new light piercing the darkness alone before being shared among ministers and people as they process into the building. This solemn entry into the church building looks back to the Exodus narrative, for it re-enacts the pilgrim procession of the Israelites from the land of bondage through the Red Sea to the promised land, led by the pillar of cloud and fire. When the deacon sings the candle's praises in the *Exsultet* he makes this clear: 'This is the night when you first saved our ancestors, freeing Israel from her slavery and leading her safely through the sea.' The Roman rite adds, 'This is the night that with a pillar of fire banished the darkness of sin'. As the pillar of cloud and of fire was for the Israelites a sign of the glory and the presence of Yahweh, so for us Christ is *the* Sign, *the* Sacrament of God's presence and of God's glory. 'The Word became flesh and lived among us, and we have seen his glory, the glory as of a father's only son, full of grace and truth' John 1:14). He is the 'the light of the world', 'the true light, which enlightens everyone' (John 8:12; 1:9).

---

[13] Pitre, *Jesus and the Last Supper*, pp. 442–3, expounds this with great clarity.
[14] *Common Worship: Times and Seasons*, p. 337.

So also, the symbol of light passed to all from the Paschal Candle speaks of both the Resurrection itself (as in the collect of the Easter Vigil Mass in the Roman rite: 'O God, who make this most sacred night radiant with the glory of the Lord's Resurrection'), and also of the sacramental communication of the power of the Resurrection in baptism. Baptism is indeed an act of *illumination*, and the Greek word *photismos* is used to describe baptism from the time of Justin Martyr in the second century. The author of the Letter to the Hebrews addresses the baptised as those who 'have once been enlightened' (Hebrews 6:4) and in Ephesians there is a fragment of one of the earliest of all Christian hymns, almost certainly a baptismal hymn: 'Sleeper, awake! Rise from the dead, and Christ will shine on you' (Ephesians 5:14). Appropriately, when baptisms take place at the Easter Vigil, as ideally they should, then it only *after* they have been baptised that the neophytes receive their own candles lit from the Paschal Candle. After Pentecost the Paschal Candle should be moved to a place near the font and used to light the baptismal candles throughout the rest of the year.[15]

The Fourth Gospel sees the Son of God as shining forth as the light of the world, guiding his people on their pilgrimage (John 8:12); it sees how he feeds and sustains them with heavenly manna (John 6:28–58) and with living water (John 4:13–14 and 7:37–9); and it sees Jesus as a new and greater Moses, fulfilling the Law (John 1:17) — also a controlling theme in Matthew's Gospel. He is a new and great Joshua, effecting entrance to the promised land and place of rest, for the name Jesus is the Greek form of the Hebrew *Jehoshua* or *Joshua*, meaning 'Yahweh saves' (cf. Hebrews 4:8). For all this, it remains difficult to grasp the ultimate element in this paschal narrative, the assumption by Jesus of the role of the paschal lamb, suffering innocently and vicariously for the redemption of the world. Why did he have to suffer in this way and why did God require it of him?

If the Incarnate Son of God had come into a world free from sin, he could indeed have made his Passage, his *transitus*, back to the right hand of his Father without the cross and without the tomb. As the Eternal Son and Word he had eternally offered the perfect oblation of love and homage to the Father, and his incarnation alone would have sufficed to join humanity to himself and draw

[15]   *The Roman Missal*, p. 496.

the whole created order into a full association with his perfect sacrifice of praise. Christ himself was without sin (Hebrews 4:15; 1 Peter 2:22); for himself he had no need to die. He came, however, into a world that had torn itself away from God by the violence of sin; he did not share the sin but he came to bear the burden of it as the Lamb of God that carries the sins of the world (1 John 29), and his acceptance of baptism at the hands of John the Baptist was an act of identification with sinful humanity in the grip of the powers of darkness. Christ came into the world in order to return to the Father, but not to return empty handed. He came to bring ransomed and liberated humanity with him (cf. Mark 10:45). This involved a fierce and bitter warfare, because the powers of darkness were not going to surrender their hold on humankind without a struggle (Colossians 2:14–15; Hebrews 2:14–15).

Significantly in this respect, the liturgy of Holy Week and Easter frequently employs the language of combat. The Easter Sequence, *Victimae Paschali*, still to be found in the Extraordinary Form of the Roman Rite and in the Ordinariate Missal, was written by Wipo in the eleventh century and well illustrates this point:

> *Death and life have contended in that combat stupendous:*
> *The Prince of life, who died, reigns immortal.*[16]

Familiar also are the two magnificent hymns by Venatius Fortunatus, Bishop of Poitiers in the sixth century; *Vexilla Regis prodeunt*,[17] used as the Office Hymn at Vespers throughout Holy Week in the Roman Breviary and *Common Worship: Daily Prayer*, and *Pange lingua gloriosi*,[18] sung at the Office of Readings during Holy Week and, most movingly, during the Veneration of the Cross on Good Friday:

Pange, lingua, gloriosi	*Sing, my tongue, the glorious battle,*
proelium certaminis,	*Sing the ending of the fray,*
et super Crucis trophaeo	*O'er the Cross, the victor's trophy,*
dic triumphum nobilem	*Sound the loud, triumphant lay:*
qualiter Redemptor orbis	*Tell how Christ, the world's Redeemer,*
immolatus vicerit.	*As a Victim won the day.*

Christ's warfare, however, was the warfare of love; he allowed all the onslaughts of the powers of hatred and darkness to be con-

---

[16] *Divine Worship, The Missal*, p. 430. *New English Hymnal*, no. 519.
[17] *New English Hymnal*, no. 79.
[18] *New English Hymnal*, no. 78.

centrated upon himself; he accepted them without resistance and without retaliation and still went on loving those who tortured and reviled him. When evil had done its very worst he still held fast, wavering not for a moment in his faithful self-oblation to the Father and in his love for us: and when he died evil could do no more to break the power of his conquering and reconciling love. 'It is finished' (John 19:30), that is to say 'it has been accomplished.'

There is a strain in Christianity which tries to understand the mystery of the Atonement by seeing God the Father as requiring to be appeased by innocent blood before he can write off humanity's debt and offer forgiveness. Others will reject any theology which can talk of the Cross as 'the lightning rod of grace that short-circuits God's wrath to Christ'.[19] Nevertheless, in the conditions of this world of sin the Cross was necessary for our redemption. In the Cross, God's wrath is not seen so much as his infinite love. What might be interpreted as God's wrath is his valuation and condemnation of human sin, which is so hideous that it crucifies the Son of God. God cannot shrug off human sin as a matter of little or no importance: 'Forgiveness may be free, but it is not cheap.'[20]

The Cross must never be separated from the Resurrection and Christ's death and resurrection must never be separated from the re-creation of humanity. It was necessary for there to be a death in order that there might be a new beginning, in order to inaugurate a new creation in the human race. In the Incarnation, Jesus became so completely one with the race of Adam that what he wished to gain for us he first gained for himself. In other words, the redemption of human nature was a drama which unfolded first in Christ. So, Christ's death was a necessary consequence of his acceptance of our fallen condition in his Incarnation. Christ had to die because the Old Adam had to die. Without death there could be no resurrection, no glorification, no New Adam of the Risen Christ and his Body the Church. Christ died not in order to exempt us from dying but in order that we might die effectively and really in his death, and so rise effectively and really in his Resurrection (1 Peter 1:3–5):

> Blessed be the God and Father of our Lord Jesus Christ! By his great mercy he has given us a new birth into a living hope through the resurrection of Jesus Christ from the dead, and into

19 Attributed to A. W. Tozer, 1897–1963.
20 Fr Hugh, SSF, *No Escape from Love* (Faith Press, London, 1959), p. 46.

an inheritance that is imperishable, undefiled, and unfading, kept in heaven for you, who are being protected by the power of God through faith for a salvation ready to be revealed in the last time.

❧ IV ❧

The Passover of Christians

It was because of God's love for humankind that Christ came into the world. From all eternity the love of God the Father has been poured out in the Holy Spirit upon the Son and returned by the Son in the Spirit to the Father. Christ took flesh in order that humankind might be incorporated into his humanity and thus be carried up to the Father in the movement of his love and the power of the Spirit. It is Christ 'by whom, and with whom, and in whom'[1] humankind is enabled to participate in the eternal dynamic of self-giving love which is the Holy Trinity. He came therefore into this world solely in order that he might return to the Father, but return bringing redeemed humanity with him. Because he came into a world of sin to unite to himself a humanity in the grip of sin, his return could be no peaceful journey, but rather a passover of mortal conflict with the powers of darkness.

This passover struggle, brought to a conclusion by our Lord in his own person (for he was utterly alone as far as any human support was concerned), was the unique and final Passover in the sense that the work of redemption effected by it has a final, once-for-all, finished quality. It is unrepeatable, and yet it is constantly at work to effect humanity's own passover so that humankind may follow the Lord through his passion and death to rise with him and sit with him and reign with him. Yet this passover of Christians is in no sense independent or distinct from Christ's passover; it is part and parcel of it. The author of the Letter to the Ephesians can speak of the action of God in raising Christ from the dead and his action in raising up humankind to newness of life as one single movement, as one single action.

---

[1] From the concluding doxology to Eucharistic Prayers B, C, F and G in *Common Worship: Services and Prayers for the Church of England*.

> But God, who is rich in mercy, out of the great love with which he loved us even when we were dead through our trespasses, made us alive together with Christ—by grace you have been saved—and raised us up with him and seated us with him in the heavenly places in Christ Jesus. (Ephesians 2:4–6).

St Paul's teaching on baptism in the Letter to the Romans is key to a deeper understanding of this identification (6:3–11):

> Do you not know that all of us who have been baptised into his death? Therefore we have been buried with him by baptism into death, so that, just as Christ was raise from the dead by the glory of the Father, so we too might walk in newness of life. For if we have been united with him in a death like his, we will certainly be united with him in a resurrection like his. We know that our old self was crucified with him so that the body of sin might be destroyed, and we might no longer be enslaved to sin. For whoever has died is freed from sin. But if we have died with Christ, we believe that we will also live with him. We know that Christ, being raise from the dead, will never die again; death no longer has dominion over him. The death he died, he died to sin, once for all; but the life he lives, he lives to God. So you also must consider yourselves dead to sin and alive to God in Christ Jesus.

In this passage is articulated more clearly than anywhere else in the New Testament, the identification of the Christian with Christ precisely in the act of his passover—his *transitus*—by way of the Cross to the glory of the Resurrection. It is on the paschal character of Christian baptism that this view of the Christian life as passover is founded.

Whatever variations there may have been in early baptismal practice, it is clear that in this passage St Paul's language is inspired by the symbolism of immersion. The etymological meaning of 'baptise' is 'dip', hence the sinner's immersion in water can be seen as symbolic death and burial. While elsewhere, notably in 1 Corinthians 6:11 and Titus 3:5, Paul or his pseudonymous disciple speaks of baptism in terms of a cleansing bath, here the function of water is not so much to wash as to drown. Paradoxically, baptism is birth by drowning and thus recalls the story of Noah and the Flood, the experience of the Israelites at the Red Sea, and the Exodus which the Lord had to accomplish at Jerusalem and which he spoke of as his baptism (Luke 12:50). So it is that the First Letter of Peter can speak of the ark of Noah as an antitype of baptism (1 Peter 3:20–1)

and St Paul can speak thus of the Israelites, 'and all were baptised
into Moses in the cloud and in the sea' (1 Corinthians 10:2). The
rite for the Public Baptism of Infants in the 1662 *Book of Common
Prayer* sets the scene with a prayer containing these words:

> Almighty and everlasting God, who of thy great mercy didst
> save Noah and his family in the ark from perishing by water; and
> also didst safely lead the children of Israel thy people through
> the Red Sea, figuring thereby thy holy Baptism.

In the Roman Rite of Baptism, the prayer for the blessing of baptismal water is rich in typological allusion:

> O God, whose Spirit in the first moments of the World's creation
> hovered over the waters, so that the very substance of water
> would even then take to itself the power to sanctify; O God, who
> by the outpouring of the flood foreshadowed regeneration, so
> that from the mystery of one and the same element of water
> would come and end to vice and a beginning of virtue; O God,
> who caused the children of Abraham to pass dry-shod through
> the Red Sea, so that the chosen people, set free from. Slavery to
> Pharoah, would prefigure the people of the baptised; O God,
> whose Son, baptised by John in the waters of the Jordan, was
> anointed by the Holy Spirit, and, as he hung upon the Cross,
> gave forth water from his side along with blood ...[2]

The *Common Worship* baptism service provides a number of seasonal prayers over the baptismal water and a standard form which
shows a debt to the Roman prayer and introduces explicitly the
Pauline reference from Romans 6:

> Over water the Holy Spirit moved in the beginning of creation.
> Through water you led the children of Israel from slavery in
> Egypt to freedom in the Promised Land. In water your Son Jesus
> received the baptism of John and was anointed by the Holy Spirit
> as the Messiah, the Christ, to lead us from the death of sin to
> newness of life. We thank you, Father, for the water of baptism.
> In it we are buried with Christ in his death. By it we share in
> his resurrection. Through it we are reborn by the Holy Spirit.[3]

The link between baptism and the death and resurrection of the
Lord was made strikingly explicit in the developed ceremonial of
the early Church. The rites of baptism were truly awe-inspiring,

[2]   Cf. *The Roman Missal*, p. 411.
[3]   *Common Worship: Christian Initiation*, p. 69.

and the operative symbolism had an immediacy and an impact which is hard to recapture today. The candidates descended to the font in semi-darkness, stripped off all their clothes and were anointed all over with oil to prepare them, like athletes, for their struggle with the Devil. Facing west to renounce the Devil and all his works, they were immersed three times in the water if the font was deep enough, or had water poured three times over their heads. They then ascended from the font towards the east, were anointed on the forehead (sealed with the Holy Spirit), clothed in white robes and given lighted candles. Thus dressed and carrying their candles, they entered the church to participate for the first time in the whole of the Eucharist and to receive Holy Communion. After receiving from the chalice of wine, they partook of two other cups, a chalice of water to signify the cleansing of the inner man, and a chalice of milk and honey mixed to celebrate their entry into the 'Promised Land'. Moreover, all this took place, where possible, in the night of Easter: the catechumens celebrated their own 'death and resurrection' in the celebration of Christ's death and resurrection.

The distinctively Pauline death–resurrection imagery of baptism is not concerned with a merely symbolic act; he speaks of the Christian's real identification with the death and resurrection of the Lord. Christ's death marked the moment of his victory over the powers of evil; death could no longer have any dominion over him, for he was at this moment freed from all the limitations and humiliations imposed upon him by his identification of himself with humanity in its fallen state. Death was for him the gateway to his glorification. So too the identification of the baptised with the death of Christ is not an identification with the physical act of disintegration but with the act in which the Lord renounce and triumphed over the old Adam, liberating the human race from the grip of the powers of sin and death. As this identification with Christ's death is not a literal anticipation of the moment of physical death, neither is identification with his resurrection a literal anticipation of the moment of bodily resurrection, but an identification with his resurrection as the creative act by which God renewed the human race in exalting and glorifying his Son and in pouring out his Holy Spirit. The baptism of Christ by John the Baptist was undoubtedly the determining historical influence upon Christian baptism and the Gospel accounts of Christ's baptism were probably shaped, or at least influenced, by the liturgical traditions of the earliest Christian congregations. From the account in Mark 1:9–11 and its parallels in Matthew and Luke it seems clear that Christ's baptism was associated with divine sonship. It would thus seem reasonable to conclude that for St Paul men and women could be spoken of as 'becoming children of God' in baptism. If in preaching St Paul can quote Psalm 2: 'You are my Son, today I have begotten you' as a reference to the Resurrection (Acts 13:33), so there is a sense that Christians can apply it to themselves as a reference to their baptism.

However, if individuals confine themselves to seeing their own Passover in terms of baptism alone sense can never be made of it. Baptism is but a part, albeit the most important part, of a unified movement of Christian Initiation which, as the description of early baptismal ceremonies given above has already hinted, also includes Confirmation and First Communion. The General Introduction to the revised rites of Christian Initiation in the Roman Ritual expresses it thus:

> Through the sacraments of Christian initiation men and women are freed from the power of darkness. With Christ they die, are buried and rise again. They receive the Spirit of adoption which makes them God's sons and daughters and, with the entire people of God, they celebrate the memorial of the Lord's death and resurrection.[4]

The movement from darkness to light enacted in the baptistry is a real removal or change effected by God. St Paul teaches that God 'has rescued us from the power of darkness and transferred us into the kingdom of his beloved Son, in whom we have redemption, the forgiveness of sins' (Colossians 1:13–14). Every other aspect of baptismal grace—forgiveness, regeneration, the conferring of character—must be seen in the light of this movement in which the new Christian is so completely identified with Christ as to be into the body of his risen and glorified humanity, identified with him moreover in his own passage through darkness to light, in his death and resurrection. As personal experience demonstrates, it is not that baptism places one immediately into a state of perfection and easy security where one has no need to fight and no risk of falling,

---

[4] *The Rites of the Catholic Church: Christian Initiation* (Pueblo Publishing, New York, 1976), p. 3.

rather in baptism one is united with Christ so that in the victorious power and energy of his risen life one may be transformed and continually live out one's baptism by being conformed to him in his warfare against evil and in his death to sin.

When the neophytes emerged from the waters of the font they were anointed again and received the laying on of hands—a rite which in a later form and detached from its Easter context has become known as Confirmation. It is difficult to appreciate the paschal character of Confirmation when it is celebrated in isolation, detached from baptism, but when, as is now increasingly the case, the sacraments of initiation are linked together in a single rite there seems to be a progression from the strictly paschal character of baptism (incorporation into Christ's death, burial and resurrection) to the more pentecostal character of Confirmation (bestowal of the gifts of the Spirit). St Augustine saw it all as part and parcel of the same process, 'When you were exorcised, it was the grinding of you. When you were baptised, it was your moistening. When you received the fire of the Holy Spirit, it was the baking of you.'[5]

An entire chapter could be dedicated to teasing out the relationship of baptism to Confirmation and full participation in the Eucharist especially in the light of the Church of England's *Common Worship* journey model of Christian Initiation, its own distinctive take on the catechumenate process now frequently used in Roman Catholic parishes. Suffice it to say that way back in 1982, the Lima Report of the World Council of Churches expressed it thus:

> In God's work of salvation, the paschal mystery of Christ's death and resurrection is inseparably linked with the pentecostal gift of the Holy Spirit. Similarly, participation in Christ's death and resurrection is inseparably linked with the receiving of the Spirit. Baptism in its full meaning signifies and effects both.[6]

What St Luke sees as two distinct moments, Easter and Pentecost, the Fourth Gospel brings together as a single event—Easter Day. As will be investigated further in Chapter xiv, *Pascha* and Pentecost form a single unity.

---

5   Augustine, *Sermo* cclxxi (Patrologia Latina 38, col. 1245).
6   *Baptism, Eucharist and Ministry*, World Council of Churches, Faith and Order Paper no. 111 (Geneva, 1982), pp. 4–6, para. 14.

Baptised, sealed with the Spirit, robed in white, the new Christians entered from the baptistery into the church itself to participate in the Eucharist and to receive Holy Communion for the first time

> *The Lamb's high banquet we await*
> *In snow-white robes of royal state;*
> *And now, the Red Sea's channel past,*
> *To Christ, our Prince, we sing at last.*[7]

St John's Gospel records that while the dead Christ hung on the cross, 'one of the soldiers pierced his side with a spear, and at once blood and water came out' (John 19:34). This remarkable incident is Johannine material without parallel in the Synoptic accounts of the Passion.[8] As the strong following verse indicates, it must have had a very great significance for the Evangelist or his immediate redactors: 'He who saw this has testified so that you also may believe' (John 19:35). An allusion to the two sacraments of Baptism and Eucharist is so immediately apparent that many commentators have felt it necessary to devote much energy to the attempt to prove that such an interpretation is inadmissible.[9]

Nevertheless, patristic exegetes worked under no such inhibition and from Tertullian on there is a strong tradition of seeing the wound in Christ's side as the birthplace of the Church and the source of the efficacy of the sacraments.[10] St John Chrysostom makes the point with some force in his Homilies on St John's Gospel. Commenting on John 19:34, he observes:

> With this too an ineffable mystery was accomplished. For there came forth water and blood. Not without a purpose, or by chance, did these two founts come forth, but because by means of these two together the Church consisteth. And the initiated know it, being by water regenerate, and nourished by the Blood and the Flesh. Hence the Mysteries (sacraments) take their beginning; that when thou approachest to that aweful Cup, thou mayest so approach, as drinking from the very Side.[11]

[7] *New English Hymnal*, no. 101, *Ad cenam Agni providi*, seventh century, trans. J. M. Neale.
[8] Barrett, *Gospel according to John*, pp. 54–6.
[9] For a summary see R. E. Brown, *The Gospel according to John XIII–XXI* (Anchor Bible, Yale University Press, New Haven, 1966), pp. 944–56.
[10] Tertullian, *De Anima*, ch. xliii (Patrologia Latina 2, col. 721).
[11] John Chrysostom, *Homilies on St John*, no. 85, in Library of the Fathers, vol. 36 (J. Parker, Oxford, 1852).

Whether St John himself intended this construction to be put upon his words remains the subject of scholarly debate. Oscar Cullman, writing in 1978 on early Christian worship, maintained that this text represents a climax in the Gospel and contains the key to the understanding of its whole purpose; that of setting forth the connection between contemporary Christian worship and the historical life of Jesus.[12] John records that Jesus himself spoke of his body as a Temple (John 2:19–22) and, echoing Isaiah (44:3), cried out: 'Let anyone who is thirsty come to me, and let the one who believes in me drink. As the scripture has said, 'Out of the believer's heart shall flow rivers of living water' (John 7:37–8). In most artistic representations of Christ crucified, the wound inflicted by the soldier's lance is shown on the right-hand side of the body, even though a knowledge of basic anatomy would lead the artist to remember the heart is on the left. The Church's liturgical meditation on and transmission of Scripture has here influenced the development of iconography—as one would hope and expect it should—the underlying notion being the fulfilment of the prophecy of Ezekiel in the Passion of Christ (47:1–2, 9):

> He brought me back to the entrance of the temple; there, water was flowing from below the threshold of the temple towards the east (for the temple faced east); and the water was flowing down from below the south (*right*) end of the threshold of the temple, south of the altar. Then he brought me out by way of the north gate and led me round on the outside to the outer gate that faces towards the east; and the water was coming out on the south (*right*) side. Wherever the river goes, every living creature that swarms will live, and there will be very many fish, once these waters reach there. It will become fresh; and everything will live where the river goes.

The rich image is taken up again in Johannine literature, in Revelation 22:1–2, where the river of life is seen 'flowing from the throne of God and of the Lamb'. All this finds appropriate liturgical expression when the rite of sprinkling holy water is performed at the beginning of the Sunday Eucharist in Eastertide with the traditional chant of *Vidi aquam*, 'I beheld water issuing out from the temple, on the right hand side, alleluia: and all to whom the

[12] O. Cullman, *Early Christian Worship* (SCM, London, 1978), pp. 114–16.

water came were saved, and they shall say: Alleluia, alleluia.'[13]

The patristic exegesis of John 19:34 points to the truth that Baptism and Eucharist both unite the believer to the mystery of the Cross. Those who are united once for all to Christ in his death and resurrection by being grafted through baptism into his body the Church are kept in this union, and constantly renewed and strengthened in it, by participating in the Eucharist wherein he commanded his disciples to remember and encounter him, as the continuing people of God, until his return. The Eucharist no less that Baptism is a paschal sacrament, for as the new paschal meal of the Church, the new passover banquet, it is the sacrament of the unity of the Body of Christ with its glorified and ascended head, the memorial of the Cross and Resurrection, the sacrifice of praise. As a sacrifice it is in no sense independent of or additional to that of Calvary; it is identical with it, for as a memorial (*anamnesis*) of the historical event it exists to bring the believing community into vital contact with the once for all event of Christ's death and resurrection. And no less than Baptism and Confirmation is the Eucharist a pentecostal sacrament for it is the Holy Spirit 'who makes the crucified and risen Christ really present to us in the eucharistic meal' and 'who makes the historical words of Jesus present and alive'.[14]

The significance of what our Lord did and said over the bread and wine on the night before he suffered is that first of all he plainly declared his coming death to be a sacrifice, with his body being given and his blood poured out for the forgiveness of sins and for the inauguration of a new covenant—a radically new kind of relationship between God and humankind. By his words and actions, he not only declared his death to be a sacrifice; he also solemnly consecrated himself to that sacrifice, acting as both priest and victim. But our Lord went one step further, for he gave the bread and the cup to his disciples, commanding them to eat and drink. By this he was drawing his followers into the closest possible association with his sacrifice; for by continuing to 'do this' through the ages

---

[13]   *Divine Worship, The Missal*, p. 1044. The rite of sprinkling holy water was introduced into the liturgy early in the eighth century, and Bede (d. 735), commenting on the *Vidi aquam* text, observed that as the door of Solomon's Temple was on the right, so it was the right side of the Saviour which was to be opened by the spear-thrust: *In Libros Regum* (Patrologia Latina 91, col. 722) and *De Templo Salomonis* (Patrologia Latina 91, col. 753–4).

[14]   *Baptism, Eucharist and Ministry*, 'Eucharist', p. 13, para. 14.

they were not only communicating in the fruits of his oblation but in the very act of oblation itself.

In asking who it is that offers the eucharistic sacrifice a choice does not have to be made between saying either that it is Christ or that it is the Church: similarly in considering the question who or what is it that is offered in the eucharistic sacrifice a choice does not have to be made between Christ and his Church. The Eucharist is precisely the sacrament of unity, of the unity of Head and members in one Body; it is the sacrament of the whole Christ, *Totus Christus*.[15] In the Eucharist it is the whole Christ that offers and the whole Christ that is offered, for it is the means whereby the barriers of time and space are transcended and Christ's members in every place and in every generation 'enter into the movement of his self-offering'.[16] At every eucharistic celebration we give ourselves to be laid upon the altar in our gifts of bread and wine and to be offered in and with our gifts in sacrifice and thanksgiving to the Father; we give our lives for Christ to say over them, as over our gifts, 'This is my body ... This is my blood'; we give our lives to be broken, and shared, and given away. Both in consecration and in communion our lives are identified with the life of Christ and our offering of ourselves with Christ's offering of himself.

The Eucharist is thus the supreme link between Christ's sacrifice and the present life of the Church—between his *transitus* and our own. The Church has nothing of her own to offer but the offering of Christ made once for all upon the Cross and accepted and vindicated in the Resurrection, and so she only dares to offer herself in and through her Head and Bridegroom and his perfected and unspotted sacrifice. As the *Final Report* of the Anglican-Roman Catholic International Commission put it:

> On the one hand, the eucharistic gift springs out of the Paschal Mystery of Christ's death and resurrection, in which God's saving purpose has already been definitively realised. On the other hand, its purpose is to transmit the life of the crucified and risen Christ to his body, the Church, so that its members may be more fully united to Christ and to one another.[17]

[15] The phrase is St Augustine's: 'This is the whole Christ: Christ united with the Church.' *In Psalmum xc, Sermo* ii (Patrologia Latina 36, col. 1159).
[16] Anglican-Roman Catholic International Commission, *The Final Report*, Eucharistic Doctrine (1971), p. 14, para. 5.
[17] *Ibid.*, para. 6.

So then, a paschal character is given not only to baptism but to eucharistic worship and through that to the whole Christian life. Death too, for the Christian, has a paschal character—an insight which had a profound effect upon the revision of funeral rites in the Western Church. In 1960, before the Second Vatican Council, François-Xavier Durrwell wrote:

> Physical death consummates sacramental death; it completes our incorporation into Christ in his redemptive act. The summit, as it were, of man's carnal weakness becomes, in his acceptance of it, the supreme means of being caught up with the Saviour in his death and therefore in his triumph.[18]

Benedict XVI, speaking to the clergy of Rome in February 2013 shortly before his abdication, spoke of the importance of Conciliar teaching and declared that its essential message was 'the Paschal Mystery as the centre of what it is to be Christian and therefore of the Christian life, the Christian year, the Christian seasons'. Given this theological presupposition, it is not difficult to understand why *Sacrosanctum Concilium*, the Constitution on the Sacred Liturgy, declared that 'funeral rites should express more clearly the paschal character of Christian death'.[19] The rites that emerged dispensed with or made optional some of the more lugubrious texts inserted in the medieval period and reintroduced a note of paschal joy and hope. Nevertheless, there remain two theologies of death at work in the Roman Missal of 1971—the first, with an emphasis upon judgement, a place with the saints, rest, light and so on, comes from the Gelasian, Gregorian and later sacramentaries; the second, placing the emphasis on the Resurrection and entry into the Paschal Mystery, reflects the exhortation in *Sacrosanctum Concilium* noted above. As a matter of pastoral practice, it is possible when requested to select formularies which have the first theology exclusively and no paschal references. Visually too, there was a change; while black remains an optional colour, many opted for the now authorised purple or even white. To reinforce yet further the paschal nature of the funeral service it was recommended that the Paschal Candle should be lit and placed at the head of the coffin.

The same spirit has been at work in Anglican revisions since the late 1960s. In the United States, the 1979 *Book of Common Prayer* of

---

[18] Durrwell, *The Resurrection*, p. 347
[19] Flannery, *Vatican Council II*, ch. III, p. 24, para. 81.

the Episcopal Church led the way, with a rubric suggesting that the lighted Paschal Candle should be carried before the coffin as it was borne into the church. A note also declares that 'the liturgy for the dead is an Easter liturgy. It finds all its meaning in the Resurrection. Because Jesus was raised from the dead, we, too, shall be raised. The liturgy, therefore, is characterised by joy.'[20] In the Church of England in 1986, *Lent, Holy Week, Easter* allowed for the Paschal Candle, moved to a place near the font after Pentecost and used at baptisms throughout the year, to be used also at funerals.[21] With the publication of *Common Worship: Pastoral Services* in 2000 it might have been expected that this provision would be made more explicit but a 'let the reader understand' position is taken with the note, '*A candle* may stand beside the coffin and may be carried in front of the coffin when it is brought into the church' (italics mine).[22] An understanding of this cryptic note had to wait until the publication of *Common Worship: Times and Seasons* in 2006 when abundant notes on the use of the Easter Candle in the Easter Liturgies include this:

> The Easter Candle should be placed in a prominent position from Easter day until Pentecost, and it is traditional for it to be lit for the principal services during this period. It should also be used at baptism and may be used at funerals throughout the year.[23]

St Paul constantly writes of Christian living and dying not in terms of the Cross alone, not in terms of the Resurrection alone, but in terms of both united together (Philippians 3:8–11):

> I regard everything as loss because of the surpassing value of knowing Christ Jesus my Lord. For his sake I have suffered the loss of all things, and I regard them as rubbish, in order that I may gain Christ and be found in him, not having a righteousness of my own that comes from the law, but one that comes through faith in Christ, the righteousness from God based on faith. I want to know Christ and the power of his resurrection and the

---

[20] *The Book of Common Prayer according to the use of The Episcopal Church* (Church Hymnal Corporation and The Seabury Press, New York, 1979), pp. 506–7. See also G. Rowell, *The Liturgy of Christian Burial*, Alcuin Club Collections no. 59 (SPCK, London, 1977), esp. ch. 6.
[21] *Lent, Holy Week, Easter*, p. 227, note 5.
[22] *Common Worship: Pastoral Services* (Church House Publishing, London, 2000), pp. 242 and 292.
[23] *Common Worship: Times and Seasons*, p. 331, note 7.

> sharing of his sufferings by becoming like him in his death, if somehow I may attain the resurrection from the dead.

These verses demonstrate the essential character of Christian living. It is knowing the fellowship of Christ's sufferings and the power of his Resurrection. St Paul writes further (Romans 8:16–17):

> We are children of God, and if children, then heirs, heirs of God and joint heirs with Christ—if, in fact, we suffer with him so that we may also be glorified with him.

And earlier in the same epistle he refers to Christ as 'Jesus our Lord ... who was handed over to death for our trespasses and was raised for our justification' (Romans 4:25).

There is a sense in which it can be said that Christians are still waiting for the final and definitive Passover, which is the *Parousia*, the return of Christ in power and glory. But if for the Jews in the Old Testament the true reality of the Passover was all in the future, it is not so for the Christian who looks back to the central act of history—no mere type or figure but the true substance of redemption—and who looks forward to resurrection not as something set totally in the future but as something begun in baptism. The new life, the new age of the Spirit, has already begun; so 'the old yeast is cleaned out' (cf. 1 Corinthians 5:7) that the Passover of Unleavened Bread may be celebrated in newness of life. That the new life has already begun is the message of one of the readings provided for Easter Day (Colossians 3:1–4):

> So if you have been raised with Christ, seek the things that are above, where Christ is, seated at the right hand of God. Set your minds on things that are above, not on things that are on earth, for you have died, and your life is hidden with Christ in God. When Christ who is your life is revealed, then you also will be revealed with him in glory.

The process of sanctification is nothing else than the transformation and transfiguration of lives by the paschal light of Christ as St Paul and St John make clear (2 Corinthians 3:18 and 1 John 3:2):

> And all of us, with unveiled faces, seeing the glory of the Lord as though reflected in a mirror, are being transformed into the same image from one degree of glory to another.

> Beloved, we are God's children now; what we will be has not yet been revealed. What we do know is this: when he is revealed, we will be like him, for we will see him as he is.

The Holy Week liturgy is concerned, as Chapters II and III have shown, with the Passover of the Jews and with the Passover of Christ. It is no less concerned with the Passover of Christians here and now, and it is engaged in the work of effecting it through the ministry of the Word and the Sacraments. As Michael Ramsey put it:

> Cross and resurrection are the grounds of the Church's origin, the secret of the Church's contemporary being, the goal of the Church's final self-realisation on behalf of the human race. The Word and the Sacraments in the midst of the Church make known to its members continually what is their origin, their secret and their goal. For the *Word* is the Word of the Cross, whereby the Church is made, renewed and judged. The *Eucharist* is the proclaiming of the Lord's death until his coming again; the setting forth before God and man of the whole drama of his life, death, resurrection and Parousia; and the feeding of his people with his broken body and outpoured blood.[24]

[24] A. M. Ramsey, *The Resurrection of Christ* (Fontana, Glasgow, rev. edn, 1961), p. 97.

$$\text{V}$$

The Mystery of the Cross

As Lent moves towards Holy Week there is a palpable change of liturgical atmosphere and devotional focus, a moving away from an emphasis on penance and baptismal preparation towards a more concentrated attention on the Cross. Since the 1969 revisions to the Roman Calendar, the term 'Passiontide' is no longer formally applied to the last two weeks of Lent. However, a hint at a former usage is found in the name for the Sunday before Easter, 'Palm Sunday of the Lord's Passion'. Pius XII's revision of the Holy Week liturgy in 1955 had drawn attention to this intensification of Lent in its final weeks by naming the Fifth Sunday *Dominica I Passionis* (First Sunday of Passiontide) and Palm Sunday became *Dominica II Passionis seu in Palmis* (Second Sunday of Passiontide or in Palms). In Roman Catholic churches and in some of those of the Anglican tradition, this change of atmosphere can be marked visually in an arresting manner. Crucifixes and images of the saints may be veiled in violet cloth from the Fifth Sunday of Lent:[1] The Roman Missal suggests:

> The practice of covering crosses and images in the church may be observed, if the episcopal conference decides. The crosses are to be covered until the end of the celebration of the Lord's passion on Good Friday. Statues and images are to remain covered until the beginning of the Easter Vigil.[2]

The custom of veiling images of the Crucified has traditionally been explained by reference to the Gospel reading on Passion

---

[1] An older usage was to veil them from the beginning of Lent; medieval English usage prescribed unbleached linen for this purpose. Some Anglican churches maintain this use of Lenten array—unbleached linen with the Instruments of the Passion painted thereon in blood red.
[2] *The Roman Missal*, p. 280.

Sunday (John 8:46–59), in which Jesus 'hid himself' from the people.[3] The tradition has much to commend it in terms of religious awareness in that the liturgical environment thus altered visually conspires to focus on the great essentials of Christ's work or redemption.[4]

More importantly, perhaps, this move towards the Cross is also effected by the lectionary choices and more particularly by the Proper Prefaces. In the Tridentine Missal and its present authorised incarnation, the Extraordinary Form, the Preface of Lent gives way to the Preface of the Cross:

> who by the tree of the Cross didst give salvation unto mankind: that whence death arose, thence life might rise again: and that he, who by a tree overcame, might also by a tree be overcome.[5]

The present Roman Rite provides two prefaces 'of the Passion of the Lord' the first of which stresses the power of the Cross and the second the victory of the Passion.[6] *Common Worship* provides an extended preface 'from the Fifth Sunday of Lent until the Wednesday of Holy Week' derived from an earlier draft of the *Missal* which alludes to the hiddenness symbolised by the Lenten veil:

> For as the time of his passion and resurrection draws near the whole world is called to acknowledge his hidden majesty. The power of the life-giving cross reveals the judgement that has come upon the world and the triumph of Christ crucified.

The short preface also highlights the mystery of the Cross in a very traditional but different way, reminiscent of the Tridentine preface but perhaps more striking:

> And now we give you thanks because, for our salvation, he was obedient even to death on the cross. The tree of shame was made the tree of glory; and where life was lost, there life has been restored.[7]

This preface presents a vision of a life-giving tree like the tree which

---

3   See also Isaiah 45.15, 'Truly, you are a God who hides himself, O God of Israel, the Saviour.'
4   Cf. P. J. Elliott, *Ceremonies of the Liturgical Year according to the Modern Roman Rite* (Ignatius Press, San Francisco, 2002), p. 67.
5   Translation provided by H. W. G. Kendrick for *Missale Anglicanum, The English Missal* (Knott, London, 1912).
6   *The Roman Missal*, pp. 588–91.
7   *Common Worship: Services and Prayers for the Church of England*, pp. 311–12.

God commanded Moses to cast into the waters of Marah to turn their bitterness into sweetness (Exodus 15:22–5); it is the tree of life of which Revelation also speaks: 'and the leaves of the tree are for the healing of the nations' (Revelation 22:2). Ultimately it looks back to the Garden of Eden and recalls that in the Cross (and the Cross is already radiant with the light of the Resurrection) there is not only a new Exodus, but a new Creation. John Donne wrote of this underlying unity:

> We think that Paradise and Calvarie,
> Christ's Crosse and Adam's tree, stood in one place;
> Look, Lord, and find both Adams met in me;
> As the first Adam's sweat surrounds my face,
> May the last Adam's blood my soule embrace.[8]

Donne's allusion is to a very ancient tradition which represents an attempt to explain why the place of Christ's crucifixion should have been called Golgotha—in Aramaic *gulgulta*, the place of the skull. The legend is that the skull in question was that of Adam, buried there by his third son, Seth. Pips from the fruit of the Tree of Life were placed under Adam's tongue at his burial. From these seeds grew two trees which were cut down to provide wood for the cross on which Christ was crucified. This cross, in turn, was raised over Adam's grave, its shaft driven downwards into the cavern where his bones lay. Thus, the blood and water pouring from the Saviour's side flowed over the head of Adam and with him the whole of humanity was cleansed. The story is rounded off in a truly poetic manner as the body of Christ is seen as a precious bloom flowering on the cross, a new blossom on old wood. This tale was retold in the thirteenth century by Jacobus de Voragine in his *Legenda Aurea* and passed into English literature as *The Golden Legend* when that compilation was translated and printed by William Caxton in 1483.[9]

The images in this story are tremendously powerful. Christ who is life, triumphs over death. His victory definitively conquers

---

[8] John Donne, 'Hymn to God, my God, in my Sickness', in his *Selected Poems* (Penguin, London, 2006).
[9] *The Golden Legend*, trans. under auspices of W. Caxton, 7 vols (J. M. Dent, London, 1900), vol. 3, pp. 169 ff. For a more recent translation see *The Golden Legend: Readings on the Saints*, trans. W. G. Ryan (Princeton University Press, Princeton, 2012).

death; for that which is dead is made eternally alive. The tree of life which had withered and died, blossoms into life on the grave of him whose sin was the cause of the whole process. Here is what St Paul so cogently explained to the Corinthians, 'since death came through a human being [Adam], the resurrection of the dead has also come through a human being [Christ]. For as in Adam all die, even so in Christ shall all be made alive' (1 Corinthians 15:21–2). This teaching is one of solidarity—the solidarity of the whole human race, solidarity in the sin of the first Adam and its consequences, and again, solidarity in the resurrection of the second Adam who is Christ. Those who are of the race of Adam share in his fall but those who are baptised into Christ's death are able to share in his life. Whereas the bones of the first Adam moulder at the foot of the Cross, the body of the second Adam blossoms into life on the wood of the tree. Adam is baptised by the blood and water from the Saviour's side and redeemed. For Christ's victory over the 'old serpent' would not have been complete had he not delivered Adam from his power. The skull and bones at the bottom of a crucifix or icon serve not only as a reference to locale but also as an indication of purpose.

The beautiful images of this legend find powerful expression in *Pange lingua*, a hymn of Venantius Fortunatus, written at the request of St Radegund in 569 to celebrate the solemn reception at Poitiers of a relic of the True Cross to be placed in her newly founded abbey church. The hymn is written in the metre of a Roman military marching song such as was used for the *Adventus* procession welcoming a military leader or ruler into a city. Rather than greeting an emperor, Fortunatus's liturgy transforms the procession into a peaceful act of worship yet still sounds an appropriately triumphant note as the victory song of Christ the heavenly King.[10] It is now used in the liturgy of the Lord's Passion on Good Friday and, in the Latin edition of the Roman Office, as the office hymn at the Office of Readings and Matins throughout Holy Week.

De parentis protoplasti	*God in pity saw man fallen,*
fraude Factor condolens,	*Shamed and sunk in misery,*
quando pomi noxialis	*When he fell on death by tasting*
morte morsu corruit,	*Fruit of the forbidden tree;*

[10] A. S. Walpole, *Early Latin Hymns* (Cambridge University Press, Cambridge, 1922).

ipse lignum tunc notavit,	*Then another tree was chosen*
damna lingi ut solveret.	*Which the world from death should free.*
Hoc opus nostrae salutis	*Thus the scheme of our salvation*
ordo depoposcerat,	*Was of old in order laid,*
multiformis proditoris	*That the manifold deceiver's*
ars ut artem falleret,	*Art by art might be outweighed,*
et medelam ferret inde	*And the lure the foe put forward*
hostis unde laeserat.	*Into means of healing made.*
Crux fidelis, inter omnes	*Faithful Cross! above all other,*
arbor una nobilis;	*One and only noble tree!*
nulla talem silva profert	*None in foliage, none in blossom,*
flora, fonde, germine.	*None in fruit thy peer may be;*
Dulce lignum, dulci clavo,	*Sweetest wood and sweetest iron!*
dulce pondus sustinens.	*Sweetest weight is hung on thee.*[11]

In a recent study of the liturgical and artistic expression of the Cross and Creation, Christopher Irvine has observed that the image of being sprinkled with Christ's blood, as were the bones of Adam, carries an echo of the blood ritual on the Day of Atonement in the temple in Jerusalem.[12] Here the ritual sprinkling performed by the High Priest, alone in the Holy of Holies, cleanses not a person or people but a place whose symbolic function is held to be somehow impeded by human sin. As Margaret Barker has pointed out, the temple was held to be a microcosm of creation, hence the annual cleansing of its Holy of Holies was effectively the ritual restoration and renewal of creation itself.[13] The iconographical tradition of the crucifixion where Christ's blood flowing from his wounds brings life and forgiveness to Adam and in him all humanity, also illustrates the significance of the Cross in the renewing and restoration of creation.[14] The cross of shame becomes the tree of glory with Christ's body as its foliage, blossom and fruit, and the place where life is lost is cleansed to become the place where life is restored. The tree planted on the hill of Calvary evokes the tree of life planted

---

[11] Translated by John Mason Neale in *New English Hymnal*, no. 78, and in a more complete version as no. 517. Unaccountably, the second of the verses quoted here is omitted in *New English Hymnal*. It can be found in *English Hymnal*, nos. 95 and 96.

[12] Christopher Irvine, *The Cross and Creation in Christian Liturgy and Art*, Alcuin Club Collections 88 (SPCK, London, 2013), p. 69.

[13] Margaret Barker, *Temple Theology: An Introduction* (SPCK, London, 2004), pp. 62–3.

[14] Irvine, *The Cross*, p. 70.

in the earthly paradise.[15]

For the Poitiers liturgical reception of the relic of the True Cross, Fortunatus wrote a second hymn in which military language is transformed into religious imagery. *Vexilla Regis prodeunt* likens the cross to the standard hung with banners borne into battle by a Roman legion but within three verses transforms the image into the Tree of Life, the diametric opposite of a military standard.

Vexilla Regis prodeunt,	*The royal banners forward go,*
fulget Crucis mysterium,	*The Cross shines forth in mystic glow,*
quo carne carnis conditor	*Where he in flesh, our flesh who made,*
suspensus est patibulo.	*Our sentence bore, our ransom paid.*
Impleta sunt quae concinit	*Fulfilled is all that David told*
David fideli carmine,	*In true prophetic song of old,*
dicendo nationibus:	*The universal Lord is he,*
regnavit a ligno Deus.	*Who reigns and triumphs from the tree.*
Arbor decora et fulgida,	*O Tree of beauty, Tree of light,*
ornata Regis purpura,	*O Tree with royal purple dight,*
electa digno stipite	*Elect on whose triumphal breast*
tam sancta membra tangere.	*Those holy limbs should find their rest.*[16]

Anna Svendsen, writing about David Jones's well-known painting called *Vexilla Regis*, explores the rich layers of theological meaning in the choice of words used in the Fortunatus hymn: they 'point to the mysterious commingling of suffering and redemption, death and life, that characterises Christ's self-offering, violent suffering, death and resurrection'.[17] Jones, whose mental health had been damaged by shell-shock in the Somme offensive of 1916, was intrigued by the transformation of images of war into images of redemption. He described how the concept of the advancing *vexilla* (banners)

> is even more poignant when we recall that the actual *vexilla* Fortunatus saw with his physical eyes were standards, imitative of past imperium, but in fact now carried before petty Merovingian dynasts at fratricidal wars of loot. Such was the sordid violence from which the poet gave the liturgy the enduring image of

---

15   *Ibid.*, pp. 137–8.
16   *New English Hymnal*, no. 79, again translated by J. M. Neale.
17   A. Svendsen, 'Procession of Peace', *Art and Christianity* 110 (summer 2022), pp. 2–4.

banners. It is the sort of thing poets are for: to redeem is part of their job.[18]

Contemporary with Venantius Fortunatus and expressing visually much the same sense of awe and mystery is the great apse mosaic in Sant'Apollinare in Classe, just outside Ravenna. Here the victory of the Cross, raised triumphant like a great jewelled throne on a star-spangled sky, initiates the transfiguration of the whole cosmos. In its place of honour, dominating the whole basilica, the richly adorned cross has been lifted high into the heavens to become the focal point of the new order. Priest and people looked towards it when praying, the point to which prayer was properly directed.[19] In this liturgical space, the Cross is seen, and its mystery only understood, in the light of the Resurrection as a pledge of creation healed, restored and made valid. The idea is very much that expressed in the apocryphal third-century *Acts of Andrew*:

> I know thy mystery for which thou art set up: for thou art planted in the earth, and securely set in the depth, that thou mayest join the things that are in the earth and that are under the earth unto the heavenly things. O Cross, device of the salvation of the Most High! O Cross, trophy of the victory of Christ over the enemies! O Cross, planted upon earth and having thy fruit in the heavens! O name of the Cross, a thing filled with all![20]

It was not just the monumental representations of the Cross which proclaimed its victory but also the miniature. Reflecting on the rapid and widespread dissemination of relics of the wood of the true cross in the fourth century, Christopher Irvine examined the iconography of a highly decorated cross reliquary, the Fieschi Morgan *Staurotheke* in the Metropolitan Museum of Art in New York.[21] A Byzantine work of the early ninth century, it is a rectangular, enamelled box, just over 10 by 7 cm in size. Its decoration, he suggests, is theologically significant, representing a way of liturgical seeing and suggestive of the intended and received meaning of the Cross. Most notable is the underside of the lid which carries

---

[18] D. Jones, 'The Eclipse of the Hymn', in *Epoch and Artist: Selected Writings by David Jones*, ed. Harman Grisewood (Faber, 2008), p. 261.

[19] S. Heid, *Altar and Church* (Schnell & Steiner, Washington, DC, 2023), p. 282.

[20] M. R. James, trans., *The Apocryphal New Testament* (Oxford University Press, Oxford, [1924] 1975), pp. 359–60.

[21] Irvine, *The Cross*, pp. 109–10.

representations of the Annunciation, the Nativity, the Crucifixion and the Harrowing of hell, a selection intended to indicate that the material of the wood of the cross it sheltered was intended to represent the whole saving work of God in Christ. Similarly, an enamelled, cross-shaped reliquary of the wood of the cross of similar date, once belonging to Pope Paschal I and now in the Vatican Museum, depicts seven episodes: Annunciation, Visitation, Nativity, Adoration of the Magi, Flight into Egypt, Presentation and Baptism. This selection is surely also intended to indicate that the Cross was regarded as a sign that made visible the whole mystery of Christ.

The terms 'Paschal Mystery' and 'Mystery of the Cross' have been used extensively thus far without an explanation of the word 'mystery' itself. It is a key word in theology and a word which can very easily be misconstrued. In devotional parlance the word 'mysteries' is often used in the plural when speaking of separate events in redemption history, as, for example, in the fifteen mysteries of the Rosary.[22] In the New Testament however the mystery is one and indivisible, whether it is spoken of as 'God's mystery', 'the mystery of his will', 'the mystery of Christ', 'the mystery of the Gospel', or simply 'the mystery' (cf. Colossians 2:2; Ephesians 1:9, 3:4, 6:19, 3:3 and elsewhere). This is not to suggest that it is wrong to use the term in the plural , since, for example, the use of the phrase the 'Holy Mysteries' to describe the Eucharist and the general use of the word *mysteria* in Greek to denote what in Latin came to be called *sacramenta* can be traced back to Pauline usage, and particularly, perhaps, to his reference to 'servants of Christ and stewards of God's mysteries' (1 Corinthians 4:1).

Mystery is a word which can be used in a purely secular context. In this sense it is something which baffles the mind, and which eludes a solution because the essential key to its understanding has been lost. A mystery in this sense is something which demands a solution, and which once solved is no longer a mystery. The word is also used sometimes to describe something which has an atmosphere of the irrational and the occult—the world of magic, ghosts and spirits Mystery in this sense can never be understood because

---

[22] Perhaps it would be more accurate to speak of twenty mysteries of the Rosary, since in 2002 Pope John-Paul II added five more, the Luminous Mysteries, to the traditional fifteen. Apostolic letter *Rosarium Virginis Mariae*, October 2002.

it completely defies all rational explanation. The New Testament idea of mystery is entirely different and is best approached via St Paul's First Letter to the Corinthians. There St Paul contrasts the preaching of the Cross—'a stumbling-block to Jews and foolishness to Gentiles'—with the wisdom of the world. He is concerned to show that though it seems to a merely worldly wisdom to be utter foolishness there is a true wisdom of God; indeed it is Christ himself who is both 'the power of God and the wisdom of God' (1 Corinthians 1:17–31). He then goes on to write further on this wisdom (2:6–10):

> Yet among the mature we do speak wisdom, though it is not a wisdom of this age or of the rulers of this age, who are doomed to perish. But we speak God's wisdom, secret and hidden, which God decreed before the ages for our glory. None of the rulers of this age understood this; for if they had, they would not have crucified the Lord of glory. But, as it is written, 'What no eye has seen, nor ear heard, nor the human heart conceived, what God has prepared for those who love him'—these things God has revealed to us through the Spirit; for the Spirit searches everything, even the depths of God.

The key idea here is of an eternal wisdom of God—God's plan of redemption and glorification for his creation—which is inaccessible to humanity except through the revelation of the Spirit and which has been made known 'in a mystery' in the Cross of Christ. This key idea is found in other epistles, as when St Paul speaks of 'the mystery that was kept secret for long ages but is now disclosed, and through the prophetic writings is made known to all the Gentiles' (Romans 16:25–6) and of 'the mystery that has been hidden throughout the ages and generations but has now been revealed to his saints' (Colossians 1:26).

St Paul borrowed this idea of a 'mystery' of wisdom, long hidden in the mind of God but now made manifest, from Jewish apocalyptic (Dan 2:18–23), where it seems to be a concept of Persian origin. The term is also found in the Qumran literature, where it is used with some of the profundity where with St Paul invests it, but he enriches it immeasurably by applying it to salvation's climactic moment: the saving Cross of Christ and its consequence—the restoration of all things in Christ. There have been hints and glimpses and prophecies of this revelation in the Old Testament, but it is only in Christ that this mystery has been brought from eternity into time to be disclosed and revealed. For Christians therefore the mystery is not something *hidden*; it is the exact opposite, it is something *revealed*. Yet having been revealed it remains a mystery, for it possesses a depth which far exceeds the grasp of human understanding: 'For now we see in a mirror, dimly' (1 Corinthians 13:12).

The Mystery of the Gospel is the whole movement of Christ's passage to the Father as the pioneer of our salvation and the first born among many brethren, a movement that stretches from the Incarnation to the *Parousia* but is concentrated in the Cross and Resurrection. The Paschal Mystery is not so much one part or element in this Mystery of the Gospel as the whole mystery seen in the light of its central and essential dimension. Michael Ramsey wrote how

> The centre of Apostolic Christianity is *Crucifixion — Resurrection*; not Crucifixion alone nor Resurrection alone, nor even Crucifixion as the prelude and Resurrection as the finale but the blending of the two ... for Life-through-Death is the principle of Jesus's whole life: it is the inward essence of the life of the Christians; and it is the unveiling of the glory of the eternal God.[23]

But the Mystery of Christ is not only revealed to the mind as a Word to be heard, pondered and obeyed; it is actually communicated as a saving reality which breaks in upon life and is made present in worship. As Dom Odo Casel taught, the encounter with the divine Mystery in the liturgy is 'the most central and most essential action of the Christian religion'.[24] For Casel, the liturgy makes present the unique, unrepeatable mystery of Christ which was realised historically in the past and is sacramentally re-presented in the liturgical commemoration. And the Mystery is not something which lies totally outside; all are included within it, since God, as the author of the Letter to the Ephesians (1:9–10) says,

> has made known to us the mystery of his will, according to his good pleasure that he set forth in Christ, as a plan for the fullness of time, to gather up all things in him, things in heaven and things on earth.

The Mystery is a mystery of unity, the nuptial mystery of Christ and his Church (Ephesians 5:32). St Paul also can say 'how great

---

[23] Ramsey, *The Resurrection*, pp. 20–1.
[24] Odo Casel, OSB, *The Mystery of Christian Worship* (Crossroad Publishing, Chestnut Ridge, New York, 1999).

among the Gentiles are the riches of the glory of this mystery, which is Christ in you, the hope of glory' (Colossians 1:27).

The Mystery is of Christ *in the Christian*, because he works out the mystery of his death and resurrection in Christian lives, leading believers along the path which he has pioneered, associating them with himself in his own passage to the Father. The Christian life, therefore, cannot adequately be described as 'the imitation of Christ'. Imitation can only be imitation from within: it is dependent upon incorporation into Christ, and without this it is both impossible and meaningless.

The Paschal Mystery of Christ's death and resurrection is rooted solidly in unrepeatable historical events and yet it makes contact with the here and now. Its reality on its deepest level transcends history and is made present in order to insert the believer into itself. In Casel's thought, the Mystery is present and active in the Church and in the Church's sacraments because the dynamic and redeeming power and energy of Christ's death and resurrection are present and active there. Moreover Christ himself is always present in his Church—present in a particular manner in the eucharistic banquet but present also in all the sacraments and in the ministry of the Word; and he is present as the risen and exalted and glorified Lord, who was once slain, and who bears even now in his body the marks of his Passion, but is now alive for evermore, reigning with the Father and the Holy Spirit in the glory of the Trinity. The sacrifice of the incarnate Christ has behind it the eternal exchange of love within the Trinity, and in particular the movement of filial love and homage rendered by the Son to the Father. Michael Ramsey could write of 'the unveiling of the glory of the eternal God' in the death and resurrection of Christ because these events give us a glimpse into the very heart of the Godhead, the exchange of love within the Blessed Trinity.

In the Liturgy of Good Friday, a large wooden crucifix is brought through the church into the sanctuary and is lifted up there for the veneration of the people: 'This is the wood of the Cross, on which hung the salvation of the world. Come, let us worship.'[25] In one permitted form of this showing of the Cross it is a veiled cross which is carried through the church and there gradually unveiled. Here is a profound truth: the Cross itself is an unveiling; it is a reve-

---

[25] *Common Worship: Times and Seasons*, p. 309.

lation of the mystery hidden and kept secret for long ages and it enables the worshipper to gaze at the deepest and most sacred of all mysteries, and not only to gaze but to be taken up to share and to participate in it. Writing not long after the Holy Week reforms of Pius XII, Charles Davis could say:

> The liturgy is the mystery of Christ made present to us. It is a symbolic representation of the saving work of Christ in which the reality of that work becomes present. How is it present? It is present in so far as it is reproduced in us by the present action of the risen Christ. Our sacramental life is an image of the life of Christ, and we are conformed to Christ in the mystery of his *transitus*. But this is also brought about, not only by the present action of Christ, but also by the active influence of the acts that made up his redemptive work. These are present by their dynamic power, so that the total mystery of Christ in its historical realisation acts on us in the liturgy and is the cause of our own participation in the mystery. The inner core of that redemptive work, since it transcends time, still exists, and hence is made present as an existing reality by means of the liturgical representation.[26]

The liturgy of Holy Week is thus not a series of dramatic ceremonies devised to kindle the imagination and assist in an annual refreshing of personal devotion to the passion and Resurrection of the Lord. It is rather more significantly the real presence of the Paschal Mystery in the here and now. As Adrian Nocent has written

> The liturgy, after all, is not simply a play. We do not take part in the liturgy in order to recall past events in an atmosphere of spiritual emotion. We take part in it in order to celebrate a mystery that the liturgy itself renders present.[27]

This is the significance of the carving on the Paschal Candle not only of a cross and the letters Alpha and Omega but also of the numerals of the current 'year of grace'. 'Christ yesterday and today,' proclaims the celebrant tracing the inscription, 'The beginning and the end, Alpha and the Omega, all time belongs to him, and all ages; to him be glory and power through every age and for ever. Amen.'[28]

---

[26] C. Davis, *Liturgy and Doctrine* (Sheed & Ward, London, 1960), pp. 73–4.
[27] Adrian Nocent, OSB, *The Liturgical Year*, 4 vols, trans. M. J. O'Connell (Liturgical Press, Collegeville, Minnesota, 1977), vol. 2, *Lent and Holy Week*, p. 187.
[28] *Common Worship: Times and Seasons*, p. 335.

Because the mystery of the Cross in its fullness shines forth as the whole Christian gospel in its concentrated essence, Holy Week and Easter must stand on a different footing from all other feasts of the Christian Year. This is to some extend illustrated in T. S. Eliot's well-known version of St Thomas Becket's Christmas sermon where he has the Archbishop say:

> I wish only that you should meditate in your hearts the deep meaning and mystery of our masses of Christmas Day. For whenever Mass is said, we re-enact the Passion and Death of our Lord; and on the Christmas Day we do this in celebration of his Birth.[29]

Many of the Fathers attributed to the Pascha the character of a mystery or sacrament; St Leo in his sermons refers several times to the *sacramentum* of the Cross or of the Pascha. During his papacy (440 to 461) there was no separate commemoration of the Crucifixion on what is now Good Friday, so that when he describes the Cross of Christ as 'both *sacramentum* and example'[30] and when he talks of the *paschale sacramentum*[31] he is pointing to one reality and one liturgical celebration—'sacramento Dominicae passionis et resurrectionis' ('the sacrament of the Lord's Passion and Resurrection').[32] In the same way, when he says that the Gospel narrative which his flock have just heard presents to them the whole paschal mystery—'totum paschale sacramentum'—he is referring to the reading of the narrative of both the Passion and Resurrection at the Easter Vigil.[33]

There is, together with an undeniable richness, a real lack of precision in this kind of 'sacramental' language, only in a somewhat difficult and obscure passage from one of St Augustine's letters is there some attempt at definition. 'A celebration of something is a sacrament only when the commemoration of the event becomes such that it is understood also to signify something that is to be received as sacred.'[34] Augustine makes a sharp distinction between a feast like Christmas, which is only the memorial or

---

[29] T. S. Eliot, *Murder in the Cathedral* (Faber & Faber, London, 3rd edn, 1935), p. 47.

[30] Pope St Leo, Sermon 72 (Patrologia Latina 54, col. 390).

[31] *Ibid.*, Sermon 47 (Patrologia Latina 54, col. 294).

[32] *Ibid.*, Sermon 51 (Patrologia Latina 54, col. 308).

[33] *Ibid.*, Sermon 72.

[34] Augustine, *Epistola 55 (Ad Inquisitiones Januarii)* (Patrologia Latina 33, col. 204).

commemoration of a past event, and Easter, which can be called a sacrament because it not only commemorates the historical event of Christ's death and resurrection but also celebrates the believer's own passage from death to life. He argues that this should be evident from the very word Pascha which is properly translated *transitus*—passage from death to life.[35]

Since the middle of the twentieth century it has become possible to use this language once again and speak of 'the Sacrament of Easter'. On the eve of the Second Vatican Council, the French liturgical scholar, Antoine Chavasse, could write:

> In celebrating the death and resurrection of Christ the Church does not simply recall a past historical event. She celebrates 'sacramentally' the mystery of salvation and in evoking the death and resurrection of Christ she actualises their mysterious power of influence. The mystery of Easter is thus at the same time the mystery of Christ, the Head, and the mystery of the Church, the Body of Christ. In the Paschal Vigil Christ applies to his Church in a more special way the saving power of his death and resurrection, and the means of his intervention is this very celebration which the Church is making.[36]

After the Council this approach was to be more authoritatively and more publicly set forth by Pope Paul VI in the *motu proprio* by which he gave approval to the reform of the liturgical year and in which he referred back to the teaching of some of his more immediate predecessors:

> These popes, together with the Fathers and the tradition of the Catholic Church, taught that the historical events by which Christ Jesus won our salvation through his death are not merely commemorated or recalled in the course of the liturgical year, even though they instruct and nourish the least educated among the faithful. These pontiffs taught rather that the celebration of the liturgical year exerts a 'special sacramental power and influence which strengthens Christian life'. We ourselves believe and profess the same truth.[37]

---

[35] Quoted by L. Bouyer, *Life and Liturgy*, p. 205.

[36] A. Chevasse, 'Le Cycle Paschal', in *L'Église en prière. Introduction à la liturgie*, ed. A. G. Martimort (Desclee & Cie, Tournai, 1961), p. 695.

[37] Apostolic Letter of 14 February 1969, *Mysterii Paschalis*, quoting *Maxima Redemptionis Nostrae Mysteria* of Pius XII in 1955. It will be noted that these two papal texts, unlike St Augustine, attribute a sacramental quality to the whole liturgical year.

Each year, as Holy Week and Easter come around once more the liturgical season should be approached as a sacrament, a grace-bearing sign which is able to effect what it signifies. The Sacrament of Easter demands from the believer a total commitment. Christians are called to live the liturgy of these days in such a way as to lay themselves open to be assimilated to the mystery it celebrates. The faithful must so fully enter into the *transitus* of Christ to the Father that they celebrate at the same time their own passage to the Father. To enter deeply into the fellowship of Christ's sufferings is to know fully and joyfully the power of his Resurrection.

⇝ VI ⇜

Passion and Resurrection

While Easter has always been a source of joy and confidence to Christians in every generation, and belief in the resurrection of Christ has always and everywhere been at the centre of Christian faith, there is nevertheless a sense in which Easter needs to be rediscovered in our time. Unlike Christmas, Easter fails to engage with the majority of the population except on the level of the mystery of a holiday whose date varies each year and is calculated on some arcane basis involving the moon and a 'golden number'. Were Easter to be fixed on the same Sunday each year, as some Church leaders seem to want, it would very soon pass unnoticed save for chocolate eggs and bunnies appearing in the shops, many months before the feast. That Christmas touches the hearts and imaginations even of those whose Christian faith is minimal or non-existent is also easily understandable as, far more than Easter, it has attracted to itself a wealth of appealing sentimentality, folk-lore, and tradition.

In Western Christendom since medieval times, the Passion of Christ has made more of an impact than the Resurrection and has come to be seen in separation from it; this is true moreover for Roman Catholics, Anglicans and Protestants. Symptomatic of this is the devotion Stations of the Cross where only relatively recently has a fifteenth station commemorating the Resurrection been added to the traditional set. Include J. S. Bach's great settings of the Passions of Matthew and John, the typical Western crucifix or crucifixion scene in painting or stained glass, such hymns as that of the great eighteenth-century Non-conformist Isaac Watts, *When I survey the wondrous Cross*—the 'Protestant crucifix in verse' as it has been called, and the whole range of Western devotional, musical and artistic expression of the theme and a distinct lack of balance can be seen. The reasons for this divorce are many and complex and

83

have never been the object of adequate systematic investigation.[1] The Latin doctrine of the Atonement, articulated most fully by St Anselm, Archbishop of Canterbury from 1093 to 1109, in his *Cur Deus Homo?*, with its emphasis on the satisfaction required by the Father of the Son, was elaborated but not fundamentally altered by the Scholastic theologians of the later medieval period. It was fully in harmony with the developed penitential system of the Western Church and shared its legalistic preoccupations. The fact that this view of the Atonement stressed the work which Christ performed as a *man* in relation to God led inexorably to a deep and tender but unbalanced devotion to the sacred humanity of Jesus and to his suffering and death, which was to be further developed in the spirituality of the Cistercians in the twelfth century and of the Franciscans in the thirteenth.[2]

After the Black Death had swept across Europe in the four-teenth century, decimating the population and leaving scarcely a single community untouched, Christian iconography and popular devotion became obsessed with the suffering and death it had wit-nessed. A profound sense of sin and penitence led to an increased emphasis on the cost of redemption and thus to an increasingly realistic portrayal of the human agony of the Saviour. Here popular piety effectively completed the process Scholastic theology had begun. The description of Christ's sufferings in the *Revelations* of St Bridget of Sweden (d. 1373) and the visions of the Passion in the *Revelations of Divine Love* of Julian of Norwich (d. *c.* 1420) represent the most influential literary expressions of this trend, the *Imitatio Christi* of Thomas à Kempis (d. 1471), its best-known devotional expression, while the Isenheim altarpiece of Matthias Grünewald (d. 1528) is one of the most memorable works of art produced under the same impulse.[3] Certainly, the Passion can make more of an impact on human sensibilities, because suffering and death

---

[1]   Gustav Aulén, *Christus Victor*, trans. A. G. Hebert (SSM SPCK, London, 1931) ,provides a masterly survey of the historical material.

[2]   See G. L. Prestige, *Fathers and Heretics*, Bampton Lectures for 1940 (SPCK, London, 1940), Lecture VIII. That, on the other hand, the full patristic theology of the Paschal Mystery and a doctrine of redemption that embraces both Cross and Resurrection were still very much living realities for the twelfth-century Cistercians has been demonstrated by Alf Härdelin in *Pâques et rédemption*, Collectanea Cisterciensia, fasc. I (Cisterciens de la stricte observance, Westmalle, Belgium, 1981).

[3]   See Irvine, *The Cross*, pp. 16–23.

are basic and common human experiences, whereas resurrection from the dead is manifestly not. But for the Christian the Passion is important because it is redemptive, and in the context of redemption it is inseparable from the Resurrection.

The dangerous divorce of Cross and Resurrection is not only a matter affecting the liturgical, devotional and imaginative life of the Church; it has also had a baleful influence on the Church's theology. For the truth of the old maxim — *lex orandi, lex credendi* — operates in both directions. Liturgy can both express and influence theology; theology can both express and influence liturgy. This mutual influence has worked for better and for worse; it can be seen at work in the history of the divorce between Passion and Resurrection and it can be seen at work also in the history of the rediscovery of their unity. One of the pioneers of the rediscovery of this theological unity, the Redemptorist theologian, F.-X. Durrwell, wrote:

> Not so long ago, theologians used to study the Redemption without mentioning the Resurrection at all. The fact of Easter was made to yield its utmost value as a piece of apologetics; but no one thought of examining it in itself as one of the inexhaustible mysteries of our salvation. Christ's work of redemption was seen as consisting in his incarnation, his life and his death on the cross. The theologians stressed the note of reparation, of satisfaction, of meritoriousness in that life and death, and generally they went no further. When the Resurrection was mentioned, it was not so much to give it any part in our salvation as to show it as Christ's personal triumph over his enemies, and a kind of glorious counterblast to the years of humiliation he had endured to redeem us. In short, Christ's resurrection was shorn of the tremendous significance seen in it by the first Christian teachers and relegated to the background of the redemptive scheme. Such blindness naturally impoverished the whole theology of the Atonement.[4]

Durrwell's book was first published in 1950 and had a considerable influence at the time and in subsequent years on liturgical renewal and theological discussion. However, some thirty years later in the eleventh French edition, he acknowledged that his criticism retained some its validity even after the radical reform of the Easter liturgy, noting that the central event in which is summed up the whole of the Faith had still not been made the object of very thorough reflection in the field of dogmatic theology.

[4]   Durrwell, *The Resurrection*, Foreword, p. xxiii.

A similar rediscovery to that of Durrwell was pioneered within the Church of England by a remarkable pair of Cambridge theologians, Sir Edwin Hoskyns and Noel Davey, although their classic presentation of their theme *Crucifixion–Resurrection* was only published posthumously in 1981.[5] But already in 1945 Michael Ramsey, who had absorbed and made his own the teaching of his master Hoskyns, had written:

> It would be absurd to say that the West lost sight of the Resurrection, for every saintly life and every achievement of Christian thinking bears witness to it, Yet there have been phases in the West when the Cross was isolated and seen without the light of Easter upon it. The tendency can be traced in art, where the crucifix with the dead Christ upon it replaced the earlier 'Majestas' crucifix with Christ crowned, robed and victorious. I can be traced in doctrine, where the sacrifice of atoning death has often been separated from the victory of the atoning Resurrection. It can be traced in worship, where the commemoration of Calvary in the liturgy has replaced the commemoration of the whole drama of God's redemption. In all this, sweeping generalisations are out of place. It is often inevitable for Christians to fix their gaze solely upon 'Jesus Christ and him crucified', to know nothing save the Cross; and when they do they are indeed near to the Resurrection. None the less there has sometimes been a concentration upon the Cross that is less than Pauline, and there is a germ of truth in Westcott's words: 'It has been indeed disastrous for our whole view of the Gospel that a late age placed upon the Cross the figure of the dead Christ, and that we have retained it there.'[6]

The rebalancing between Passion and Resurrection and the consequent 'rediscovery' of Easter has been the fruit of a number of convergent movements of renewal in the Church. It has been due to the Biblical Theology movement of the 1940s and 1950s and the renewed attention paid to the basic *kerygma* of the Apostolic Church. It has been due also to the renewed study of the Greek and Latin Fathers and a wider interest in and better understanding of their teaching. It has obviously been due in a very large measure indeed to the Liturgical Movement and to three aspects of it in

[5] E. Hoskyns and N. Davey, *Crucifixion–Resurrection: The Pattern of the Theology and Ethics of the New Testament*, ed. Gordon Wakefield (SPCK, London, 1981).
[6] Ramsey, *The Resurrection*, p. 117. He quotes from Westcott's *The Revelation of the Risen Lord* (London, Macmillan, 1881).

particular; that concerned with historical research, that concerned with the articulation of a liturgical theology, and that concerned with a pastoral care for seeing that the liturgy really communicates its message to the faithful. In this connection it is right to single out one particular name, that of Dom Odo Casel of the Benedictine Abbey of Maria-Laach, whose whole life was dedicated to the understanding and propagating of the theology of the Christian Mystery and who had sought to retrieve for the Church the belief that Christ in the Paschal Mystery was present in every liturgy: he died with singular appropriateness on the night of Easter 1948 just after he had proclaimed as deacon the *Exsultet*, the good news of the light of Christ.[7]

Another influence has been the Ecumenical Movement. Christian writers of all traditions have contributed to the rediscovery of the indissoluble unity between Passion and Resurrection and the reformed and renewed Holy Week liturgy of the Roman Rite has been adopted or adapted not only by Anglicans and Lutherans, but more widely in the Reformed and Free Church traditions.[8] It is also important to realise that this movement in the Western Churches has been due in some measure to renewed contact with the Orthodox Churches of the East, which have not suffered from the divorce between the Cross and the Resurrection introduced in the West. These Churches have kept and guarded the essential unity of the two in their theology, liturgy and devotion. Their Holy Week liturgy has to some extent suffered from changes that obscure its full impact (see below, pp. 109–14), but it has never ceased to be a potent and dominant influence in forming the faith and devotion of the Orthodox faithful. It has been a revelation to many Western Christians to attend the great Easter midnight service and to feel the intense faith and jubilation expressed in this magnificent rite. The Orthodox were for centuries accustomed to living as a minority within wider cultures antipathetic to their Christian belief; they were—and in the Middle East still are—used

---

[7]   An appraisal of Casel's often controversial views can be found in Klauser, *A Short History of the Western Liturgy*, trans. John Halliburton (Oxford, Oxford University Press, 2nd edn, 1979), pp. 24–30. See also Patrick Malloy, *How Firm a Foundation: Leaders of the Liturgical Movement* (Liturgical Training Publications, Chicago, 1990), pp. 50–6.

[8]   See, for example, the Holy Week Services in *The Methodist Worship Book* (Methodist Publishing, London, 1999), pp. 235–65.

to suffering and persecution, and to situations in which the liturgy has been the sole teaching vehicle permitted to them. For them, as for the early Christians, the conviction of Christ's resurrection has been the sustaining power in their life and witness. 'Christ is risen! He is risen indeed!'

Today Christians in the West have also had to accustom themselves to living as a minority in a world not just indifferent to faith but increasingly hostile to it. The lively and intelligent faith required if witness in today's society is to carry any conviction needs to be fed, of course, by regular attendance at divine worship but, most especially, by participation in the paschal celebration of the Christian Mystery. Even with the more transparent and accessible rites now shared by many worshipping traditions, the keeping of Lent, Holy Week and Easter requires considerable effort. It is not easy for the clergy to build up and maintain a really corporate keeping of Holy Week in their parishes and congregations, nor for the faithful to give up the time required for real engagement with the liturgy and a proper and recollected observance of the *Triduum*. As Chapter 1 has attempted to demonstrate, this focused engagement with the Paschal Mystery needs to begin on Ash Wednesday because the whole of Lent is an indispensable preparation for a right celebration of the Cross and Resurrection. Nothing is more important in the Christian life than participation in the unbroken liturgical movement of the *Triduum*. The whole movement of renewal in the Church and its essential commitment to mission should find its concentrated essence in the restored Easter Vigil and its new awareness of the Resurrection.

This lesson is beginning to be assimilated. This process has been helped by nearly fifty years of experience of and reflection upon the 1970 revision of the Holy Week rites in the *Roman Missal*. Liturgical revision in the Anglican Communion over the same time span has been predicated upon the belief that, with only the usual doctrinal reservations, the Roman way with Holy Week is the right way. The Church of England now has good, officially commended, liturgical material for the period from Ash Wednesday to Pentecost in *Common Worship: Times and Seasons* modelled on the Roman Rite and sister provinces within the Communion have similar provision. It has been helped by the opening up of Christian imagination to the powerful symbolism of the Holy

Week rites by poets and artists.[9] Interestingly, it has been helped
too by the work of anthropologists and sociologists. As early as
1908, Arnold van Gennep isolated and named a category of ritual
in all cultures called 'Rites of Passage'.[10] These are the transitional
rituals which accompany changes of place, state, social position
and age in a culture. The rites can be seen to have a basically threefold, processual structure consisting of separation, liminality and
reaggregation. The correspondence with Christian Initiation is
immediately obvious but this insight also makes clear how deep-
seated is the appeal behind such ideas as *transitus*, Passover, Exodus and pilgrimage. In addition, the work of the psychologist C.
G. Jung, who located the special power of symbols—including
those used in the Paschal liturgy—in pre-conscious attitudes or
even the human collective unconscious, and of the theologian
Paul Tillich, who related Jung's symbols to religious experience,
has led to an increase in awareness amongst all Christians both of
the continuing potency of the traditional paschal symbols and of
the deep resonances they evoke even in those who at a conscious
level would claim to have become impervious to the Christian
message. It might also be said that there is a growing understanding by Christians in the Evangelical tradition that the dismantling
of the age-old ceremonies at the Reformation was due not only to
Reformation theology but also to another very potent influence
in the sixteenth century; the 'Gutenbergian revolution', brought
about by the invention of printing towards the end of the fifteenth
century, which led many people to become intoxicated with the
power of words and to imagine that all teaching had to be communicated verbally and orally. In our own time, the age of television,
mass advertising, and social media developments, it has become
clear once more that words, spoken or printed, are not enough for
communicating a message.

As outlined in Chapter 1, the new catechumenate paths recommended in both Roman Catholic and Anglican Initiation Rites have
reinvigorated the understanding of Lent for many people. Here the
rediscovery of Easter extends to a reappraisal and much-needed

9 Richard Harries, *The Image of Christ in Modern Art* (Ashgate Publishing,
   Farnham, 2013).
10 Arnold van Gennep, *The Rites of Passage* (Routledge & Kegan Paul, London,
   1960).

revaluation of the importance of the Lenten journey of which it is the goal. As the introduction to the new Roman *Rite of Christian Initiation for Adults* puts it:

> The whole initiation has a paschal character, since the initiation of Christians is the first sacramental sharing in the death and rising of Christ and since, moreover, the time of purification and enlightenment or illumination ordinarily takes place during Lent, with the postbaptismal catechesis or mystagogia during the Easter season. In this way Lent achieves its full force as a profound preparation of the elect and the Easter Vigil is considered the proper time for the sacraments of initiation.[11]

The process has, to a certain extent, also worked in the other direction where in certain communities a new interest in the Adult Catechumenate, born of changing demographics, the decline in infant baptism and the development of new approaches to mission and evangelism, has led to the rediscovery of Lent, Holy Week and Easter in all their richness.

For all this, congregations are often thin at the Easter Vigil and earlier in the week. As early as 1988, the Congregation for Divine Worship in Rome became anxious about the celebration of the *Triduum*:

> In some areas where initially the reform of the Easter Vigil was received enthusiastically, it would appear that with the passage of time this enthusiasm has begun to wane. The very concept of the vigil has almost come to be forgotten in some places with the result that it is celebrated as if it were an evening Mass, in the same way and at the same time as the Mass celebrated on Saturday evening in anticipation of the Sunday. It also happens that the celebrations of the Triduum are not held at the correct times. This is because certain devotions and pious exercises are held at more convenient times and so the faithful participate in them rather than in the liturgical celebrations.[12]

This may be because the presentation of the rites is too often unimaginative and lacking in drama. The revised rites for the Vigil, Roman Catholic, Anglican and Methodist, have the potential to engage those who attend with both the clear symbolism of the

---

[11] *Rite of Christian Initiation of Adults*, Introduction, para. 8.
[12] Congregation for Divine Worship and the Administration of the Sacraments, *Paschalis Solemnitatis* (Vatican, January 1988), para. 3.

opening Service of Light and the unfolding narrative of the Vigil as it leads to the proclamation of the Resurrection and its joyful alleluias. However, the whole service needs to be planned and presented carefully, with an intelligent use of the church building, if it is to make maximum impact. Even the most thorough formation of the faithful regarding the paschal mystery as the centre of the liturgical year and of the Christian life will be of little effect if the liturgy itself is anti-climactic, disappointing and dull. It also may be that attendance is poor at the Vigil because, in a manner of speaking, many people are still Calvary-Christians for whom Good Friday is still the climax of Holy Week and Easter a sort of epilogue. The unitive nature of the *Triduum* must not just be preached but also experienced and participated in as a continuous liturgical celebration, well presented, and reverently offered. As J. D. Crichton wrote when all this was new:

> The paschal celebration of the Lord's passion and resurrection at Eastertime is the culminating point of the whole Liturgical Year, it has absolute precedence over all other feasts and celebrations, it is put first in the list of precedence and, to re-establish that it is a unitary celebration of the one Passover, it has been renamed. It is not merely the *Sacrum Triduum* (lit. 'sacred three days') but the *Paschal Triduum* and 'begins with the Evening Mass of the Lord's Supper (on Maundy Thursday), is centred upon the Pascha Vigil and ends with Vespers on Easter Day'. Thus is restored to us in its full significance the most ancient celebration of the Christian Church. The impression has finally been removed that we were merely celebrating three holy days that 'commemorated' the last events of Christ's life. The three days form a whole in which the Church celebrates the whole paschal mystery which is reflected (and participated in) in different ways throughout the period.[13]

At the level of theological reflection also there are signs of a malaise. The Jesuit writer Gerald O'Collins has observed:

> Through being non-symbolic, non-experiential and non-liturgical, many recent Christologies have not appreciated and furthered the communication of the risen Christ. Often they have been especially good at using scriptural and historical scholarship. But to the extent that they have persistently refused to explore relevant symbols, reflect imaginatively on profound human

---

[13] J. D. Crichton, *Christian Celebration* (Chapman, London, 1981), Part I, 'The Mass', pp. 108 ff.

experience, and draw on the Church's liturgy, they have failed to play their part in communicating successfully the presence of the risen Lord.[14]

And again, he writes:

> How many Western European, North American or Latin American theologians draw on liturgical sources and devotional practices to explore and present the saving 'work' and divine identity of Jesus Christ? And yet it is forms of worship, with the music and the visual art which accompany them, that primarily transmit to believers what they experience and know about the risen Lord. Liturgy is the great vehicle of tradition which evokes and hands on belief in him as living and present ... The liturgy clearly supports starting with the paschal mystery and centering Christological thinking there ... Thus any Christology which follows the witness of Christian worship will centre itself on the paschal mystery. That would enable it to communicate more effectively with believers who express and experience their faith primarily in terms of Christ's dying and rising.[15]

Perhaps, therefore, we still need a radical revolution in outlook and mentality before this centrality of the paschal mystery and of its liturgical celebration really takes hold of the faithful. Such a revolution must be brought to pass, and the paschal mystery moved to the centre of consciousness of the whole Church and of every Christian. Cause and effect, chicken and egg, the liturgical celebration of the Great and Holy Week, which is the subject of Part Two of this study ought to be the key to solving this problem but alas, when poorly understood and badly performed it may be one of its causes.

---

[14] Gerald O'Collins, SJ, *Jesus Risen* (DLT, London, 1987), p. 201.
[15] *Ibid.*, pp. 203–4.

PART TWO

THE LITURGY OF THE GREAT AND HOLY WEEK

VII

Reform and Renewal

In the wider movement of liturgical renewal in the twentieth century, Roman Catholics and Anglicans were often moving at the same pace as well as in the same direction. In the heady days after the close of the Second Vatican Council ecumenism and liturgical renewal went hand in hand, each driving the other into closer co-operation. The International Consultation on English Texts was formed in 1968 and produced a collection of agreed English language texts for the ordinary of the Mass which were adopted in the authorised translation of the *Roman Missal* in 1973 and in Church of England authorised liturgies after Series III in the same year and thence into the *Alternative Service Book* of 1980 and *Common Worship* in 2000. Sadly, with the issuing of the instruction *Liturgiam Authenticam* by the Congregation for Divine Worship and the Discipline of the Sacraments in 2001, dynamic equivalence ceased to be considered a legitimate principle for translating from the Latin and 'the original text, insofar as possible, must be translated integrally and in the most exact manner, without omissions or additions in terms of their content, and without paraphrases or glosses'.[1] The common texts were abandoned by Rome in favour of a more literal approach and in 2010 a new English translation of the amended Latin text of the third *editio typica* Missal of 2008 was authorised. Aside from the abandonment of an ecumenical approach to liturgical revision and common texts which is regretable in itself, the end result of attempting to confine the English language in the tight garments of Latinate word order has been felt by many to be uncomfortable.

---

[1] *Liturgiam authenticam*, On the use of Vernacular Languages in the Publication of the Books of the Roman Liturgy (Rome, 18 March 2001), section 20.

While this recent revision may be seen by some as a backward step, the reform of liturgical texts in the last century was pioneered by the Roman Catholic Church, beginning with the Holy Week services. In 1951 Pope Pius XII promulgated a revised Easter Vigil for use at night as an optional alternative to the Vigil ceremonies and First Mass of Easter celebrated, according to the rubrics then in force, on Holy Saturday morning. Hitherto, those few who attended at this early hour heard the Deacon singing eloquently—albeit in Latin—of the glories of this *vere beata nox*! According to the same rubrics, the Mass of the Lord's Supper on Maundy Thursday and the Solemn Commemoration of the Passion on Good Friday were also celebrated in the morning with their respective *Tenebrae* offices on the previous afternoon. In the liturgical calendar these days were ranked merely as ferias and their ceremonies were generally celebrated by the clergy alone as a necessary duty to be accomplished out of obedience, while the faithful contented themselves with non-liturgical devotions—an hour before the Blessed Sacrament on Thursday, for example, and Stations of the Cross on Friday. The retimed and revised Easter Vigil proved popular, and authorisation was extended for four more years while a commission worked on a thoroughgoing revision of the entire liturgy of Holy Week. The commission's proposals were approved by the Pope in 1955 and published in the decree *Maxima redemptionis nostra mysteria* to come into effect on the Palm Sunday of the following year.[2] These reforms made some obvious changes to the timing of services and to the rites of Palm Sunday, notably to the blessing of palms and the procession, and to the Easter Vigil, with the reduction of the Old Testament readings from twelve to four and the introduction of a vernacular renewal of baptismal promises. Few changes, however, were made to the text and rubrics of the *Triduum* so that the essential character of the traditional Holy Week services was not radically altered. This version of the liturgy of Holy Week was incorporated into Pope John XXIII's revision of the Tridentine Missal in 1962 and thus is that which is currently authorised—albeit with special permission required—under the terms of *Summorum pontificum* whereby Pope Benedict XVI granted permission for the more frequent celebration of what he described

---

[2]   H. A. P. Schmidt, *Hebdomada Sancta* (Herder, Rome, 1957), pp. 222–31.

as the Extraordinary Rite.[3] The reforms incorporated in the 1970 Missal of Paul VI were considerably more far-reaching, as will be seen in the discussion of the individual services later in this volume.

Whereas the Roman Catholic Church began its liturgical revision process with the liturgy of Holy Week and Easter, the Church of England gave these rites no such priority. One of the most obvious weaknesses of the 1980 *Alternative Service Book* was its failure to provide in any clear or coherent way for the Holy Week services. Not until six years later was this lacuna rectified with the publication of the volume of services and prayers for *Lent, Holy Week, Easter*, commended by the House of Bishops.[4] This did not have the same degree of canonical authority as the *Alternative Service Book* and, unlike the Roman Rite Holy Week Order, was more in the nature of 'a *directory* from which choices may be made'; it was 'a manual to be used with selectivity, sensitivity and imagination'.[5] It was only in 2006 that this material was finally edited, revised, supplemented and arranged in a more coherent form as part of the *Common Worship* project and published as commended material in the *Times and Seasons* volume.[6]

There are obvious reasons for this contrasting approach. The Easter Vigil, the Palm Sunday procession, the Altar of Repose on Maundy Thursday, and the Mass of the Presanctified with the Veneration of the Cross on Good Friday were all suppressed in the Church of England during the sixteenth century and found no place in the successive editions of *The Book of Common Prayer*. The Passion readings were retained in Holy Week and vestigial Solemn Prayers on Good Friday but, notoriously, the only indications of paschal joy on Easter Day were the Easter Anthems, ordered to be sung instead of the Venite at Matins, and a proper preface to the Prayer of Consecration in the Holy Communion service. The revival, or partial revival, of the traditional Holy Week rites towards

---

3   Benedict XVI, *Motu Propriu—Summorum Pontificium* (Rome, 2007). 'It is ... permitted to celebrate the Sacrifice of the Mass following the typical edition of the Roman Missal, which was promulgated by Blessed John XXIII in 1962 and never abrogated, as an extraordinary form of the Church's Liturgy.' Pope Francis has severely limited the conditions governing this permission.

4   *Lent, Holy Week, Easter,* 'Services and Prayers'.

5   *Lent, Holy Week, Easter,* Introduction, pp. 1–2.

6   *Common Worship: Times and Seasons,* pp. 257–503. The Holy Week and Easter material was later made available in an altar (president's) edition in 2011.

the end of the nineteenth century by clergy of advanced ritualist sympathies was regarded as both flagrantly illegal and deeply superstitious by their opponents. It is only in the latter part of the last century that moderate and evangelical Anglicans have come to look with a more favourable eye on these services as they have become increasingly sacramentally and liturgically conscious.[7]

Other Churches of the Reformation, though equally burdened by their history, were not quite so slow in responding to the rediscovery of Easter. It is interesting to note that rather earlier than the Church of England Liturgical Commission, the Joint Liturgical Group, which included representatives of the Free Churches, the Church of Scotland, and a Roman Catholic observer, produced *Holy Week Services* in 1968, with a second, fuller edition in 1983.[8] The Holy Week liturgy of the ecumenical community of Taizé in France had a considerable influence on the Reformed Churches of Europe while in the United States, inspired by the new rites introduced in the 1977 *Book of Common Prayer* of the Episcopal Church,[9] the United Methodist Church produced *From Ashes to Fire*, a book of supplementary material to enrich worship from Ash Wednesday to Pentecost.[10]

For Roman Catholics the problem was quite different; they had a Holy Week liturgy, but it was not feeding and inspiring the thinking or the praying of either the laity or the clergy in the way it should. The problem was not only one of language (Latin) but also, as we have seen, one of inconvenient and counter-intuitive timing. So, the Liturgical Movement, begun (in so far as such a thing can be dated) in Belgium before the First World War under the leadership of Dom Lambert Beauduin, was bound sooner rather than later to feel particularly frustrated by what might be called the Babylonish Captivity of the Easter Vigil. The pressure for change

[7] This process can be traced in a number of publications from the late 1970s, notably: David Austerberry, *Celebrating Holy Week* (Mowbray, London, 1982); Peter Akehurst, *Keeping Holy Week*; and Trevor Lloyd, *Celebrating Lent, Holy Week and Easter* (Grove Books, Bramcote, Nottingham, numbers 41 and 93, 1976 and 1985).

[8] Joint Liturgical Group, *Holy Week Services* (SPCK/Epworth Press, London, 1968 and 1983).

[9] *The Book of Common Prayer and Administration of the Sacraments* ... (Church Hymnal Corporation, Seabury Press, New York, 1979).

[10] *From Ashes to Fire*, Supplemental Worship Resources 8 (United Methodist Church of America, Abingdon, Nashville, 1979).

came both from the world of liturgical and historical scholarship, particularly that of Dom Odo Casel of Maria Laach, who published in Germany an important study of Easter in the Patristic Church in 1934,[11] and from that of pastoral liturgy. It is significant that in 1945, in the first year of publication, the influential French review *La Maison-Dieu* contained a plea for the restoration of the Vigil. So, the reforms instituted by Pius XII in 1951 and 1955 not only put an end to the anomaly of a nocturnal celebration performed in full daylight and altered the timings of the other services but responded to the growing pressure to make full provision for the active participation of the laity, including — a straw in the wind — the use of the vernacular for the renewal of baptismal vows at the vigil and other changes that were later to be more generally applied. In 1955 it also became permissible to choose the ferial Lenten Mass in preference to a saint's feast, a move which went some way to restoring the integrity of the Great Forty Days. If it is true, as Hermann Schmidt observed, that Easter is the heart of the liturgy, *Pascha est cor liturgiae*, then the reform of the liturgical books of the Roman rite began at the right place.[12]

[11] Dom Odo Casel, OSB, 'Art und Sinn der ältesten christlichen Osterfeier', *Jahrbuch für Liturgiewissenschaft* 14 (1934), pp. 1–78.
[12] Schmidt, *Hebdomada Sancta*.

VIII

The Beginnings of Holy Week

Reference was made in Chapter I of this study to the suggestion that at the time of the First Council of Nicaea, the Pascha was a single, unitive celebration of the Death, Resurrection and Glorification of Christ, held during the night of Easter. Later in the fourth century at Jerusalem, a historical sequence celebrating the separate moments of the Passion story in chronological order was introduced (see above, p. 10). Turning to the description of Holy Week as it is celebrated today, it is appropriate first to explore this change in a little more detail. First, a note of caution: the particularly rich deposit of contemporary or near-contemporary documents—eye-witness descriptions, catechetical material, and lectionary evidence—from fourth-century Jerusalem has led some scholars, notably Dom Gregory Dix,[1] to over-emphasise a Jerusalem-inspired change from an early, unitive, eschatological celebration of Easter to a new, historical, rememorative Paschal liturgy throughout Christendom. Thomas Talley,[2] and more recently Robert Taft and John Baldovin,[3] have argued that this change cannot be explained satisfactorily simply as a radical shift from eschatological orientation to a historical one. A sense of liturgical progression through the events of Holy Week can be found in the worship of the Syrian Church in the first half of the third century, and as Jungmann has demonstrated, the Roman liturgy always kept its eyes on the whole mystery of the

---

[1] Gregory Dix, OSB, *The Shape of the Liturgy* (Dacre Press, London, 1945), ch. 11.
[2] Talley, *Origins of the Liturgical Year*, pp. 39 and 232.
[3] Robert Taft, 'Historicism Revisited', in *Beyond East and West: Problems in Liturgical Understanding* (Rome, Edizioni Orientalia Christiana, 2nd edn, 1977), pp. 42–9; John Baldovin, *The Urban Character of Christian Worship*, OCA 228 (Pontifical Oriental Institute, Rome, 1987), pp. 90–3.

Passion and never completely abandoned a unitive approach.[4] Nevertheless, it is impossible to understand Holy Week as the Church celebrates it in the twenty-first century without some understanding of the Jerusalem background.

An essential element in that background was the sprawling complex of buildings erected on the orders of the Emperor Constantine and dedicated in 335 to shelter and enshrine the sites of Christ's Crucifixion, Entombment and Resurrection. These key locations had been rediscovered, identified and excavated, possibly under the supervision of his mother, St Helena. Aligned roughly west to east, it consisted of a great rotunda, the Anastasis, which enclosed an aedicule containing the tomb of Christ—detached from the surrounding rock in the preliminary excavations. This great, domed structure, resting on a circle of huge columns, was not completed until several years after Constantine's death in 337.[5] Equal in splendour was the Martyrium, a large five-aisled and galleried basilica with an atrium and porch opening from the main street. Between these two structures was a colonnaded courtyard with the rock of Calvary in a chapel at its southeast corner. Attached to the northern side of the Anastasis rotunda was accommodation for the bishop and his clergy and to the south a baptistry. It is worth quoting in full the earliest description of this complex we have, given by Eusebius of Caesarea in his *Vita Constantini*, left incomplete at his death in 339.

> First of all, he adorned the sacred cave itself, as the chief part of the whole work, and the hallowed monument at which the angel radiant with light had once declared to all that regeneration which was first manifested in the Saviour's person. This monument, therefore, first of all, as the chief part of the whole, the emperor's zealous magnificence beautified with rare columns, profusely enriched with the most splendid decorations of every kind. The next object of his attention was a space of ground of great extent, and open to the pure air of heaven. This he adorned with a pavement of finely polished stone and enclosed it on three sides with porticos of great length. For at the side opposite to the cave, which was the eastern side, the church itself was erected; a noble work rising to a vast height, and of great extent both in

4   Josef A. Jungmann, SJ, *The Early Liturgy*, trans. F. A. Brunner (DLT, London, 1960), p. 261.
5   E. J. Yarnold, SJ, *Cyril of Jerusalem* (Routledge, Abingdon, 2000), pp. 15–17.

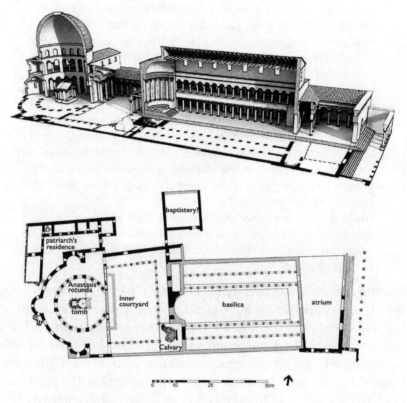

Figure 1. Cross section and plan of the Constantinian
church of the Resurrection in Jerusalem

length and breadth. The interior of this structure was floored
with marble slabs of various colours; while the external surface
of the walls, which shone with polished stones exactly fitted
together, exhibited a degree of splendour in no respect inferior
to that of marble. With regard to the roof, it was covered on the
outside with lead, as a protection against the rains of winter. But
the inner part of the roof, which was finished with sculptured
panel work, extended in a series of connected compartments,
like a vast sea, over the whole church; and, being overlaid
throughout with the purest gold, caused the entire building
to glitter as it were with rays of light. Besides this were two
porticos on each side, with upper and lower ranges of pillars,
corresponding in length with the church itself; and these also
had their roofs ornamented with gold. Of these porticos, those
which were exterior to the church were supported by columns
of great size, while those within these rested on piles of stone
beautifully adorned on the surface. Three gates, placed exactly

east, were intended to receive the multitudes who entered the church. Opposite these gates the crowning part of the whole was the hemisphere, which rose to the very summit of the church. This was encircled by twelve columns (according to the number of the apostles of our Saviour), having their capitals embellished with silver bowls of great size, which the emperor himself presented as a splendid offering to his God. In the next place he enclosed the atrium which occupied the space leading to the entrances in front of the church. This comprehended, first the court, then the porticos on each side, and lastly the gates of the court. After these, in the midst of the open marketplace, the general entrance-gates, which were of exquisite workmanship, afforded to passers-by on the outside a view of the interior which could not fail to inspire astonishment. This temple, then, the emperor erected as a conspicuous monument of the Saviour's resurrection and embellished it throughout on an imperial scale of magnificence.[6]

Passing reference has already been made to Egeria, the late-fourth-century pilgrim nun, who was an eyewitness to Church life in the Jerusalem of St Cyril and a worshipper in this great building (see above, p. 13). At this point she comes into her own. In 1884 an incomplete, eleventh-century manuscript, unnoticed for seven hundred years, was discovered in the library of the Pia Fraternita dei Laici in Arezzo in Italy; it is part of a travel diary known now to liturgical scholars as *Itinerarium Egeriae* or now more usually as *The Pilgrimage of Egeria*.[7] The diary was written by a nun who was most probably called Egeria and who seems to have come from the province of Galicia on the Atlantic coast of Spain. Writing for her sisters back home, she compiled this account of her pilgrimage to the Holy Land and the Near East in the penultimate decade of the fourth century. Of particular importance is her very detailed description of the events of 'the Great Week' as kept in Jerusalem. It is clear that she describes these events in such detail for the members of her community because they would have been totally unfamiliar to them; this becomes obvious when she comes to the Easter Vigil which she does *not* describe, simply recording that 'the paschal vigil is done in the same way as with us' and only describing one addition, a detail peculiar to Jerusalem. As Talley

---

[6] Eusebius, *Vita Constantini* 3.36–40 (Patrologia Latina 8, col. 58 ff.).
[7] Egeria, trans. McGowan and Bradshaw.

observes, 'her failure to find anything more noteworthy about the paschal vigil is precious information indeed. Such omission means that the Jerusalem practice concerning which we have such rich information was, for all practical purposes, just what was considered normal in her own country'.[8]

The origin of our Palm Sunday can be found in her description of a ceremony held in the early evening:

> And when the eleventh hour begins, there is read that passage from the Gospel where children with branches meet the Lord, saying, 'Blessed is the One who comes in the name of the Lord'. And immediately the bishop rises and all the people go forward from there entirely on foot from the summit of the Mount of Olives. For all the people [go] before him with hymns and antiphons, continually responding, 'Blessed is the One who comes in the name of the Lord'. And there are very many children in these places — including those who cannot walk on foot; because they are to be carried, their parents carry them on their shoulders — all carrying branches, some of palm, others of olive; and so the bishop is led in the same way as the Lord was led then. And from the summit of the Mount to the city and from there through the whole city to the Anastasis all, even any who are noble ladies and gentlemen, lead the bishop entirely on foot, responding thus, going very slowly lest the people become tired, and so at a late hour arrive at the Anastasis.[9]

As far as Maundy Thursday is concerned, Egeria describes two celebrations of the Eucharist in the late afternoon or early evening. The second seems to have been the more solemn of the two and it occurs at the place she calls *behind the Cross*, a chapel enclosing an outcrop of rock that was believed to be Golgotha. She notes that this is the only day of the year that the Eucharist is celebrated at that place 'and everyone receives Communion'. After this celebration 'everyone hurries to return to their home to eat' and then begins a continuous round of prayer and vigil, stations being held with appropriate readings and prayers at the Mount of Olives and in the Garden of Gethsemane and in the city for the narrative of Christ's trial before Pilate. Some then go home 'to sit down a little while' at the bishop's suggestion, while the less fatigued go to pray at the Column of the Flagellation.

8   Talley, *Origins of the Liturgical Year*, p. 51.
9   Egeria, trans. McGowan and Bradshaw, p. 168.

Without any real break the observance of Good Friday begins. The faithful are summoned to be present in the chapel behind the Cross at 8 o'clock in the morning and the bishop's chair is placed there:

> A table covered with a linen cloth is placed before him; the deacons stand around the table and a silver-gilt casket is brought in, in which is the holy wood of the cross; it is opened and [the wood] is brought out; both the wood of the cross and the inscription are placed on the table. So, when it has been placed on the table, the bishop, sitting, grips the ends of the holy wood with his hands, and the deacons who stand around guard it. It is guarded thus because the custom is that all the people coming one by one, both faithful and the catechumens, bowing to the table, kiss the holy wood and pass through. And because, I don't know when, someone is said to have bitten off and stolen a piece of the holy wood, therefore it is now thus guarded by the deacons who stand around lest anyone dares to come and do so again. Thus all the people pass through one by one, all bowing, touching the cross and the inscription first with their forehead, then with their eyes, and then kissing the cross, they pass through.[10]

This obviously takes a long time, from 8 o'clock to midday, at which time a three-hour liturgy of the Word is held in the open courtyard between the Chapel of the Cross and the Anastasis. It concludes when 'that passage from the Gospel of John is read where he gives up his spirit'. There is then a further service in the Martyrium, after which all go to the Anastasis:

> And when they have come there, the passage from the Gospel is read where Joseph asks for the Lord's body from Pilate [and] places it in a new tomb. When this has been read, prayer is made, the catechumens are blessed, then [the faithful, and then] the dismissal is done.[11]

On reading her account, one can only admire the resilience of Egeria and her fellow worshippers, most of whom would have been fasting all week, participating in what was clearly an extremely exhausting and emotionally draining experience.

It would be easy to conclude from Egeria's account that our present Holy Week and so many of its ceremonies could only

[10] *Ibid.*, p. 176.
[11] *Ibid.*, p. 178.

have originated in Jerusalem, and almost certainly as a result of the keen pastoral and pedagogical sensitivity and imagination of a great teaching bishop, St Cyril of Jerusalem, whose Lenten 'open classes' for catechumens and any others who care to attend she had already described. Moreover, we might be led to believe they could have only developed after the Constantinian Peace of the Church, which led to the excavation of the Holy Places and the subsequent building programme. Certainly, the rediscovery of the Holy Places resulted in their being opened up for the devotion of the faithful, not just the Christian community in Jerusalem, but also the waves of pilgrims which these developments encouraged. The new accessibility of the actual sites where the separate events of the Passion had taken place could not have failed to affect liturgical performance. The impression made on the pilgrims—notably on Egeria herself—by Holy Week and Easter spent in Jerusalem may help to account for the eventual spread of some of the special ceremonies of the Jerusalem liturgy to other parts of the Christian world. However, recent scholarship has raised the question as to whether in fact the Jerusalem ceremonies were simply imitated elsewhere. Initially, there was a reluctance in some places even to adopt the idea of a *triduum* and where it was adopted what went on did not necessarily always resemble the particular customs of the Jerusalem church.[12] Tidy answers, like those proposed by Dix, are not generally the most accurate when tracking post-Nicene liturgical development, which in most cases tended to be evolutionary rather than revolutionary. Liturgical trends, observes Paul Bradshaw, 'were not suddenly instituted by individual influential figures (like Cyril) in response to the changed situation of the Church in the post-Constantinian world'.[13]

Nevertheless, one factor certainly contributing to this evolution has already been mentioned, the rapid dissemination of relics of the True Cross to other Christian centres (see above, p. 73). Possession of such treasures was held to justify the adoption in such places of the Jerusalem rite of veneration. The pre-eminent example of this is the Roman basilica called Santa Croce in Gerusalemme (Holy Cross in Jerusalem). The earliest account of this church, actually called

---

[12] Bradshaw and Johnson, *Origins*, pp. 64–5.
[13] See P. F. Bradshaw, *The Search for the Origin of Christian Worship* (SPCK, London, and Oxford University Press, New York, 2nd edn, 2002), pp. 65–7.

Jerusalem, comes from a fourth-century biography of Sylvester I, the pope who had the satisfaction of seeing Rome transformed from a pagan into a Christian city through the generosity of the Emperor Constantine. The emperor opened a basilica in the Sessorian Palace which he named Jerusalem on account of the relic of the Cross placed within the church in a golden reliquary. Little of the Constantinian basilica remains today save eight great granite columns in the otherwise baroque nave, but the subterranean chapel of St Helena, beneath the modern Relic Chapel, was originally part of the Palace. Here the pavement rests directly on earth brought by St Helena from Jerusalem, the debris from her excavations on the site of Golgotha and the tomb of Christ. Although it took some time at the end of the seventh or the beginning of the eighth century for the rite of the Veneration of the Cross at this basilica to establish itself as part of the papal liturgy (thanks to the influence of a succession of oriental popes), it was a comparatively short step which then led from the veneration of a relic of the True Cross to the veneration of a simple cross and to the consequent spread of the practice to churches which did not possess a relic. In a similar way, it was a comparatively small step to free the Palm Sunday procession from its exclusive connection with its original geographical context.

By the end of the fifth century in much of Christendom the separate events of Christ's redemptive *transitus* were celebrated as distinct festivals. The influence of the Jerusalem liturgy and the ceremonies associated with it had possibly contributed to the gradual emergence of a serial, historical commemoration of these events in Holy Week. By deliberately reconstructing the final events in Jesus's life in a week of celebration, the worshipper was led not merely to recall those actions, but also, in some mysterious way, to share in them because, as Leo the Great had already observed, 'all that was visible of the Redeemer has passed over into the sacraments'.[14] Hence the tremendous appeal of the Holy Week ceremonies and the desire today to revive them or reclaim them for the whole Church, Eastern and Western, Catholic and Reformed.

[14]   Leo, *Sermo* lxxiv (Patrologia Latina 54, col. 398A).

IX

The Eastern Tradition

If it is possible to trace elements in the evolution of the Western Holy Week liturgy from the Jerusalem services described by Egeria, it is less easy to trace it precisely where the evidence ought to be more clear, in the rites of the Eastern Churches. The limited scope of this study precludes an examination of the liturgical complexity and theological richness of the Holy Week and Easter liturgies of the Eastern Orthodox and Oriental Orthodox Churches, but it does seem appropriate at this point to discuss briefly the present Holy Week and Easter services of the Byzantine Rite. Easter is considered the 'Feast of Feasts' and one hundred days are dedicated to its proper celebration, roughly corresponding to Western Lent and Eastertide—fifty before Easter Day for preparation, the *Triodion*, and another fifty after it for commemorating the glorification of the Lord, the *Pentecostarion*.

The Saturday before Holy Week is called the Saturday of the Holy and Righteous Lazarus[1] and worship begins with the phrase: 'Six days before the Passover Jesus came to Bethany, the home of Lazarus, whom he had raised from the dead' (John 12:1). One of the *troparia* sung on this day and on Palm Sunday links together these two mysteries in joyful anticipation of the Resurrection and the Parousia.

> Giving us before thy Passion an assurance of the general resurrection, thou hast raised Lazarus from the dead, O Christ our God. Therefore, like the children, we also carry tokens of victory, and cry to thee, the Conqueror of death, Hosanna in the highest; blessed is he that comes in the name of the Lord.

---

[1] According to Egeria the Jerusalem Church celebrated the liturgy on this day at the Lazarium, the church of Lazarus at Bethany.

Palm Sunday itself has a blessing and distribution of palms at Matins but no procession. Although the procession seems once to have been part of the day's celebration—there is evidence that it existed in the eleventh century in Constantinople—it has fallen into disuse.[2] Many of the most striking and well-attended ceremonies are in fact associated with the Offices in the Great Week rather than the eucharistic liturgy. Thus, on the Monday, Tuesday and Wednesday, although the Liturgy of the Presanctified Gifts is celebrated, the main emphasis is on Matins.

Monday's Matins, sung by anticipation on Palm Sunday Evening, commemorates both the patriarch Joseph as a type of the righteous man, and the fig tree which was cursed by the Lord (Matthew 21:19)—an interesting link with the pre-Reformation English name for this day, Fig Monday. The service begins with the Hymn of the Bridegroom:

> Behold the Bridegroom comes in the midst of the night—beware, therefore, O my soul, lest thou be borne down in sleep and lest thou be shut out from the Kingdom. I see thy bridal hall adorned, O my Saviour, and I have no wedding garment. O giver of light, make radiant the vesture of my soul and save me.

An icon of Christ the Bridegroom may be processed around the church and, anticipating the sufferings of Christ, the choir sings: 'Thy sublime sufferings, on this day, shine upon the world as a light of salvation.'

Tuesday Matins commemorates the parable of the Ten Virgins (Matthew 25:1–13) and on Wednesday, the commemoration is of the anointing of Christ with precious ointment by the woman in the house of Simon, the leper. On this evening the 'Hymn of Cassiane', probably a work of Patriarch Photius, is sung. It begins:

> The woman who had fallen into many sins recognised thy Godhead, O Lord; Woe to me, saith she; receive the sources of my tears, O thou who doth gather into clouds the water of the sea. Who can trace out the multitude of my sins and the abysses of my misdeeds? O thou whose mercy is unbounded.

The sacrament of the anointing of the sick is usually celebrated on the evening of Wednesday in Holy Week. As Metropolitan Kallistos

2   Kallistos Ware and Mother Mary, ed., *The Lenten Triodion* (Faber & Faber, London, 1978), p. 58.

Ware has written:

> All are anointed, whether physically ill or not; for there is
> no sharp line of demarcation between bodily and spiritual
> sicknesses and this sacrament confers not only bodily healing
> but forgiveness of sins, thus serving as a preparation for the
> reception of Holy Communion on the next day.[3]

Thursday sees the Eucharist celebrated according to the Liturgy of
St Basil, offered more properly after Vespers, but nowadays more
usually in the morning. In some cathedrals this will be followed by
the Washing of Feet if the bishop is celebrating and in patriarchal
churches the Holy Chrism is consecrated. During this Liturgy in
parish churches, the priest prepares the *Amnos*, the reserved Sacrament, which is kept throughout the whole year for communion of
the sick. The Blessed Sacrament is reserved in Orthodox churches
throughout the year. On this day, having been to confession or
having received the sacrament of Unction, the faithful receive Holy
Communion. The choir sing:

> Receive me today, O Son of God, as a partaker of thy Mystic
> Feast; for I will not speak of the Mystery to thine enemies, I will
> not kiss thee as did Judas, but as the thief I will confess thee.
> Lord, remember me when I come into thy Kingdom.[4]

Also on Thursday evening, by anticipation, Matins of Holy and
Great Friday is celebrated. It is a long vigil service, lasting about
five hours, and as its name suggests—The Office of the Holy and
Redeeming Passion of our Lord Jesus Christ—it focuses on the
reading of the 'Twelve Gospels', a narrative of the Passion derived
from all four Gospels and interspersed with troparia. The sequence
of readings follows this order:

1. John 13:31 to 18:1
2. John 18:1–29
3. Matthew 26:57–75
4. John 18:28 to 19:16
5. Matthew 27:3–32
6. Mark 15:16–32
7. Matthew 27:33–54

[3] *Ibid.*, p. 60.
[4] The website of the Greek Orthodox Church of America gives access to a
new translation into English of all the regularly used liturgical texts of the
Orthodox Church: https://www.goarch.ord/chapel/texts

8. Luke 23:32–49
9. John 19:38–42
10. Mark 15:43–7
11. John 19:38–42
12. Matthew 27:62–6.

After the fifth reading an image of the Crucified is processed round the church, while the priest chants the antiphon:

> Today is hung upon the Tree he who did hang the land in the midst of the waters. A crown of thorns crowns him who is King of angels. He is wrapped about with the purple of mockery who wrapped the heavens with clouds. He received buffetings who freed Adam in Jordan. He was transfixed with nails who is the Bridegroom of the Church. He was pierced with a spear who is the Son of the Virgin. We worship thy Passion, O Christ. Show also unto us thy glorious Resurrection.

Good Friday is a strictly aliturgical day; there is no celebration of the Eucharist, not even the Liturgy of the Presanctified Gifts. The Orthodox Liturgy is familiar with the rite of the Veneration of the Cross; this takes place on the third Sunday of Lent and on the Feast of the Exaltation of the Holy Cross on 14 September but not on Good Friday. Today, at Vespers, the Cross is replaced by the *epitaphion*, a cloth painted or embroidered with a representation of the body of the Christ as it was when taken down from the Cross. A mourning hymn is chanted as the *epitaphion* is carried from the altar in procession around the church:

> When Joseph of Arimathea took thee, the life of all, down from the Tree dead, he buried thee with myrrh and fine linen, rejoicing. Glory to thy humiliation, O Master, who clothest thyself with light as it were with a garment.

It is then placed, as it were, inside the Sepulchre, a wooden bier in the midst of the church, surrounded by flowers, which symbolises the Tomb of Christ. There it remains for the faithful to venerate. Compline follows immediately upon this service: its popular title is the Lamentation of the Most Holy Mother of God and highlights a striking contrast with the Western tradition, which finds no place for the sorrows or joys of our Lady in strictly liturgical material for Holy Week and Easter, except for one of the Good Friday Tenebrae responsories (*Caligeraverunt oculi mei*) and the recitation of the *Regina Coeli* after Compline in Eastertide.

Matins of Holy Saturday, celebrated on Friday evening, sees another procession with the *epitaphion*, carried this time around the outside of the church exactly as at a funeral. The *trisagion* (Holy God, holy and strong, holy and immortal, have mercy upon us) is sung at this point to a slow and solemn melody, as at the burial service. A note of Easter assurance is sounded early in the service with this *troparion* so redolent of the triumphant atmosphere of the traditional Resurrection icon:

> Going down to earth, O Life immortal, thou hast slain hell with the dazzling light of thy divinity. And when thou hadst raised up the dead from their dwelling place beneath the earth, all the powers of heaven cried aloud: Giver of life, O Christ our God, glory to thee.

On the morning of Holy Saturday Vespers is celebrated and the Liturgy of St Basil. This rite is in fact the present-day descendant of the Easter Vigil, although now celebrated on Saturday morning as a result of the same pressures that caused the Vigil to be celebrated at this time in the West until the reforms of Pius XII. There is a series of fifteen prophetic readings from the Old Testament including the Exodus account of the crossing of the Red Sea. The baptismal reference of the rite is made clear from the beginning of the eucharistic liturgy with the chant 'As many of you as were baptised into Christ have put on Christ, alleluia!' but at least in the currently received practice of the Russian Church, which dissociates the pastoral offices from the celebration of the Eucharist, no baptisms now take place at this service. There is no liturgical moment of the Resurrection in this service. Just as the now familiar icon of the Resurrection shows Christ, not leaping from the tomb as in the West, but trampling on death and the gates of hell, so the exact moment of his rising from the dead remains for ever mysterious. We know only that he who was dead is now alive, raising up mankind with himself. As St John Chrysostom triumphantly proclaims in his great Paschal Homily still read today as part of the Easter liturgy:

> He who came down into Hades despoiled Hades; and Hades was embittered when it tasted of his flesh. It received a body and encountered God. It received mortal dust and met Heaven face to face. It received what it saw and fell whither it saw not. O death, where is thy sting? O Hades, where is thy victory? Christ is risen and thou are overthrown. Christ is risen and the

demons have fallen. Christ is risen and the angels rejoice. Christ is risen and there is none dead in the tomb. For Christ is raised from the dead and become the first fruits of them that slept. To him be glory and power from all ages to all ages. Amen.[5]

The great Easter liturgy itself, celebrated at midnight between Saturday and Sunday, consists of Easter Matins and the Eucharist according to the Liturgy of St John Chrysostom. Although it is not the Easter Vigil, it has become *the* Easter Liturgy, the one and only eucharistic liturgy of Easter day, and it is a popular and crowded celebration marked not only with a degree of real joy and genuine and overflowing exuberance but also with 'a sense of an event powered from beyond the realm known to us'.[6]

> It is the day of Resurrection, O people; let us be enlightened.
> It is the Passover, the Lord's Passover. For from death to life
> and from earth to heaven Christ our God has brought us over,
> singing the hymn of victory.

However different the Eastern and Western liturgical traditions now appear, in both the Church of God is celebrating in this great and holy week the whole of the Paschal Mystery, refusing to allow its unity to be broken up, even if each day is given over to one aspect of it. The unitive and the eschatological are not swallowed up in the rememorative but we continue to proclaim the Lord's death until he comes and acclaim a past event, a present reality and a future expectation.

---

[5] See Fr Panayiotis Papageorgiou, 'The Paschal Catechetical Homily of St. John Chrysostom: A Rhetorical and Contextual Study', *The Greek Orthodox Theological Review* 43 (1998), pp. 93–100.

[6] F. Rutledge, *The Crucifixion. Understanding the Death of Jesus Christ* (Eerdmans, Grand Rapids, 2015), p. 61.

X

From Palm Sunday, The Passion of the Lord, to Maundy Thursday

The Roman calendar reforms of 1969 abolished Passion Sunday, which since the seventh century had been the name for the fifth Sunday of Lent and transferred the name back to Palm Sunday. As in the Gelasian Sacramentary, this now has the Latin title, *Dominica in Palmis, De Passione Domini* which is virtually untranslatable into English—the 2010 edition of the Roman Missal in English renders it, 'Palm Sunday of the Passion of the Lord'. Nevertheless, the restoration of the words 'Of the Passion of the Lord' to the ancient title Palm Sunday is significant. Early evidence suggests that well before there was a blessing of palms or procession in the Roman rite this was the day when the Passion narrative from St Matthew's Gospel was read.[1] The powerful Passion sermons of St Leo the Great, pope from 440 to 461, in which he speaks of the 'indescribable glory of the Passion' as Christ's victory, were preached on this day.[2] The liturgical combination of the joyful entry into Jerusalem and the proclamation of the Passion underlines the Easter significance of all that follows in Holy Week. Palm Sunday celebrates Christ's triumphal entrance into the Holy City to accomplish the Paschal Mystery; in going thus to his death he begins his *transitus*, his return in glory to the Father. Images and crucifixes veiled from the preceding Sunday have already contributed to the atmosphere in church and there is another immediate visual difference in the liturgy of this day since the colour of the vestments used changes

---

[1] A. Bugnini and C. Braga, 'Ordo Hebdomadae Sanctae Instauratus', *Ephemerides Liturgicae* 70 (1956), p. 87–8.

[2] J. W. Tyrer, *Historical Survey of Holy Week*, Alcuin Club Collections 29 (Oxford University Press, Oxford, 1932), p. 74. J. D. Crichton, *The Liturgy of Holy Week* (Goodliffe-Neale, London, 1971), p. 11.

from the violet of Lent to the red which will also be used on Good Friday. Passion red expresses neither the unrestrained joy of white nor the dominant penitence of violet but a delicate blend of joy and sorrow, of triumph attained through suffering.

Palm Sunday's distinctive ceremony, the Commemoration of the Lord's Entry into Jerusalem, should take place before the principal Eucharist of the day and consists of the blessing of palms and a procession together. One of the guiding principles of the 1955 reform of the Palm Sunday liturgy was to transfer the focus of the rite from the blessing of palms, which had become disproportionately lengthy, to the procession, rescuing it from having become a mere appendage to the blessing and restricted to the clergy and servers. Consequently, it is a mistake today to separate the two parts either by multiplying the blessing of palms before other celebrations or by omitting the procession altogether, for the palms are blessed entirely in order that they may be carried in the procession. To many people the essence of Palm Sunday has been found in going to church to get a palm cross, but to encourage this attitude by distributing them at services other than the main one or separately from the procession is to deflect attention from the real significance of the ceremony and to risk debasing it to the level of the trivial, the sentimental or even the superstitious. This latter attitude had perhaps been encouraged somewhat by the first of the multiplicity of prayers of blessing of the *missa sicca* in the pre-1955 rite which asked for all who received a palm 'that they may obtain thereby protection both in body and soul: and that, by thy grace which in a figure is shewn forth herein, may effectually be healed unto everlasting salvation'.[3] In any case, whatever the devotional appeal today of the dry, woven, palm cross, in procession they have hardly the same symbolic significance as the real green branches of box, yew or willow used in England before the Reformation.[4] In some parts of the country willow branches, with their spring covering of catkins, are still known as 'Palm'. Sprigs from these branches can still be taken away after the service and used to decorate crucifixes or pictures in the home. Whereas in the old rite palms were first

[3]   Translation from *The Anglican Missal* (The Society of SS Peter and Paul, London, 1946), p. 291.
[4]   For a lively description of the pre-Reformation procession in England see *The Early Works of Thomas Becon*, ed. J. Ayre (Parker Society, Cambridge, 1843).

blessed and then distributed, in the new rite it is assumed that the people are carrying palm *branches* from the outset. The implication in the 1969 Roman order that the people have brought the branches to church with them is made explicit in the preliminary notes to the Church of England Liturgy of Palm Sunday in *Common Worship: Times and Seasons* and to the service in the *Methodist Worship Book*.[5]

The procession, with or without palm branches, is of primary importance as it is the first of the commemorative liturgical actions in Holy Week whereby the Church involves herself in the redemptive movement of Christ's return to the Father. It is highly desirable that the congregation should assemble for the beginning of the service at some suitable place distinct from the church so that the procession can move from one to the other and be clearly seen to effect a solemn entry into Jerusalem. Whilst such a procession embodies an element of the dramatic, as do so many of the Jerusalem liturgical ceremonies, it does not require the distracting participation of a donkey. It is not just a piece of play acting or make-believe designed to stimulate the imagination or heighten devotion, the Holy Week ceremonies are not there to *impress* but rather to *involve*. This sort of procession is a real act of witness—involving the whole congregation, not just the clergy, servers, and choir—whereby those embarking on Holy Week can pledge their loyalty to Christ, enrol themselves among his followers and publicly commit themselves to follow him along the *Via Dolorosa* of his sufferings to the triumph of his Resurrection. This is made abundantly clear in the brief, didactic introductions provided in the *Common Worship* and *Methodist Worship Book* orders (which are modelled on that in the Roman rite) for the president to use as he or she invites the people to take a full part in the celebration:

> Dear brothers and sisters in Christ, during Lent we have been preparing by works of love and self-sacrifice for the celebration of our Lord's death and resurrection. Today we come together to begin this solemn celebration in union with the Church throughout the world. Christ enters his own city to complete his work as our Saviour, to suffer, to die, and to rise again. Let us go with him in faith and love, so that, united with him in his sufferings, we may share his risen life.[6]

[5] *Common Worship: Times and Seasons*, p. 268, and *The Methodist Worship Book*, p. 236.
[6] *Common Worship: Times and Seasons*, p. 270.

As soon as this explanatory introduction has been read, the people hold up their branches and fronds to be blessed. The prayer in *Common Worship* sees the palms as signs of Christ's victory and both Roman and Anglican prayers stress the eschatological theme which is so noticeable in the new rites. The emphasis in the Roman blessing has shifted dramatically from that found in the pre-1955 string of blessing prayers, which virtually consecrated the palms, so that in the present choice of two prayers both of which really focus on the people who are about to set forth in procession rather than on the palms they are to carry.

The scene is now set for the reading of the Palm Gospel which used to be invariably Matthew 21:1–9 but which now may be taken from any of the Synoptic accounts: Matthew 21:1–11, Mark 11:1–10 or Luke 19:28–40 (John 12:12–16 is a permitted alternative in year B). The president or deacon then bids the procession go forth and so it moves to the church where the Eucharist is to be celebrated. The procession is a procession of praise to Jesus the Messiah and so antiphons, psalms, and hymns of praise are sung as it moves along. It is Christ the King who is acclaimed in these chants, the words of which do not restrict themselves to the Lord's entry into Jerusalem before his passion. The Church's praises speak also of the resurrection and ascension of Christ, his entry into the *heavenly* Jerusalem, and in so doing the liturgy looks forward to the final fulfilment of the paschal mystery in the *Parousia*. This is the sense of the Old Testament background: 'The Lord has proclaimed to the end of the earth: Say to daughter Zion, 'See, your salvation comes; his reward is with him, and his recompense before him' (Isaiah 62:11); 'Rejoice greatly, O daughter Zion! Shout aloud, O daughter Jerusalem. Lo, your king comes to you, triumphant and victorious is he, humble and riding on a donkey, on a colt, the foal of a donkey' (Zechariah 9:9) — this passage is part of that appointed as the first lesson in the Third Service lectionary for this day in *Common Worship*; 'the Lord whom you seek will suddenly come to his temple' (Malachi 3:1). This, too, is the reason why the Palm Sunday narrative was appointed in the *Book of Common Prayer* as the Gospel for Advent Sunday; it is a foretaste of the final entry of Christ with the whole company of the redeemed into the fullness of his kingdom. 'Lift up your heads, O gates! and be lifted up, O ancient doors! that the King of glory may come in' (Psalm 24:7).

All this would seem to show that the Commemoration of the Lord's Entry into Jerusalem is not just the historically and sequentially correct way in which to begin the observance of Holy Week, but it is also theologically the richest and most appropriate. Accordingly, it was regarded as of such importance by the compilers of the 1969 Roman rite that they direct that it must preface every public Mass on Palm Sunday. To cope with all pastoral circumstances, they provide three forms: the Procession, or normative commemoration, described above and followed closely by *Common Worship*; the Solemn Entrance, which is to be performed within the church only when circumstances do not permit an extended procession; and a Simple Entrance, in which the commemoration is made with an antiphon and psalm. The rubrics continue hopefully, 'It is desirable that, where neither the Procession nor the Solemn Entrance can take place, there be a sacred celebration of the Word of God on the messianic entrance and on the Passion of the Lord, either on Saturday evening or on Sunday at a convenient time'.

There is no longer any discontinuity between the process and the Eucharist, no change from red to violet vestments as there was in the first stage of the reform under Pius XII. The Mass begins almost abruptly; the celebrant, having as it were made a more solemn entrance than usual, venerates the altar, omits the penitential rite, and begins the Mass with the Collect, much as would have happened in the early days of the Church.

The liturgical emphasis is now firmly on the Passion, but even here the Resurrection is never out of sight. The Collect, essentially the same in Roman and Anglican traditions and probably composed by St Leo, presents the model of Christ's humility expressed in his suffering and asks that through following his example we may be made worthy to participate in his Resurrection. The first two readings — Isaiah 50:4–7(9a) and Philippians 2:6(5)–11 — by providing an interpretative context, form a preparation for the solemn reading of the Passion which is read from a different Synoptic account in each year of the three-year cycle. The reading from Isaiah, taken from the third of the Servant Songs, is a poetic description of the Lord's humiliation and suffering in obedience to his Father's will culminating in his ultimate vindication; the 'Kenotic Hymn' from Philippians 2 makes this even more explicit — God has highly exalted the Man who humbled himself in obedience even to the point of giving his life on the Cross and given him the name that is above every other name.

The liturgy of Palm Sunday now to be found in the Roman, Anglican, and Methodist service books perfectly expresses the essential balance between rememorative and unitive celebrations of the Paschal Mystery. It avoids focusing on details and incidents which might present a one-sided view of the Passion in terms solely of suffering and offers instead the very different insight expressed in the earliest apostolic sermon, 'let the entire house of Israel know with certainty that God has made him both Lord and Messiah, this Jesus whom you crucified' (Acts 2:36b). The Passion—'this Jesus whom you crucified'—can only be understood in the light of Resurrection-Exaltation—'God has made him both Lord and Messiah'—and so its liturgical celebration must, in the words of Adrian Nocent, 'give a complete and rounded theological vision of the mystery of Christ. It tells that this mystery is not a mystery of death alone but a mystery of life that triumphs over death. This vision is important for a proper conception of the spiritual life.'[7]

Palm Sunday inaugurates the Great and Holy Week, but the first three ferial days of the Week, Monday, Tuesday, and Wednesday are distinguished neither by special ceremonies nor today by any attempt to link them chronologically with particular events in the story of the Passion of Christ. Nevertheless, there remains in popular devotion an attempt to attribute events in the heightening drama of the lead up to the Passion as related in the Gospels to each of the three days. Hence Monday is known by some as 'Fig Monday' when the Lord cursed the barren fig tree (Matthew 21:18–22), Tuesday is 'Temple Tuesday' when in righteous anger he cleansed the temple of its traders and moneychangers (Matthew 21:12–13), and Wednesday is 'Spy Wednesday' referring to the action of Judas in undertaking to betray Jesus to the temple authorities, becoming thereby a spy in the midst of the disciples (Matthew 26:14–16). In the earliest years from which evidence exists, the only weekday services were Liturgies of the Word or *synaxes* on Wednesdays and Fridays.[8] Before the 1970 reforms, the Wednesday Mass retained certain primitive features from this era, notably two Old Testament readings, a vestige of the time when on this day a 'stational Mass', following on from the *synaxis* or even conjoined with it, was cel-

---

[7]   Nocent, *The Liturgical Year*, vol. 2, p. 201.
[8]   K. Niederwimmer, *The Didache: A Commentary* (Fortress Press, Minneapolis, 1998), p. 8.

ebrated at St Mary Major. In the middle of the fifth century, Pope Leo the Great's Passion sermons, begun, as noted above, on the Sunday, were concluded at this Mass. Today however, each of these three days is given two readings only in the Roman lectionary, the first being from Isaiah; *Common Worship* gives the same readings and responsorial psalms but provides additional readings from the New Testament epistles and alternative Gospel readings. The *Roman Missal* provides a different collect for each day but following the *Book of Common Prayer* the *Common Worship* provision assumes the use of the Palm Sunday collect on these three days. The 1979 American *Book of Common Prayer*, however, does provide a collect for each day, one of which will be familiar to many English Anglicans through Eric Milner White's *A Procession of Passion Prayers*.[9] It is worth mentioning at this point that it is not appropriate at Morning Prayer on Maundy Thursday in the Anglican rite to use the collect provided for the evening Eucharist; *Common Worship* directs the use of the Palm Sunday collect.

The *day* of Thursday in Holy Week is the last day of Lent; the Paschal *Triduum* does not begin until the evening, but that fact explains the absence of any eucharistic celebration on the morning of that Thursday. The only exception allowed is the Mass of the Chrism, normally celebrated by the Diocesan Bishop in the Cathedral on this morning but often, for pastoral reasons, anticipated on one of the earlier days of Holy Week. However, the so-called Gelasian Sacramentary,[10] which may in part represent usage in Rome before the year 700, provides three Mass formulae for Thursday. The second and third of these represent the masses which are familiar today, the Chrism Mass (*Missa Chrismatis*) and the Evening Mass of the Lord's Supper (*Missa ad Vesperum*), but the first has disappeared from use. It was the occasion for the public reconciliation of penitents (*Ordo agentibus publicam poenitentiam*) the ejection of whom, *cum lacrymis*, was a feature of the ancient Ash Wednesday rite (see above, p. 15). The old English name for Maundy Thursday,

9   E. Milner White, *A Procession of Passion Prayers* (SPCK, London, 1962). Similarly, the 1979 American *Book of Common Prayer*, again like the Roman rite, provides a proper collect for every day in the Easter Octave.
10   L. C. Mohlberg, *Liber Sacramentorum Romanae Aeclesiae Ordinis Anni Circuli*, Rerum Ecclesiasticarum Documenta, Series Maior, Fontes IV (Herder, Rome, 1960).

'Shere Thursday', represents an echo of this custom, 'shere' being a now-obsolete word meaning pure or clean.[11]

If the first Mass of Maundy Thursday has long since disappeared and the Rite for the Public Reconciliation of Penitents on this day has gone from the *Pontificale Romanum*, the last day of Lent remains an appropriate day for the Sacrament of Reconciliation and many may still wish to make their confession on the very threshold of the solemn celebration of the mystery of redemption. Today is indeed a day of reconciliation, for the sign of the remission of sin and of reconciliation with God in the new covenant is the fraternal banquet of the Lord's Supper. It should also be remembered that the circumstances of today's celebration give particular emphasis to the role of the Eucharist as the sacrament of unity, and that it is sin which disperses and divides and scatters abroad the people of God (John 11:52). Penance is thought of as perhaps the most 'private' of all the sacraments, as indeed in a sense it is, but it does have an important public and communal dimension (see above, p. 16). Sacramental reconciliation with God and his Church on this day is as fitting an adaptation of today's ancient ceremony as the receiving of ashes on Ash Wednesday is of that day's former rite. 'It is fitting that the Lenten season be concluded, both for the individual Christian as well as for the whole Christian community, with a penitential celebration, so that they may be helped to prepare to celebrate more fully the Paschal Mystery.'[12] Not everyone will be able to go to confession on Maundy Thursday itself, but pastoral provision should be made in Holy Week, preferably before the Mass of the Lord's Supper rather than on Good Friday or Easter Eve. The formula of absolution in the Roman rite underlines the paschal character of this sacrament:

> God, the Father of mercies, through the death and resurrection of his Son has reconciled the world to himself and sent the Holy Spirit among us for the forgiveness of sins; through the ministry of the Church may God give you pardon and peace, and I absolve you from your sins in the name of the Father, and of the Son, + and of the Holy Spirit.

Common Worship: Christian Initiation provides orders for both a

---

[11] Tyrer, *Historical Survey*, p. 80.
[12] *Paschalis Solemnitatis*, section 37.

Corporate Service of Penitence and the Reconciliation of a Penitent and these offer a number of authorised absolution formulae.[13] The second of these absolutions, while not entirely satisfactory as it omits the crucial words 'I absolve you', nevertheless provides the same paschal resonance:

> God, the Father of mercies, has reconciled the world to himself through the death and resurrection of his Son Jesus Christ, not counting our trespasses against us, but sending the Holy Spirit to shed abroad his love among us. By the ministry of reconciliation entrusted by Christ to his Church, receive his pardon and peace to stand before him in his strength alone, this day and evermore.

If the reconciliation of penitents speaks of the sacrament of penance, then the consecration of the Holy Oils performed by the bishop in the cathedral church at the *Missa Chrismatis* (or *Chrismalis*) speaks particularly of the sacraments of baptism, confirmation, ordination, and the anointing of the sick. Indeed, the sacraments of initiation, celebrated so appropriately in the early days of the Church at the Easter Vigil, required great quantities of Holy Oil—for the all-over pre-baptismal anointing of the neophytes with the Oil of the Catechumens and for their post-baptismal anointing with the Oil of Chrism. The nearest available day for the consecration of these oils by the bishop was the Thursday in Holy Week, Good Friday being clearly out of the question and Easter Eve itself a eucharistic *dies non*; hence the second of the Mass formulae for this day found in the Gelasian Sacramentary. But there is more than a merely historical and practical justification for this practice because celebrating on this day the inauguration of the New Covenant in the institution of the Eucharist, the Church is celebrating the mystery from which all the other sacraments take their origin and towards which they are all directed—the mystery of the Body of Christ, which is at the same time the mystery of the Church and the mystery of the Eucharist. Hence in the celebration of the Chrism Mass as radically reformed by Paul VI[14] there are two centres of interest: holy order, seen in the proper context of the priestly nature of the whole People of God, and the consecration of the Holy Oils which are at the service, as it were, of the priestly and sacramental ministry of the Church.

---

13 *Common Worship: Christian Initiation*, pp. 288–9.
14 Only the *Secreta* (Prayer over the Gifts) survives from the old Gelasian Mass formula.

The celebration of the Chrism Mass should be seen as one of the most important diocesan occasions of the year and thus take place at a time and, if not in the cathedral, at a place convenient for the greatest number of priests and people. The new rite is a celebration of the common priesthood in Christ which the bishop and priests share and so it is important that the diocesan clergy are present in truly representative numbers to concelebrate with their bishop and renew their priestly commitment. By celebrating this Eucharist with their bishop the clergy and people give real expression to the unity which binds together the many separate celebrations in parishes and other communities throughout the diocese. The ministerial priesthood is an essential part of the royal priesthood of all the baptised, which it exists to serve and enable. Therefore, this celebration should not be allowed to become an exclusively clerical occasion as is made clear in the Greeting in the *Common Worship* rite (from Revelation 1:6): 'Jesus Christ has made us a kingdom of priests to serve his God and Father.' This is more explicit in the proper preface in the Roman rite:

> For by the anointing of the Holy Spirit you made your Only Begotten Son High Priest of the new and eternal covenant, and by your wondrous design were pleased to decree that his one Priesthood should continue in the Church. For Christ not only adorns with a royal priesthood the people he has made his own, but with a brother's kindness he also chooses men to become sharers in his sacred ministry through the laying on of hands. They are to renew in his name the sacrifice of human redemption, to set before your people the paschal banquet, to lead your holy people in charity, to nourish them with the word and strengthen them with the Sacraments. As they give up their lives for you and for the salvation of their brothers and sisters, they strive to be conformed to the image of Christ himself and offer you a constant witness of faith and love.[15]

This preface sums up an entirely new element in the Chrism Mass, introduced in the reforms of Paul VI: the renewal of priestly commitment to Christ and the service of his body, the Church. This takes place after the sermon which should be preached by the bishop, and which should urge the priests to be faithful in fulfilling their office in the Church. The *Common Worship* rite, catering

---

[15] *Roman Missal*, 2010 translation, pp. 326–7.

for those who might be persuaded to attend more readily by the opportunity to renew their ministerial commitment than by the consecration of the Holy Oils, provides forms of renewal which can include lay ministers and deacons as well as priests and an occasion for the bishops of the diocese to be questioned by a lay person on the vows they made at their consecration.[16]

The second element in the Chrism Mass, the consecration of the Holy Oils for use throughout the diocese in the year ahead, is accomplished in a splendid ceremony furnished with texts and chants of great richness. Ideally the oils are carried into the presence of the bishop by three deacons, followed by lay people carrying the elements to be used for the Mass.[17] After the procession is over, the Roman rite allows for the blessings to occur in one of two ways: in accordance with traditional practice, the blessing of the Oil of the Sick may take place before the end of the Eucharistic Prayer, and the blessing of the Oil of Catechumens and the consecration of the Chrism after the distribution of communion; for pastoral reasons, however, all the oils may be blessed together following the Liturgy of the Word. The *Common Worship* order places the three blessings after the exchange of Peace and before the preparation of the altar.

In the Roman rite, the oils are blessed with formulae which clearly indicate the purpose for which they are to be used. First comes the blessing of the Oil of the Sick as 'a safeguard for body soul and spirit'. The power of Christ should be seen as active in the anointing of the sick, making present and real for them the healing he practised when here on earth. The Oil of Catechumens, formerly known as the Oil of Exorcism, is blessed next for use before baptism. The prayer asks that those to be baptised may receive 'divine wisdom and power that they may understand more deeply the Gospel of Christ'. Finally, the Oil of Chrism, mixed with fragrant oil of flowers is consecrated to be used at ordinations and in the sacraments of initiation. Before saying the prayer of consecration, the bishop breathes upon the opening of the vessel of the Chrism. Chrism is a sign of the Holy Spirit, and this action by the bishop recalls Jesus' Resurrection appearance to the disciples in which 'he

---

[16] *Common Worship: Times and Seasons*, pp. 282–7.
[17] An ancient Latin hymn for the procession with the oils, translated by Bishop Richard Rutt, has found favour with many Anglican dioceses and a place in *New English Hymnal*, no. 512, and *Common Praise*, no. 131.

breathed on them and said to them, 'Receive the Holy Spirit' (John 20:22). The Roman rite provides two options for the consecratory prayer. In the first option, the Prayer of Consecration asks God 'to sanctify with [his] blessing this oil in its richness, and to pour into it the strength of the Holy Spirit, with the powerful working' of Christ. The second option provides a rich description of the uses of holy Chrism: 'Pour out in abundance the gifts of the Holy Spirit on our brothers and sisters anointed with this oil; adorn with the splendour of holiness the places and things signed by sacred oils; but above all, by the mystery of this oil, bring to completion the growth of your Church'. Chrism is the oil of priesthood, both general—for those incorporated into Christ's priestly people at baptism—and particular—for those ordained to share in the ministerial priesthood of Christ—and those priests present and concelebrating with the bishop extend their hands for this prayer.

For the bishops of the Church of England and those other Anglicans who use its liturgical resources, *Common Worship* provides three, *berakhah*-shaped prayers of blessing for the oils. A deacon presents each oil to the bishop who, with typical Anglican caution, calls down a blessing not on the oil itself but on those who will receive it in anointing. Those anointed with the Oil of the Sick are blessed so that they may be 'made whole in body, mind and spirit', and 'restored in [God's] image'. The 'oil for the signing of the cross at baptism' is a sign of the candidates' 'defence in their fight against sin, the world and the devil'. Those anointed with the Oil of Chrism are blessed with 'a sign of joy and gladness as they share in the royal priesthood of the new Covenant'.[18] This latter prayer carefully ignores the fact that traditionally the Chrism is used not only for the anointing of persons but also of things such as altars, church buildings and the like.

For those unable to be present at the Chrism Mass, the significance and importance of the Holy Oils should be emphasised by the rite of reception of the oils into the parish church at some suitable time, preferably at the beginning of the Mass of the Lord's Supper. The *Common Worship* provision firmly links the reception of the oils to the evening Liturgy of Maundy Thursday and to the celebration of the Paschal Mystery as the presiding minister says:

[18]   *Common Worship: Times and Seasons*, pp. 288–9.

> Brothers and sisters, on this most holy night we enter into the three days of the celebration of our Lord's paschal victory, his death and resurrection. Those of our community who are to be baptised this Eastertide will be made one with Christ, dying to sin and rising to newness of life in him. As we begin, therefore, we receive from our bishop the holy oils blessed and set apart for the sacramental life of our parish.[19]

It used to be customary for the bishop to address some words to the concelebrant clergy on the care of the Holy Oils before dismissing them at the end of the Chrism Mass. The oils from the previous year should be disposed of reverently by adding them to the oil in a lamp, where such things still exist, or by pouring them onto cotton wool or some such and burning them. The oils for the year ahead should be carefully stored, preferably in an aumbry specially set aside for them. In cathedrals, where diocesan supplies of consecrated oils are kept for replenishing parish stocks, and in pilgrimage centres, where quantities of the Oil of the Sick are required for services of health and healing, it is a commendable practice to reserve the oils in a specially designed shrine or chrismatory where they can be seen and become a focus for prayer and meditation.[20]

---

[19] *Ibid.*, p. 292.
[20] The Anglican Cathedral in Norwich reserves the oils in a hanging chrismatory, located appropriately over a medieval Seven Sacraments Font in a side chapel. Materials explaining the use of the oils in sacramental ministry are provided with aids to prayer and meditation.

XI

Maundy Thursday Evening.
The Mass of the Lord's Supper

Before discussing the rite and ceremonies of Maundy Thursday evening it is important to clarify what is meant by the Paschal *Triduum* (*Triduum Sacrum* or *Triduum Paschale*) because the reform of liturgical year in the Roman Rite has given a uniquely privileged place to these three days of Christian paschal celebration:

> Since Christ accomplished his work of human redemption and of the perfect glorification of God principally through his Paschal Mystery, in which by dying he has destroyed death, and by rising restored our life, the sacred Paschal Triduum of the Passion and Resurrection of the Lord shines forth as the high point of the entire liturgical year. Therefore the pre-eminence that Sunday has in the week, the Solemnity of Easter has in the liturgical year. The Paschal Triduum ... begins with the evening Mass of the Lord's Supper, has its centre in the Easter Vigil, and closes with Vespers (Evening Prayer) of the Sunday of the Resurrection.[1]

The Church of England began to address the provision of Holy Week rites in the 1980s after the publication of the *Alternative Service Book 1980* and, as already has been noted (see above, p. 97), published a collection of material in 1986 under the title *Lent, Holy Week, Easter. Services and Prayers*. In the introduction to the Maundy Thursday evening Eucharist it also addresses the important point made in the Roman Calendar Norms but in a rather less precise manner. Although the word *triduum* does not appear (it did appear in the first draft, but it was pointed out in General Synod that it would need some explanation and so it was dropped), it is replaced

---

[1] *The Roman Missal*, 'Universal Norms for the Liturgical Year and the General Roman Calendar', sections 18 and 19, p. 132.

by the word *continuum*:

> Maundy Thursday marks a new beginning, the beginning of the
> end. From this point on, our Christian worship is a continuum
> through to Easter morning. The Jewish beginning of the day
> (in the evening) unites the events of Maundy Thursday with
> the death of Christ the next afternoon.[2]

It is much to be regretted that when the *Lent, Holy Week, Easter*
services were edited and supplemented for the *Common Worship:
Times and Seasons* volume, the author of the excellent seasonal introductions to each section preferred in the introduction to Passiontide
and Holy Week to adopt a rather wider focus, asserting that 'over
time, the *Pascha* developed into the articulated structure of Holy
Week and Easter' and made no mention of a *triduum*. Nevertheless,
the idea of a continuity of liturgical action is suggested:

> Through participation in the whole sequence of services, the
> Christian shares in Christ's own journey, from the triumphal
> entry into Jerusalem on Palm Sunday to the empty tomb on
> Easter morning.[3]

Though the term *triduum* is of great antiquity, its exact application
has varied. The significance attached to 'three days' and 'the third
day' goes back to the New Testament, the Creeds and the earliest Christian tradition. Some early commentators and preachers
found reference to Christ's passion, death and resurrection in the
prophetic words of Hosea (6:1–2) in the Old Testament:

> Come, let us return to the Lord; for it is he who has torn, and
> he will heal us; he has struck down, and he will bind us up.
> After two days he will revive us; on the third day he will raise
> us up, that we may live before him.

Origen certainly believed that the events of the Pascha occupied
three days in fulfilment of this prophecy:

> Now listen to what the prophet says: 'God will revive us after
> two days, and on the third day we shall rise and live in his
> sight.' For us the first day is the passion of the Saviour; the
> second on which he descended into hell; and the third, the day
> of resurrection.[4]

---

[2]   *Lent. Holy Week. Easter*, p. 179.
[3]   *Common Worship: Times and Seasons*, p. 259.
[4]   Origen, *Homilia in Exodum* 5.2 (Patrologia Graeca 12, col. 297); see Cantalamessa,

Words are attributed to our Lord in the Gospels which bring together the events of the *Triduum* (Matthew 20:18–19):

> See, we are going up to Jerusalem, and the Son of Man will be handed over to the chief priests and scribes, and they will condemn him to death; then they will hand him over to the Gentiles to be mocked and flogged and crucified; and on the third day he will be raised.

At first the great Vigil was the unitive celebration of Christ's passion and Resurrection with no separate commemoration on the days preceding it was, however, preceded by the strict paschal fast of one or two days, with priority given to the Saturday rather than the Friday. The two day fast before the Night of Easter already gives us a *triduum*—Friday, Saturday and Sunday; so St Ambrose can speak of 'the sacred *triduum* within which he suffered, lay in the tomb, and arose, the three days of which he said: "Destroy this temple and in three days I will raise it up"',[5] and St Augustine can similarly write of 'the most holy *triduum* of the crucified, entombed and risen one' ('sacratissimum triduum crucifixi, sepulti, resuscitati').[6] As discussed in some detail earlier, the liturgical elaboration of the three days with ceremonies designed to give particular articulation to the themes of each day is considered to have begun in Jerusalem in response to the crowds of pilgrims who began to arrive there in the late fourth-century with the expectation of celebrating *Pascha* in the very places where the events of Christ's Passion and Resurrection were believed to have taken place (see above, p. 107).

It was not so much the introduction of the distinct celebrations of Maundy Thursday and Good Friday which broke the unity of the Sacred *Triduum* as the later displacement of the proper times of their celebration; the moving of the Mass of the Lord's Supper to Thursday morning and, even more fatally serious, the shifting of the Great Vigil of Easter to the morning of Holy Saturday, with the consequent anticipation on the previous evening of Matins and Lauds (*Tenebrae*) of Thursday, Friday and Saturday. This involved a loss of the sense of chronological authenticity, what the Second Vatican Council called *veritas temporis* (in real time) and led to

---

    Easter, p. 55.
5   *Epistola* 23, 12–13 (Patrologia Latina 16, col. 1030).
6   *Epistola* 55, 24 (Patrologia Latina 33, col. 215).

the *Triduum Sacrum* being reckoned as the last three days of Holy Week—Thursday, Friday, and Saturday. In theory this still included the celebration of the Resurrection, but the inclusion was far from evident and the unifying factor of the night and day of Easter being both part of the *Triduum* and of the Great Fifty Days was lost. The *Triduum* was seen as more a preparation for Easter than as embracing Easter, more of a *triduum* of the Passion than as the Paschal *Triduum*.

There was an element of innovation in Pope St Paul VI's reform—both in the use of the title Paschal (or Easter) *Triduum* and in its beginning now with the Mass of the Lord's Supper on Thursday evening—but while in the profoundest sense it marked a return to the principle expressed in the ancient *Triduum*, the cohesive liturgical unity it inaugurated may not have been quite understood as such in late antiquity.[7] The same reform also specifies that Lent comes to an end on Maundy Thursday before the ushering in of the Easter *Triduum*. The new *Triduum* is indeed a continuum; although each day has its distinct emphasis, yet it is the Paschal Mystery in its unity that is celebrated throughout.

Outwardly, the Evening Mass of the Lord's Supper is a celebration of the Eucharist much like any other but with certain ceremonies peculiar to this one evening. However, it is a eucharistic celebration which succeeds in expressing with particular force certain aspects of the eucharistic mystery which are not always so evident in other celebrations. It is clearly a joyful and festive gathering of the People of God around the Table of the Lord. The institution of the Eucharist is a cause for joy and celebration, so the liturgical colour is white or gold and the Gloria in Excelsis is sung. Where it is the tradition to veil crucifixes, the High Altar cross should be veiled in white. On this day the multiplication of celebrations is discouraged and Masses without a congregation forbidden, and—with the exception of the Chrism Mass—there should normally be only one Mass, sung and with a sermon, in every church. The bishop or the parish priest or the senior priest of the community should preside 'with the full participation of the whole local community and with all the priests and ministers exercising their office' as the rubrics of the Roman rite express it.

---

[7]   H. Buchinger, 'Was there ever a liturgical Triduum in antiquity? Theological idea and liturgical reality,' *Ecclesia Orans* 27/3 (2010), pp. 257–70.

During this celebration moreover the regrettable custom, strongly discouraged in the *General Instruction* of the *Roman Missal*, of giving Holy Communion from the Reserved Sacrament rather than from hosts consecrated there and then at the Mass is expressly forbidden: the tabernacle, aumbry or pyx is already empty and the Blessed Sacrament has been removed to a 'remote place' where it will remain until after the Easter Vigil.

The themes of the celebration are indicated in the rubric after the Gospel in the Roman rite:

> The priest gives a homily in which light is shed on the principal mysteries that are commemorated in this Mass, namely, the institution of the Holy Eucharist and of the priestly Order, and the commandment of the Lord concerning fraternal charity.

Most Anglicans will probably feel uneasy about the reference to the 'institution of the priestly Order'. The Last Supper is emphatically not seen in the best theology today of any tradition as the occasion of the 'ordination' of the Twelve to the priesthood by virtue of the command of the Lord, 'Do this in remembrance of me'. The rubric, however, does not commit Anglicans to any such theology; it points them to the kind of link between Eucharist and priesthood which was expressed in 1981 in the *Final Report* of the Anglican-Roman Catholic International Commission:

> Because the eucharist is the memorial of the sacrifice of Christ, the action of the presiding minister in reciting again the words of Christ at the last supper and distributing to the assembly the holy gifts is seen to stand in sacramental relation to what Christ himself did in offering his own sacrifice. So our two traditions commonly use priestly terms in speaking about the ordained ministry.[8]

Before examining further themes in the Last Supper and Footwashing, there is one other theme, less prominent today that formerly but nevertheless still present and worthy of some comment. An ancient name for this day is 'the day of tradition'[9] and both *traditio* in the Latin and *paradosis* in the Greek of the New Testament have a double meaning. In the context of this day's celebration, they refer both to Christ's *handing over* of his life to the Father and *passing*

---

[8] Anglican-Roman Catholic International Commission, *The Final Report*, Ministry and Ordination II, 13, p. 35.

[9] Cf. H. Thurston, SJ, *Lent and Holy Week* (Longmans, London, 1904), p. 286.

on his Body and Blood to his Church and to his being *handed over* to his enemies by Judas.[10] Formerly there was reference to Judas in the very ancient Collect of the Roman rite, where he is set in contrast to the penitent thief:

> O God, from whom both Judas received the punishment of his guilt, and the thief the reward of his confession, grant unto us the effect of thy propitiation: that, as in his passion Jesus Christ, our Lord, gave unto each the divers rewards of his merits; so he may deliver us from the transgressions of our old nature, and bestow upon us the grace of his resurrection.[11]

In the old rite the kiss of peace was also omitted because of the betraying kiss of Judas but today it is only in the Eastern rite that Judas is mentioned (except in the Gospel reading) in a thrice repeated *troparion* which also refers to the penitent thief:

> *Receive me today, O Son of God,*
> *as a partaker of thy Mystic Feast;*
> *for I will not speak of the Mystery to thine enemies;*
> *I will not kiss thee as did Judas;*
> *but as a thief I will confess thee:*
> *Lord, remember me when thou comest in thy Kingdom.*[12]

In the Roman rite of today, the Collect speaks of the Supper entrusted to the Church by Christ 'when about to hand himself over to death' ('morti se traditurus'); the second reading, found also in Anglican and Methodist provision, from the First Letter to the Corinthians, makes clear the double meaning of *paradosis-traditio* when St Paul speaks of *handing on* what he had received and goes on to speak of the night on which Jesus was betrayed or, more properly, *handed over*; a clause added on this one occasion to the Roman Canon (the First Eucharistic Prayer) refers to the day 'on which our Lord Jesus Christ was handed over for our sake' (*pro nobis est traditus*) ; finally the Communion antiphon in its Latin original, quoting the Old Vulgate of 1 Corinthians 11:24, speaks of the Body of Christ that 'will be given up for you' (*tradetur*).

---

[10] For a study of this theme in great theological and spiritual depth, cf. W. H. Vanstone, *The Stature of Waiting* (DLT, London, 1982).
[11] Trans. from *The English Missal*. This collect, *A quo et Iudas*, was probably written by Pope St Leo in the mid–fifth century.
[12] *The Lenten Triodion*. See also M. Perham and K. Stevenson, *Waiting for the Risen Christ, A Commentary on Lent, Holy Week, Easter* (SPCK, London, 1986), p. 54.

The dominant theme in this opening celebration of the *Triduum* is the Supper of the Lord, but the Supper seen not exclusively as the institution of the Eucharist but experienced in the context of a paschal celebration which cannot but embrace the whole mystery of redemption. The Roman rite Entrance Antiphon, drawn from Galatians 6, presents this wider context at the outset: 'We should glory in the Cross of our Lord Jesus Christ, in whom is our salvation, life and resurrection, through whom we are saved and delivered.' The paschal background is emphasised by the first reading (identical in the Roman rite, the *Common Worship* and *Methodist Worship Book* provision) from the twelfth chapter of Exodus; instructions for the Passover meal. It is the themes of the Supper and Eucharist which dominate the Collect, the first two readings and responsorial psalm, the Proper Preface, the Communion Antiphon and the Postcommunion prayers in both rites as well as the words adapted from the Jewish Passover meal which introduce the Preparation of the Gifts in the *Common Worship* material (see above, p. 36). Above all there is the fact that the way in which thanks are given for the gift of the Eucharist is by making eucharist; the Supper is not only remembered but celebrated.

The remaining theme, Christ's commandment to love one another, is the theme of the Gospel, which, in Roman, Anglican and Methodist rites, is the story from John 13 of the washing of the disciples' feet by the Lord. This may be followed, after the sermon, by the ceremony of the Washing of Feet. The action is described in the Roman rubric: those 'who have been chosen, are led by the ministers to seats prepared in a suitable place. Then the priest (removing the chasuble if necessary) goes to each one, and with the help of the ministers, pours water over each one's feet and then dries them.' Many parish clergy hesitate to introduce this ceremony, fearing that it will seem unreal, theatrical, embarrassing, even unsettling. Worse still are those who decide to wash hands rather than feet and extend the ceremony to everyone present, thus negating the whole point of the exercise and abandoning its scriptural basis. Few parishes, once they have made the decision to follow the rubrics, will ever want to go back on it. It is experienced as a powerful and moving, thoroughly down to earth, act of service and a renewal of the community's understanding of the grace of priestly ministry. It is salutary also for the priest, for whatever he does symbolically here he must also do in day to day service to the community. Nevertheless, both the Gospel reading, and the ceremony seem to many to introduce into the liturgy a new and puzzlingly different, even distracting theme.

While baptism stands at the borderline of the Church and the world, the Eucharist, as the sacrament proper to the Church alone, is, as a matter of principle, not a public event. Thus, the first Christians celebrated it behind closed doors: 'Listen! I am standing at the door, knocking; if you hear my voice and open the door, I will come in to you and eat with you, and you with me' (Revelation 3:20). For some centuries afterwards, the *disciplina arcani* kept the liturgy and doctrine of the Eucharist strictly secret. While this was perhaps most rigorously observed from the third century in encounters between Judaism or paganism and Christian apologists, it may be why those writings of the New Testament intended for the general public, like the Gospel of John, make no mention of the words of institution of the Eucharist. In its account of the Last Supper, the Fourth Gospel substitutes a story which none of the Synoptics record, the narrative of the footwashing. John is in no way anti-sacramental, for although he omits any reference to the institution of either baptism or the Eucharist, his Gospel is full of allusions to both, and his whole approach to the mystery of Christ is deeply sacramental. And if the Church has chosen this passage to be the liturgical Gospel for this celebration it is because this story complements — and in no way contradicts — the reading from St Paul about the institution of the Eucharist.

The washing of the disciples' feet is a sign which, as is to be expected in the Fourth Gospel, has more than one level of meaning and interpretation. At one level it is a reminder that Christ came as a *servant*, and that Christians are called to live and act as servants of one another in a Christ-like manner. At another level it is a reference to baptism: 'Unless I wash you, you have no share with me' (John 13:8). This is clearly beyond the level of a moral lesson about mutual love and service; this is dealing with the cleansing power of Christ's sacrificial death upon the cross, to which the footwashing points, applied to the Church through the waters of baptism. Footwashing was at one time associated with the baptismal liturgy in parts of Western Christendom, either during the rites of initiation at the Easter Vigil, as in Milan in the time of St Ambrose, or on this day, as in parts of North Africa in the time of St Augustine, essentially as a preparatory rite for those about to be baptised but open to others also. By extension, the Church of England's 2007 *Common Worship* rite for the ordination of deacons includes provision for the ordaining bishop to wash the feet of the newly ordained, who are called to model Christ-like service to the Church.[13] At a deeper level still in the context of the Maundy Thursday rite, this reveals the presence of him who discloses his essential identity as one 'who, though he was in the form of God, did not regard equality with God as something to be exploited, but emptied himself, taking the form of a slave, being born in human likeness. And being found in human form, he humbled himself and became obedient to the point of death—even death on a cross' (Philippians 2:6–8).

To explore further how the footwashing narrative casts light upon the Eucharist it is necessary to start from the traditional English name for the day—Maundy Thursday. This is likely to derive from the Latin *mandatum novum*, meaning a new commandment.[14] 'I give you a *new commandment* that you love one another' says Jesus later in the same chapter of John, 'Just as I have loved you, you also should love one another' (John 13:34). And it is this new commandment which is the unifying theme of the Mass of the Lord's Supper, of this opening rite of the *Triduum Sacrum*. For the mystery celebrated on this night and throughout the whole *Triduum* is supremely one of love; it is about total, sacrificial, self-giving love. On this night Jesus Christ gave himself in total self-giving love to the Father and in total self-giving love to his fellow human beings. This handing over of his life to death is signified by Jesus by his words and actions over the bread and the cup, but so too is the double movement of his offering—*to* God and *for* mankind. He gives thanks to his Father over the bread and the cup, but he also addresses his disciples. His body is *for* them, the new covenant in his blood is *for* them. Nothing is withheld of love and obedience from the Father; nothing is withheld of love and service from mankind. The gift is total, free, and unconditional; he 'loves to the end' (John 13:1).

---

[13] *Common Worship: Ordination Services* (Church House Publishing, London, 2007), pp. 29 and 137.

[14] A more recent etymology suggests 'maundy' derives not from *mandatum* but from *mendicare*, meaning to beg, but this seems unlikely. See J. Monti, *The Week of Salvation: History and Traditions of Holy Week* (Our Sunday Visitor, Huntingdon, Indiana, 1993), pp. 108–17.

The double movement of love is also an essential aspect of the eucharistic mystery. Each member of the eucharistic assembly is taken up into the movement of Christ's own self-offering to the Father when the Mass is offered, and at the same time is renewed in his or her commitment to all others within the common life of the Body of Christ. The gathered faithful can say 'we *are* the Body of Christ' and in receiving Holy Communion can say, with St Augustine, 'Amen' to the mystery they have become.[15] The *Final Report* of the Anglican-Roman Catholic International Commission, discussing that pregnant Greek word *koinonia* which means communion, fellowship, participation in a common life, 'koinonia with one another is entailed by our koinonia with God in Christ. This is the mystery of the Church'.[16] In this particular Maundy Thursday celebration of the Eucharist, and by extension in every other celebration of the Eucharist, all are intimately involved in the double movement of the love of Christ.

> We are called to respond to a double challenge: can we refuse the *mandatum novum* of brotherly love, can we refuse to share the peace of Christ, can we refuse to wash one another's feet? And can we refuse to be taken up by Christ and offered with him to the Father? Both are costly, risky and dangerous: we can refuse both, but we cannot accept the one without the other. Holy Communion—Holy *koenonia*—is communion with God in Christ and communion with one another.[17]

In the Rule of St Benedict, a whole chapter, chapter 53, is devoted to the reception of guests in the monastery. Benedict writes:

> All guests who present themselves are to be welcomed as Christ, for he himself will say: 'I was a stranger and you welcomed me' (Matthew 25:35). Proper honour must be shown 'to all, especially to those who share our faith' (Galatians 6:10) and to pilgrims... All humility should be shown in addressing a guest on arrival or departure. By a bow of the head or by a complete prostration of the body, Christ is to be adored because he is indeed welcomed in them... The abbot shall pour water on the hands of the guests, and the abbot with the entire community, shall wash their feet... Great care and concern are to be shown

[15] Sermon 27.2 (Patrologia Latina 38, col. 1247).
[16] Anglican-Roman Catholic International Commission, *The Final Report*, Introduction, para. 5.
[17] R. T. Greenacre, unpublished Holy Week address, 1987.

in receiving poor people and pilgrims, because in them more particularly Christ is received.[18]

The hymn *Ubi caritas et amor*, suggested for during the footwashing in *Common Worship* and for use at the offertory procession in the Roman rite, was actually composed for use at the footwashing in the Benedictine Abbey of Reichenau in about 800.[19] Many will be familiar with the Latin words and the traditional plainsong melody through the arrangement for choir by Maurice Duruflé; *Common Worship* provides an excellent English translation by James Quinn, SJ, and a simple setting by Gregory Murray, OSB, can be found in many hymnals.[20]

Unlike the *Common Worship* provision, the Roman lectionary and the Methodist provision omits verses 27 to 29 from the evening's second reading from 1 Corinthians 11 so the really key link between the footwashing and the Eucharist is lost. St Paul warns about receiving Blessed Sacrament unworthily: 'For all who eat and drink without discerning the body, eat and drink judgement against themselves' (1 Corinthians 11:29). Failure to discern the Lord's Body in the consecrated bread and wine brings judgement but no less worthy of judgement is the failure to discern in fellow members of the Body the real presence of Christ. C. S. Lewis was aware of this:

> Next to the Blessed Sacrament itself, your neighbour is the holiest object presented to your senses. If he is your Christian neighbour he is holy in almost the same way, for in him also Christ ... is truly hidden.[21]

The same point was made with greater force by Frank Weston, Bishop of Zanzibar, in a speech delivered to the Anglo-Catholic Congress of 1923, when he pointed out to Anglicans:

> You have got your Mass, you have got your Altar, you have begun to get your Tabernacle. Now go out into the highways and hedges ... God out and look for Jesus in the ragged, in the naked, in the oppressed and sweated, in those who have lost hope, in those who are struggling to make good. Look for Jesus.

18 *The Rule of St Benedict*, ch. 53, , in Parry, *Households of God*, pp. 257–9.
19 Cf. Perham and Stevenson, *Waiting for the Risen Christ*, p. 161.
20 For example, *New English Hymnal*, no. 513.
21 C. S. Lewis, 'The Weight of Glory', in *They Asked for a Paper* (Bles, London, 1962), p. 211.

> And when you see him, gird yourselves with his towel and try
> to wash their feet.[22]

In the narratives of the passion of Christ, after the Last Supper came the Agony in the Garden of Gethsemane so from the beginning of the separate observance of Maundy Thursday there has been a strong instinct to prolong the Eucharist by a watch of prayer.

> It is the night of Gethsemane, of our Lord's agonised prayer,
> of Judas's kiss, of the arrest; the night of the trial before the
> Sanhedrin, and of Peter's triple denial before cockcrow, Jesus
> did not sleep this night, and his disciples only fitfully, for he
> did not hesitate to rouse them from their slumbers—*Watch
> and pray*. There is severity in his voice when he comes to them
> the third time and asks, 'Are you still sleeping and taking your
> rest?' (Mark 14:41). He seems particularly to have required
> companionship on this night.[23]

Egeria describes how the night was observed in Jerusalem with the evening Eucharist and a vigil at the Eleona church, the Imbomon and then at Gethsemane itself (see above, p. 105).[24] In the Orthodox Churches of the East there is a watch of prayer on this night in the Byzantine manner (see above, pp. 111–12). In the West a particular significance has gathered around this watch because of the need to give Holy Communion on Good Friday from the Sacrament consecrated at this evening's Mass, a need which is discussed below in the section on the Good Friday liturgy. In what follows the detailed provisions of the Roman rite are described, but it should be noted that from the material provided in *Common Worship* exactly the same observance can be derived. There is more than a hint of 'Let the reader understand' (Mark 13:14) in the somewhat hermetic language of the notes referring to the Watch on Thursday and the administration of Holy Communion on Friday in the *Common Worship* provision but the necessary framework and texts are there.[25] The Maundy Mass concludes with the Prayer after Communion and a solemn procession with

22 Sermon, 'Our Present Duty', *Report of the Anglo-Catholic Congress, London, July 1923* (SSPP, London, 1923), p. 211.
23 J. T. Martin, *Christ our Passover* (SCM, London, 1958), pp. 29–30.
24 See Egeria, trans. McGowan and Bradshaw, pp. 172–5.
25 Even more hermetic is the rubric in the *Methodist Worship Book*, which hints 'The elements that remain are covered with a white cloth', implying, perhaps, communion the following day.

cross, lights and incense is formed to accompany the Blessed Sacrament, carried by the principal celebrant, to a specially prepared altar (the Altar of Repose), while the great eucharistic hymn of St Thomas Aquinas, *Pange lingua gloriosi corporis mysterium* ('Of the glorious body telling, O my tongue, its mysteries sing') is sung. The Altar of Repose is specially, but soberly, decorated with lights and flowers and situated in a suitable side chapel which will provide the venue for a watch of prayer at least until midnight. Meanwhile the High Altar and sanctuary are stripped of all ornament so that the altar is left completely bare and any crosses which cannot be removed are veiled. *Common Worship*, following a tradition established in several well-ordered cathedrals, suggests that verses from Lamentations are read or preferably, sung, while the altars are stripped. There is a moving musical setting of these words by Sir Edward Bairstow, written for York Minster, which is particularly effective as the sanctuary is rendered desolate and bare.

There is a two-fold character to this watch on Maundy Thursday evening. First, it is of course a watch before the Blessed Sacrament and therefore has the character of a prolonged meditation upon and thanksgiving for the great gift of the Eucharist instituted on this night. Abuses, however, are guarded against. Roman instructions in *Paschalis Solemnitatis* underline the fact that the Altar of Repose serves for Good Friday communion by insisting that this 'transfer of the Blessed Sacrament may not be carried out if the Liturgy of the Lord's Passion will not be celebrated in that same church on the following day'; they also make clear that the Sacrament is to be reserved in a closed tabernacle or pyx and under no circumstances exposed in a monstrance.[26] Admirers of the Sarum rite, prevalent in England up until the Reformation, and the often highly decorated Easter sepulchres provided for that rite in many medieval churches, will be sad to read here also:

> The place where the tabernacle or pyx is situated must not be made to resemble a tomb, and the expression 'tomb' is to be avoided. The chapel of repose is not prepared so as to represent the 'Lord's burial' but for the custody of the eucharistic bread that will be distributed in Communion on Good Friday.

[26] *Paschalis Solemnitatis*, paras. 54–6.

Moreover the candles and flowers arranged to honour the Blessed Sacrament are to be removed at midnight even if the watch itself continues right through the night.

Secondly, the Watch of Prayer has gathered around it all the events which the Gospel narratives associate with this night. It can and should take place, as in the Methodist provision, even if the Blessed Sacrament is not being reserved at an Altar of Repose and it should commemorate all the events of this sacred night. Parishes may well want to establish a rhythm, with long periods of silent adoration punctuated by readings from the Gospels and corporately led prayer and meditation. *Paschalis Solemnitatis* recommends readings from St John's Gospel, chapters 13 to 17; *Common Worship* provides for readings from these same chapters with accompanying psalms and a Gospel of the Watch (Luke 22:31–62 in Year A; Matthew 26:30–end in Year B; Mark 14:26–end in Year C); the *Methodist Worship Book* presents a table of shorter, consecutive readings from the Passion narratives from Matthew in Year A, from Mark in Year B and from Luke in Year C. This emphasis on the Watch springs not only from a Jerusalem-like desire to follow the chronology of the Passion and the desire to watch with Christ at least on hour but also by the need to underline the unity and continuity which bind together Maundy Thursday and Good Friday, the Supper and the Cross.

A rich feast of liturgical material, rites and ceremonies is available for the proper celebration of Maundy Thursday, the beginning of the *Triduum*, in the authorised or approved services of the Roman, Anglican and Methodist Churches. Nevertheless, some communities, not content with this provision, have sought out alternative forms of worship and engagement with the events of these three days, forms which, it has to be said, are not entirely in harmony with the unitive sweep of the traditional services. The most popular of these observances both involve a communal meal. *Lent, Holy Week, Easter*, acknowledging what was already going on in some Anglican parishes in the evangelical tradition (where it was apparently proving valuable), cautiously provided an outline for an *agape* within the context of a celebration of Holy Communion.[27] This order, using the terminology of the *Alternative Servide Book*, suggests that 'the main course of a simple meal'

[27] *Lent, Holy Week, Easter*, pp. 97–8

might be eaten after the Ministry of the Word, a second course after the exchange of Peace and then a segue into the Ministry of the Sacrament. There is no suggestion of the Foot Washing in this order. *Common Worship* decided against including this provision largely because the whole concept of the Christian *agape* has been subject to scholarly scrutiny and found wanting. Helpfully, Paul Bradshaw has written:

> The whole concept of the *agape* is a very dubious one. It has served as a useful vague category in which to dump any evidence for meals that scholars did not want to treat as eucharistic, regardless of whether the text itself described the meal as an *agape* of by some other title . . . What is particularly vital to note is that there is no evidence at all, except perhaps in the case of Tertullian, for early Christian communities that practised both a Eucharist and at the same time something else called an *agape*, but rather that where the latter use is used for a meal, it seems to be the name of the only form of Christian ritual meal existing in that community, the equivalent of what other Christian groups might call 'the Eucharist' or 'the Lord's Supper'. So, for example, Ignatius of Antioch appears to regard the words 'Eucharist' and *agape* as synonymous.[28]

The other non-liturgical Maundy Thursday observance to gain some currency is the so-called Christian Seder or Passover meal sometimes also held in conjunction with the Eucharist. No authorised order for this insensitive piece of cultural appropriation has been produced by the mainline denominations but in 2008 when the *Using Common Worship* guides were produced, the Council of Christians and Jews were publishing online guidance for those involved in organising such events. This material has since disappeared. In the run up to Holy Week 2021, the Church House Communications Unit of the Church of England issued an unauthorised and unattributed order for a Christian Seder which, after an outcry, was swiftly removed from the website. Quite simply, it is important to realise there can be no such thing as a 'Christian Seder'. To claim that there is and to ritualise it in the context of the celebration of Holy Week not only disrespects the faith traditions of today's Jewish community but also contradicts the evidence of the New Testament texts and Christian history. As we celebrate

---

[28] P. F. Bradshaw, *Eucharistic Origins* (SPCK, London, 2004), pp. 29–30.

the institution of the Eucharist and recall The Lord's command to 'do *this* in memory of me', we can be certain that '*this*' was not a Seder. It was not a Seder because there is no evidence that such a thing existed in Jesus's day. The more convincing evidence is that it was developed as a Passover commemoration after the destruction of the Jerusalem temple and the consequent abandonment of the sacrificial cult.[29]

[29]   Rabbi David Golinkin, *The Origins of the Seder* (The Schechter Institute of Jewish Studies, Jerusalem, 2006).

☞ XII ☜

Good Friday.
Friday of the Passion of the Lord

Until recently—and still up to a point today—the liturgy of the Church has been far from providing a unanimous focus for the devotion of Western Christians on Good Friday. Neither the unreformed Roman rite, the so-called Mass of the Presanctified, celebrated on Friday morning in Latin and with the reception of Holy Communion confined to the celebrant, nor the more austere *Book of Common Prayer* provision of Mattins, Litany and Antecommunion were found to be adequate channels of popular devotion. Because on the whole the People of God were not being fed by the liturgy, the gap was filled with non-liturgical services of various kinds, particularly in the Roman Catholic Church with Stations of the Cross and in both Anglican and Roman traditions with the preaching of the Three-Hour Devotion. This latter has enjoyed a surprising popularity in the Church of England considering that it originated with the Jesuits in Peru towards the end of the seventeenth century.[1] Although many of these non-liturgical devotions—including in our own day ecumenical acts of witness—have proved of immense value to countless Christians, they have lacked the objective and corporate character which only liturgical worship can give. There is moreover on this day of all days a need for liturgical *action*; for the Church needs not only to hear and ponder the Word of the Cross and render the verbal homage of love and faith and penitence, but also to express in concrete liturgical action her response to the divine initiative in the Cross and her union with it. So nothing ought to be allowed to challenge the priority of the liturgy of the day. Various experiments have been tried in Anglican churches

---

[1]   Cf. Thurston, *Lent and Holy Week*, ch. ix.

to produce a 'Liturgical Three Hours' in which some or all of the authorised liturgical services are interspersed with addresses and times for silent meditation.[2] Some Anglican churches in the Catholic tradition have found it effective to combine into three hours Stations of the Cross, for which a form is provided in *Common Worship: Times and Seasons* (pp. 236–56), with an hour of addresses, meditation and hymns, immediately followed by the Liturgy, timed to begin at 3.00pm.

The Good Friday Liturgy preserves an austere, early style of worship and employs some of the oldest texts still in current use. In this there are dangers and the introduction to the Holy Week material in *Common Worship* contains a warning:

> This solemn season ... rehearses the deepest and most fundamental Christian memories. At the same time, the services and ceremonies of Holy Week have in the course of Christian history been the occasion of, or have actively encouraged, hostility towards the Jews. The '*Ioudaioi*' of St John's Gospel have all to easily been identified with 'the Jews' as a whole, or more specifically those Jews who were neighbours of a Christian church. This places a double responsibility on those who lead the keeping if Holy Week today: to be faithful to the act of collective memory, but also to be sensitive to the ways in which an unreflecting use of traditional texts can perpetuate a strain of Christian anti-Semitism.[3]

The Celebration of the Lord's Passion falls into three main sections; it is the combination into a single whole of three rites which were originally distinct and not necessarily celebrated in the order in which they are now found. There is first of all the *Synaxis* or Liturgy of the Word, concluding with the Solemn Prayers or General Intercession. This is followed by the Veneration of the Cross, a rite which clearly proclaims its oriental origin deriving, as has been discussed above, from the fourth-century Jerusalem usage described by Egeria of venerating the relic of the True Cross at Golgotha. The *Common Worship* order, following *Lent, Holy Week, Easter*, places the Solemn Prayers after the Veneration [Proclamation] of the Cross (as does the *Methodist Worship Book*). The argument being that it is 'much more logical and effective for the Proclamation of

---

[2] See, for example, *The Chichester Customary* (SPCK, London, 1948), pp. 36–8.
[3] *Common Worship: Times and Seasons*, p. 259. See also below, p. 154.

the Cross, where it is used, to follow the Passion Narrative'. The effect of this revised order is that the prayers of intercession are offered, as it were, before the cross unveiled and placed upon the altar. This reversal might work where there is no Communion, as in the Ambrosian Rite, but the traditional order of the three sections is preferable and permitted in *Common Worship* by note. The final action is the rite of Holy Communion from the Reserved Sacrament, for which hosts consecrated on Maundy Thursday evening are used. Following the Gospel chronology, the liturgy is to take place in the afternoon, at about three o'clock, unless strong pastoral reasons suggest a later hour.

The most important of the reforms introduced into the rite in 1955 was the restoration of a general communion; the unrevised rite of the Mass of the Presanctified (a confusing title, at best, since the Mass is not celebrated) had since 1622 allowed only for the communion of the celebrant. The historical background is complex and calls for some explanation. It is well known that the unbroken Catholic tradition of both East and West has never admitted a eucharistic celebration on Good Friday and that the same held true of Holy Saturday until the Mass of the Easter Vigil came in the West to be anticipated first on Saturday evening and finally on Saturday morning. An even earlier tradition, however, extended this abstinence to the reception of Holy Communion, as is made clear in a famous letter from Pope Innocent I (401–17) to Decentius:

> It is quite clear that the Apostles during these two days both were in mourning and also hid themselves from the Jews. And further there is no doubt they fasted on the aforesaid two days to such a degree that the tradition of the Church requires entire abstinence from the celebration of the Sacraments on these two days.[4]

It is for this reason that the Byzantine liturgy which provides for the Liturgy of the Presanctified (a public distribution of communion from the Reserved Sacrament after Vespers) on the weekdays if Lent makes no such provision on Good Friday; the fast is not even broken by the reception of Holy Communion.[5] This primitive rule

[4] *Epistola* xxv.4 (Patrologia Latina 20, col. 276); cf. Tyrer, *Historical Survey*, p. 119.
[5] At one time, however, the Liturgy of the Presanctified was celebrated on Holy Friday in the Byzantine tradition. There is evidence of its use at Constantinople in the mid-eleventh century, but the practice had died out by 1200. See *The Lenten Triodion*, p. 62.

has also been maintained by the Church of Milan; the Ambrosian rite provides only for a Liturgy of the Word and the Veneration of the Cross.[6] For a long time the same rule was observed in Rome and even when provision for Holy Communion from the Reserved Sacrament (at first in both kinds) began to be made in order to meet the pressure of popular devotion, the pope and his deacons at first made a point of abstaining. In the later Middle Ages the situation was reversed, when, in the time of Innocent III, it was the pope alone who made his communion. In 1953, after the restoration of the nocturnal Easter Vigil in 1951, an International Liturgical Congress was held in Lugano to prepare for the promulgation of the revised Order for Holy Week of 1955. The experts were divided as to what solution should be proposed for Good Friday, though all agreed that there was no justification for the celebrant alone communicating and that the confusing ceremonies of the Mass of the Presanctified should not be continued. Dom Bernard Capelle argued for a general communion; Joseph Jungmann and Balthazar Fischer wanted to abolish communion altogether, pointing to the usage of Milan. It was Capelle's view that prevailed.

Some Anglicans have argued in favour of a full eucharistic celebration on Good Friday and in 1986 *Lent, Holy Week, Easter* envisaged the possibility of three routes through the material it provided: a celebration of the Eucharist, a distribution of Holy Communion from the Reserved Sacrament, or an Antecommunion only. *The Methodist Worship Book* of 1999 makes no provision for communion though, as mentioned above, there is the merest hint that the Sacrament might be reserved for this purpose from the night before. *Common Worship* in 2006 assumes that there will be a general communion from the Sacrament reserved from the Maundy Thursday evening Eucharist. At one time, a motive which led Anglicans to press for a Good Friday Eucharist was doubt as to the legitimacy of general communion from the Reserved Sacrament. This has become less of an issue since the pastoral pressures of shortage of clergy combined with multi-parish benefices has led in recent years to a more ready acceptance of Extended Communion as a way of ensuring the regular reception of Holy

[6] The revised Ambrosian Missal provides a rite which begins with the Liturgy of the Word, continues with the Veneration of the Cross and ends with the Solemn Prayer and a Blessing.

Communion by the faithful. There can be no doubt that this practice is not only ancient but ecumenical. It derives from the primitive practice of the faithful taking the sacrament to their homes at the end of the Sunday Eucharist in order to communicate themselves at home during the week. Provision for reservation was made in churches and communion from the Reserved Sacrament was given an organised liturgical structure in the Byzantine rite earlier than in the Roman. From pre-Nicene days such communion outside of Mass has normally been in one kind only which does not weaken the Anglican principle of insisting on communion in both kinds being distributed at the Eucharist. Indeed, on this occasion there is perhaps no reason why the Sacrament cannot be reserved on the Altar of Repose in both kinds which would represent a return to the former Roman usage as described in the Gelasian Sacramentary.

Another element in Anglican arguments for a Good Friday Eucharist has been the appeal to post-Reformation history. There is evidence that the Eucharist was celebrated on this day in some places in the seventeenth century and more frequently in the eighteenth and early nineteenth centuries.[7] An Irish clergyman visiting London on Good Friday 1775 noted, 'Dr Dodd did not read the Communion service rubrically, for he kneeled at the beginning, and tho' it was a fast day, he and his coadjutors wore surplices'.[8] The exclusive concentration of the *Prayer Book* Consecration Prayer on the Passion of our Lord and the generalised Protestant view of the time that the Lord's Supper was a privileged way of remembering the Lord's death favoured the practice (although it was to be found among High Churchmen of the time). The practice went into decline in the later nineteenth century under Tractarian influence, which led to the desire to return to Catholic tradition and to a fuller and richer eucharistic theology.

Today, some Anglicans though conscious of the liturgical provision now in general use, would still argue that there are no real theological reasons against offering the Eucharist on Good Friday. In order to appreciate the profound theological insight behind the traditional Catholic rule it is necessary to set Good Friday in the

---

[7]   Cf. J. G. Bishop, 'The Anglican Tradition', in *A Manual for Holy Week*, ed. C. P. M. Jones (SPCK, London, 1967), pp. 43–5.

[8]   J Wickham Legg, *English Church Life from the Restoration to the Tractarian Movement* (Longmans Green, London, 1914), p. 227.

closest possible association with Maundy Thursday and with the Easter Vigil—the continuum of which *Lent, Holy Week, Easter* spoke. It is no mere historical accident that Holy Communion is given on Good Friday from the Sacrament consecrated on Maundy Thursday evening. Egeria witnesses to the fact that in fourth-century Jerusalem Thursday and Friday constituted a single celebration of unbroken unity. The Supper of the Lord was celebrated at Calvary on Thursday, the only occasion in the year when it was celebrated there, to demonstrate the unity of the eucharistic sacrifice and that of the Cross. The Supper and the Cross are so closely linked that they form a single act of sacrifice and cannot be understood without reference to each other. The Cross gives meaning to the Supper, but the Supper also gives meaning to the Cross. The Cross is not a defeat but a victory because that which gives it its true meaning is not the act of execution on Friday, but the offering Jesus made of himself at the Last Supper on Thursday. The paschal celebration within the Easter *Triduum* is, and in the offering of the liturgy should be seen to be, essentially indivisible. There is no celebration of the Eucharist on Good Friday because the Church waits to give thanks for the Cross until she can give thanks for it together with the Resurrection in the one great unitive eucharistic celebration of the Easter Vigil.

The first of the three sections of the Good Friday Liturgy, the Synaxis, is of the simplest and most austere character. The silent procession into the church and prostration of the ministers before the stripped and bare altar and the solemn singing of the Passion do make a dramatic impact, but the emotion is restrained and the emphasis is upon the word. In this meditative dialogue the worshipper feeds upon God's word and responds in faith, in words themselves drawn from Scripture. The first two readings provided in the Roman rite are Isaiah 52:13–53:12 with part of Psalm 31 and Hebrews 4:14–16, 5:7–9 with a chant from Philippians 2. *Common Worship* provides the same reading from Isaiah but with Psalm 22 and either the same passage from Hebrews or 10:16–25. The pre-reform Roman rite had lessons from Hosea 6 and Exodus 12 which, together with the Johannine narrative of the Passion and Resurrection, formed part of the pre-Nicene Easter Vigil in Rome before ever there was any liturgy of the word on Good Friday.[9]

---

[9]   Dix, *Shape of the Liturgy*, p. 440.

It is by no means accidental that the solemn reading of the Passion according to St John is reserved for the liturgy of Good Friday, for it is the Johannine account that stresses the victory of the Cross and paints a picture of *Christus regnans in cruce*. Michael Ramsey, writing in his *Narratives of the Passion*, makes this clear:

> In the Passion story of St John the glory dominates. In the garden the soldiers fall to the ground awestruck (18:6). In the judgement hall Pilate is the broken prisoner and Jesus is the judge (18:33–8). Majestically Jesus carried his own cross to Calvary, going where he wills to go as one who has power to lay down his life (cf 10:17–18). Before he dies he cries that the divine purpose is accomplished (19:30), and he entrusts his own spirit to the Father. Dying as the king, Jesus is no less than the Passover lamb. Pilate delivers him to die at the moment when the lambs are being prepared for sacrifice (19:14). The king and the sacrificial victim are one Christ. Thus the Johannine story of the Passion both reflects and creates the imagery in the Church of One who is both lamb and king, victim and conqueror. *Vexilla regis prodeunt*—'The royal banners forward go.'[10]

When the reading of the Johannine Passion was restored to Good Friday in the 1978 American Lutheran *Book of Worship*, the Lutheran theologian Krister Stendhal made a similar point from another angle:

> The majestic death of Jesus according to the Gospel of John reminds us of earlier Christian art. Long before there were crucifixes with the suffering Jesus, plagued by the crown of thorns, the Jesus of Bernard of Clairvaux and Paul Gerhard [the seventeenth-century German author of the hymn 'O Sacred head, sore wounded'] there was the triumphant crucifix with the victorious Jesus standing in royal and priestly garb, hands outstretched in the blessing embrace of the world.[11]

In the sermon which follows the reading of the Passion the preacher should bear in mind the warning of another distinguished Lutheran theologian, the Swedish bishop, Gustaf Aulén:

> Good Friday appears in its right perspective only when it is seen in the light of Easter. If the note of triumph is not present in preaching on the passion, this preaching has lost its Christian character.[12]

---

[10] A. M. Ramsey, *The Narratives of the Passion* (Mowbray, London, 1962), p. 24.
[11] Cf. Maxwell E. Johnson, 'The Paschal Mystery: Reflections from a Lutheran Viewpoint', *Worship* 57/2 (March 1983), pp. 134–50.
[12] G. Aulén, *The Faith of the Christian Church* (Fortress Press, Philadelphia, 1960), pp. 217–18. More recent reprints are available.

The ministry of the Word has, as it were, placarded the cross of Christ before the minds and imaginations of those present. After this the members of the congregation are invited to unite their wills to the will of him who 'opened wide his arms for us on the cross'[13] by joining in intercession for the needs of the Church and the World. As the opening monition in the *Common Worship* order puts it:

> God sent his Son into the world, not to condemn the world, but that the world might be saved through him. Therefore we pray to our heavenly Father for people everywhere according to their needs.

The Solemn Prayers (whose origins are of great antiquity) are an impressive exercise in corporate intercession: first a bidding, then the congregation's silent prayer, then a collect recited by the celebrant, whose outstretched arms may serve as a reminder of the arms of Christ stretched out upon the cross in order to draw and embrace all humanity to himself. The unreformed pre–1970 text of the *orationes sollemnes* in the Roman rite contained a petition 'For the conversion of the Jews' which used language which would cause offence today. Along with some of the other petitions, it has been comprehensively rewritten 'lest anyone find reason for spiritual discomfort in the prayer of the Church'.[14] *Lent, Holy Week, Easter* followed suit and substituted two prayers, one for 'God's ancient people, the Jews' which prays for greater understanding between Christian and Jew and the 'grace to be faithful to his covenant', and another addressed to the 'Lord God of Abraham' which prays for much the same thing. *Common Worship* reproduces these exactly and the *Methodist Worship Book* in much the same way.

The central section of the Liturgy, the Veneration of the Cross, is the most dramatic and there is a noticeable change of style from the sober and restrained austerity of Roman *gravitas* to a mood of vivid, poignant, eloquent emotion. In this creative Franco-Germanic reworking of the fourth-century Jerusalem rite, developed in the ninth and tenth centuries, the Cross of Christ is no longer placarded

---

13   *Common Worship*, Core Volume, Eucharistic Prayer B of Order One; cf. Eucharistic Prayer II of the *Roman Missal*. The phrase is taken directly from *The Apostolic Tradition* of Hippolytus.

14   Cf. A. Bugnini, *The Reform of the Liturgy, 1948–1975* (Liturgical Press, Collegeville, 1990), p. 798.

only before minds and hearts and wills but now also right before the eyes of the congregation. 'It was before your eyes that Jesus Christ was publicly exhibited as crucified!' writes St Paul to the Galatians (Galatians 3:1) and now, liturgically, 'they will look on the one whom they have pierced' (John 19:37 and Zechariah 12:10). A crucifix is brought through the church to the sanctuary escorted by lighted candles; three times it is solemnly held up before the people inviting their response of worship, and then all come— celebrant, ministers, congregation—to kneel before the cross and kiss it. There is no idolatry in this kiss or superstition—whatever Archbishop Cranmer might have thought when abolishing 'creeping to the cross' —for in the veneration of an icon the honour paid to the image passes to the prototype. But neither is this kiss a light matter either, for so much is implied in this one simple gesture.

To embrace the Cross is to make an act of faith in Christ and his Cross, an act of faith that is also an act of gratitude, of penitence and love. In the *Reproaches* (*Improperia*) which are traditionally sung during the Veneration and which, inspired by Scripture (eg Micah 6:3–4), seem to be of Gallican or Spanish origin, Christ himself in dialogue with his faithless people challenges them to make this response: 'O my people, what have I done to you? Wherein have I offended you? Answer me!' The reply, in the words of the Greek *trisagion*, is both an act of faith and a cry for mercy: *Hagios ho Theos, Sanctus Deus; Hagios Ischyros, Sanctus Fortis; Hagios Athanatos, eleison hemas, Sanctus Immortalis, miserere nobis* (Holy God, Holy and Mighty, Holy and Immortal, have mercy upon us).

> The embrace is also a welcoming of the Cross into our lives; we welcome it as the tree of life but knowing it also to be an instrument of death and shame, which Christ himself endured for the joy that was set before him. We too must be ready to endure the weight and shame of the Cross at some very real cost to ourselves; we have soberly and lucidly to recognise this as we embrace the Cross with a kiss. We have made our pledge and we cannot complain if we are then called upon to honour it. Our glorification of the Cross on Good Friday subtracts nothing from its realism.[15]

In the Veneration, homage is paid not to a corpse but to a reigning sovereign. The whole ceremony is performed in the light of the

---

[15]   R. T. Greenacre, unpublished Holy Week address, 1986.

Johannine presentation of the Gospel: the Cross is held up erect and candles burn on either side. For the Cross is a throne as well as an altar and we are taking part in the act of homage at a Coronation. In the English Coronation Rite those who do homage go up to the throne, kneel and swear allegiance and then kiss the sovereign's cheek or hand. There is a clear analogy here to what is done on Good Friday, but the kiss is that of a faithful subject not that of the traitor Judas.

The traditional text of the Reproaches was criticised by the then Bishop of Birmingham, Dr Hugh Montefiore, in the General Synod debate on the Holy Week liturgy in February 1985 on the grounds that it was anti-Semitic. *Lent, Holy Week, Easter*, published the following year, therefore contained an entirely new text in which the Lord reproaches his people for failing to respect creation, their fellow humans, and the environment, and thus misses the point somewhat. These Eco-Reproaches survived into *Common Worship* but only as an alternative to a far better set which capture the spirit of the traditional text while carefully avoiding anything which might be construed as anti-Semitic. There is no doubt that many Anglican parishes will continue to use the traditional version as found in the Roman Missal or in the *New English Hymnal* (no. 516) not least because of the many excellent musical settings available. Properly understood, there is nothing anti-Semitic about the Reproaches. In this text, as in the *Exsultet* ('This is the night when you first saved our ancestors, freeing Israel from her slavery'), an identity is claimed between the People of God of the Old Covenant and the People of God of the New; in the Reproaches the Lord is engaged in a dialogue with his people, challenging those present at the liturgy to faith, love, and repentance and reproaching them with examples of infidelity taken from the past history of the People of God. As Pope Pius XI was to say in answer to Nazi anti-Semitism, 'we are all spiritually Semites'; all are one with 'our ancestors' in an inheritance both of shame and of glory, the one cannot be claimed without the other.

Alongside the Reproaches in the Roman rite two other chants are provided which emphasise the glory and the triumph of the Cross; they are the ninth-century antiphon *Crucem tuam* ('We adore your Cross, O Lord, we praise and glorify your glorious Resurrection, for behold, because of the wood of a tree joy has come to the whole world') and the magnificent hymn of Venantius Fortunatus, *Pange lingua* ('Sing, my tongue, in exultation of our banner and device') with its refrain *Crux fidelis* ('Faithful Cross').[16] *Common Worship*, in addition to two versions of the Reproaches, offers three further anthems, one of which uses *Crucem tuam* as an antiphon before and after Psalm 67. *The Methodist Worship Book* offers a fairly traditional set of Reproaches and a responsory of scriptural verses interspersed with an antiphon, 'We praise and adore you, O Christ: for by your cross and precious blood you have redeemed us'.

The Good Friday liturgy has inspired composers of many periods and religious traditions to write fine music to enrich its celebration, settings of the St John Passion for the Liturgy of the Word, for example, and of the Reproaches for the rite of the Veneration of the Cross. Great poets have been similarly inspired by the paradox of an instrument of painful death transformed into a sign of glory and have both responded to the liturgy of Good Friday and enriched it. In the second half of the sixth century, Venantius Fortunatus wrote three hymns celebrating the triumph of the Cross: *Pange lingua gloriosi*, *Vexilla regis prodeunt*, and *O Crux splendidior*, two of which have found a permanent home in the liturgy of Holy Week. Venantius was educated in Ravenna and cannot but have been moved by the great *Crux gemmata* in the mosaic decoration of the apse of Sant' Apollinare in Classe, which must have been glitteringly new in his day. Christopher Irvine has written of *Pange lingua*:

> Although the hymn rehearses the actual physical suffering of Christ on the cross, specifically mentioning the nails, the vinegar, the spear, the cross emerges as a throne from which the royal Christ reigns as the one who was victorious over the destructive and distorting power of sin and evil. So the cross is presented as an emblem of victory, the standard of the heavenly King. This poetic trope of the unfurling banners of the King provided the imagery in which Christians throughout the first millennium visualised the cross.[17]

This imagery, and maybe even this very hymn of Fortunatus, inspired a masterpiece from the earliest years of Christian poetry in England, *Dream of the Rood*, parts of which appear to be inscribed in runes on the eighth-century Northumbrian Ruthwell Cross. The

---

[16] A better translation is at *New English Hymnal*, no. 517. See also above, p. 70.
[17] Irvine, *The Cross*, pp. 118–19.

complete poem, which appears in a tenth-century compendium now in the Capitular Library in Vercelli, speaks of the Cross as a 'most wondrous tree', 'the tree of glory', 'this ardent beacon', 'the tree of a Ruler'.

> *I saw then the Saviour of mankind*
> *Hasten with great zeal, as if he wanted to climb up on me.*
> *There I did not dare, against the word of the Lord,*
> *Bow or break, when I saw*
> *The corners of the earth tremble I might have*
> *Felled all the enemies; even so I stood fast.*
> *He stripped himself then, young hero—that was God almighty –*
> *Strong and resolute; he ascended on the high gallows,*
> *Brave in the sight of many, when he wanted to ransom mankind.*
> *I trembled when the warrior embraced me; even then*
>   *I did not dare to bow to earth,*
> *Fall to the corners of the earth, but I had to stand fast.*
> *I was reared a cross. I raised up the powerful King,*
> *The Lord of heaven; I did not dare to bend.*[18]

The poem was possibly written by a Northumbrian monk, certainly an ecclesiastic as it is full of allusions to scripture and liturgical resonances, and it charts the transformation of the wooden tree into a bejewelled and glittering object of veneration through the heroic work of the victorious Christ. There are hints of the Good Friday liturgical Adoration of the Cross and of the power of the cross to heal and save: 'On me the Son of God suffered for a while; because of that I am glorious now, towering under the heavens, and I am able to heal each one of those who is in awe of me.'[19]

All this serves as a reminder that the Cross unveils the love of God; there, there is not only the sacrifice of the man Jesus, but also the divine initiative coming close is redeeming love. 'In Christ God was reconciling the world to himself' (2 Corinthians 5:19); 'God proves his love for us in that while we still were sinners Christ died for us' (Romans 5:8). The Cross is only a challenge because it is first and foremost a gift, a liberation, and a revelation.

It is because the strongest emphasis must rest on what God has done for man rather than man's response to God that the liturgy moves on from the veneration to the final section of the rite, the dis-

[18] Elaine Treharne, trans., *Old and Middle English: An Anthology* (Blackwell Publishers, Oxford, 2000).
[19] See Irvine, *The Cross*, p. 119.

tribution of Holy Communion. The Blessed sacrament is brought without ceremony from the place of repose to the altar and all say together the Lord's Prayer and receive Communion. The rite then concludes with a collect and a prayer over the people before all depart in silence leaving the cross and candles on the bare altar. Christ's death is the limitless well-spring of life for his Church which proclaims this today by inviting the faithful to consume his body on the day of his death. The closest union with Christ is a sacramental union; in Holy Communion he takes the initiative, entering into hearts and lives and bringing with him his life-giving Cross and all the graces of his Passion.

> *He endured the nails, the spitting,*
> *Vinegar and spear and reed;*
> *From that holy Body piercéd*
> *Blood and water forth proceed:*
> *Earth and stars and sky and ocean*
> *By that flood from stain are freed.*[20]

---

[20] *Pange lingua*, v. 7 *New English Hymnal*, no. 517. The original reads: 'En acetum, fel, arundo, / sputa, clavi, lancea: / mite corpus perforatur, / Sanguis, unda profluit / terra, pontus, astra, mundus, / quo lavantur flumine!'

⤙ XIII ⤚

Holy Saturday,
The Easter Vigil and Easter Day

Holy Saturday, also known as Easter Eve, has its own unique character. 'Torn—quite properly—between contrite memory and expectant hope',[1] it has its own importance in the carefully balanced structure of the Paschal *Triduum*. As Alan E. Lewis has written, it is

> that day between the days which speaks solely neither of the cross nor of the resurrection, but *simultaneously* remembers the one and awaits the other, and guarantees that neither will be heard, or thought about, or lived without the other.[2]

It has tended to be neglected partly because the pressure to anticipate the Easter Vigil found in both the history of Eastern and Western Christendom meant that one passed almost directly from Good Friday to Easter Day without the necessary and meaningful pause of Holy Saturday; and partly because it has become a day given over to decorating the church with flowers and, at least until recently, to the celebration of weddings. It has also been neglected because it is an 'aliturgical' day when the Eucharist is not celebrated. Difficult to come to terms with theologically and liturgically because, as it were, we already know the end of the story, it is important not 'to compromise the uniqueness of its position between cross and resurrection by absorbing it as simply an extension of Good Friday or an anticipation of Easter'.[3] It is essentially a day of waiting; a fast, but a fast kept in a spirit of quiet confidence and joyful hope. 'On Holy Saturday' the rubrics

---

[1]   A. E. Lewis, *Between Cross and Resurrection, A Theology of Holy Saturday* (Eerdmans, Grand Rapids, 2003), p. 2, note 1.

[2]   *Ibid.*, p. 4.

[3]   *Ibid.*, p. 2, note 1.

of the Roman rite explain, 'the Church waits at the Lord's tomb in prayer and fasting, meditating on his Passion and Death and on his Descent into hell, and awaiting his Resurrection. The Church abstains from the Sacrifice of the Mass, with the sacred table left bare.'[4]

Most probably to reflect the provision in *The Book of Common Prayer*, the *Alternative Service Book 1980* provided a Proper for Easter Eve with a proper preface and post-communion sentence. In 1986, *Lent, Holy Week, Easter* stepped in to bring some clarity to the situation with the firm reminder that

> according to ancient custom there is no celebration of the Eucharist on Easter Eve. The orders of Morning and Evening Prayer offer adequate liturgical provision for the day ... It is particularly important that Evening Prayer should be treated, by the style of its celebration, as belonging to the Eve, and not as the first service of Easter, anticipating the Easter liturgy itself.[5]

This note is helpfully repeated in the introduction to the Easter Liturgy in *Common Worship*. There has never been any provision for a Liturgy of the Word in the Roman rite on this day, but the Ambrosian rite does provide for an Ante-communion with the same Gospel (Matthew 27:57–66) as that found in the *Book of Common Prayer*.

The Roman Office of Readings provides for today a reading 'from an ancient homily for Holy Saturday' which powerfully evokes the unique character of this day and provides a powerful reminder of the traditional Easter iconography of the Harrowing of Hell, fine examples of which are to be found in the former church of St Saviour-in-Chora in Istanbul (for a while the Karije Museum but now once again a mosque), the Hosios Loukas monastery in Distomo, Greece, and St Mark's Basilica in Venice. It begins:

> What is happening? Today there is a great silence over the earth, a great silence and stillness, a great silence because the King sleeps; the earth was in terror and was still, because God slept in the flesh and raised up those who were sleeping from the ages. God has died in the flesh, and the underworld has trembled. Truly he goes to seek out our first parent like a lost sheep; he

---

4 *The Roman Missal*, p. 374
5 *Lent, Holy Week, Easter*, p. 223, repeated in *Common Worship: Times and Seasons*, p. 323.

wishes to visit those who sit in darkness and in the shadow of death. He goes to free the prisoner Adam and his fellow prisoner Eve from their pains, he who is God and Adam's son. The Lord goes into them holding his victorious weapon, his cross. When Adam, the first created man, sees him, he strikes his breast in terror and cries out to all: 'My Lord be with you all.' And Christ in reply says to Adam: 'And with your spirit.' And grasping his hand he raises him up, saying, 'Awake, O sleeper, and arise from the dead, and Christ shall give you light.'

Whether the Anglican priest-poet George Herbert, familiar certainly with the works of many of the Early Fathers, ever saw an Eastern icon of the Resurrection or the mosaics of Venice remain open to speculation;[6] nevertheless, in his poem *Easter* he too calls to mind the atmosphere both of this passage and the *Anastasis* icon:

> *Rise heart, thy Lord is risen. Sing his praise*
> > *Without delayes.*
> *Who takes thee by the hand, that thou likewise*
> > *With him may rise . . .*

And in his later poem *The Dawning*:

> *Arise sad heart: if thou dost not withstand,*
> > *Christ's resurrection thine may be:*
> *Do not by hanging down break from the hand,*
> > *Which as it riseth, raiseth thee:*

If there is one essential characteristic of the Easter Vigil it is that, like the Jewish Passover, it is a nocturnal celebration: 'That was for the Lord a night of vigil, to bring them out of the land of Egypt. That same night is a vigil to be kept for the Lord by all the Israelites throughout their generations' (Exodus 12:42). St Augustine can express the common mind of the Latin and Greek Fathers when he preaches to his congregation:

> In exhorting us to imitate his example, St Paul the Apostle, besides enumerating his many other outstanding virtues, mentions also that he often spent the night in watching (2 Corinthians 11:27). How much more assiduously, then, ought we to keep watch on this particular vigil, which is we may say, the mother of all sacred vigils, when the entire world is committed to keeping a night watch ... Therefore let us watch and pray, that both

---

[6] It is not impossible that Herbert visited Venice. Certainly his friend Nicholas Ferrar did.

outwardly and inwardly we may celebrate this vigil. God speaks to us in the readings of his holy word. Let us speak to God in our prayers. If we listen in docility to his sayings, he whom we petition takes up his dwelling in our hearts.[7]

Yet it is precisely the question of the timing of the Vigil that presents so many pastoral problems today. It is no longer what it was originally, an all-night vigil ending with the Eucharist at cockcrow. While it is true that contemporary congregations do not have the same appetite or endurance for such vigils as their predecessors, yet it can hardly be denied that unless the Vigil lasts for two hours at the very least it fails to qualify for the name of a vigil, a watch. *Paschalis Solemnitatis* includes a sharp reminder:

> The entire celebration of the Easter Vigil takes place at night. It should not begin before nightfall; it should end before daybreak on Sunday. This rule is to be taken according to its strictest sense. Reprehensible are those abuses and practices which have crept into many places in violation of this ruling, whereby the Easter Vigil is celebrated at the time of day that it is customary to celebrate anticipated Sunday Masses.[8]

The symbolism of the New Fire and of the Paschal Candle needs to be taken seriously; it can only be fully respected and appreciated when the celebration takes place in darkness. Although there is a custom particularly associated with Germany of celebrating the Vigil in the early hours of the morning, in most places the Vigil will be timed to end at or shortly before midnight.

Sensing that there are many and various pastoral circumstances in which the Easter Liturgy will be celebrated and that there might be resistance to a nocturnal service (even amongst those happy to attend a Midnight Eucharist at Christmas), or complaints that what amounts to an extended liturgy of the word followed by a Eucharist with baptisms and the renewal of baptismal commitment would prove too long, *Common Worship* provides a great deal of liturgical material—some one hundred and two pages—and a number of possible routes through it designed to cover almost every eventuality. Most important among these are two ways of celebrating the full Easter Liturgy, the first of which, labelled A, follows the

[7]   Augustine, Sermon 219 (Patrologia Latina 38, col. 1087); cf. P. T. Weller, *Selected Easter Sermons of St Augustine* (Herder, St Louis Missouri, 1959), pp. 79–81.
[8]   *Paschalis Solemnitatis*, para. 78.

traditional pattern which begins with the Service of Light and then continues with the Vigil of readings—it is this version which will be discussed more fully below. The second pattern, Pattern B, has been described as a 'storytelling approach' and begins with the Vigil of readings which is then followed by an extended Service of Light that brings the 'story' to its climax with the Gospel of the Resurrection.

For the Vigil, integral to both patterns, extensive lectionary material is supplied: Genesis 1 and Exodus 14 are obligatory, followed by twenty-two further possible readings from which five thematic paths may be constructed. The third mode of presentation for the Easter Liturgy material is a Dawn Service, presented as notes and an outline only. The deviser of this liturgy, carried away perhaps by an over romanticised view of *al fresco* worship, suggests a number of contexts for this early morning liturgy such as a hilltop, near a cave, a graveyard, a garden or on the bank of a river or stream. The notes also recommend a 'light touch' arrangement of all the main elements in the Easter Liturgy for this service, following Pattern B. Two other re-mixes of the core material are suggested, a mid-morning Eucharist on Easter Day and a Service of the Word, which somehow sidesteps the obligation of communicant Anglicans to receive Holy Communion on this day. The provision of this material in *Common Worship* is motivated by a real desire to enable as many people as possible to express the joy of Easter in liturgical worship with at least its roots in the tradition, but priests and people should not see this as an excuse not to observe the Vigil in its integrity even in the face of resistance and apathy. In many urban areas it will be possible for a number of parishes and communities to join together to celebrate the Vigil in the most suitable church building. Where this is done only one Paschal Candle should be used for the Service of Light but at the conclusion of the Eucharist the candles of other communities can be lit from the principal candle and carried out by their clergy or other representatives in the procession from the altar. Practically speaking, this flame can then be carried back to individual parish churches in an enclosed lantern.

Three preliminary points of a general nature need to be made at the outset before any discussion of the structure of the Easter Vigil and its constituent sections. First of all, it is vital to remember the truth which has been the major theme of this study, that the Easter

Liturgy is still the celebration of the whole mystery of redemption in its unity and integrity. If the separate commemoration of the Crucifixion on Good Friday has meant that the Gospel reading at the Vigil is now the account of the Resurrection only and no longer the narrative of the Passion, death and Resurrection, yet still—to cite only a few examples—the *Exsultet*, the readings from the Old Testament and the Letter to the Romans, the baptismal liturgy and the Proper Preface emphasise the fact that it is the Christian Passover being celebrated, the *transitus* of God's people and of his Messiah. The Vigil is of crucial importance because it is both the climax of Holy Week and the inauguration of the Great Fifty Days of Easter—Pentecost; it is the hinge which connects and unites the two.[9] Since Christian theology and devotion have been so impoverished by the divorce between the Cross and the Resurrection, between Lent and Easter, it is necessary to persevere in the difficult but rewarding task of restoring to its full influence in the life of the Church the one liturgical celebration which proclaims with the fullest and most uncompromising clarity the New Testament unity of the two.

Secondly, it is helpful perhaps at this point to reflect on the nature of the symbolism used in the Holy Week ceremonies and pre-eminently in the Easter Vigil. Theatrical realism is avoided— although much medieval elaboration (of the Palm Sunday procession, for example) tended in this direction. The Holy Week liturgy is not a kind of drama designed to *impress*; its first concern is always to *involve*. It often succeeds in being both extremely dramatic and wonderfully impressive if celebrated with imagination and care, but this is never the main consideration. The symbolism of Holy Week makes sparing use of the directly representational and concentrates on certain fundamental biblical and sacramental archetypes and images—fire, light, water, oil, bread and wine. The liturgical symbol of the Resurrection is neither the popular and harmless 'Easter Garden' of modern fashion nor the Easter Sepulchre of the medieval English rites (in which a crucifix and consecrated host were 'buried' on Good Friday and from which

9   The text of the Easter Vigil as first reformed in 1951 was given the title *Ordo Sabbati Sancti*, but in the present Roman Rite it is made quite clear that the Vigil does not belong to Holy Saturday but rather to Easter Sunday (*Domenica Paschae in Resurrectione Domini*) and in *Common Worship* it is the Easter Liturgy *par excellence*.

they were 'resurrected' on Easter morning);[10] rather it is the Paschal Candle whose symbolism is all the more powerful for being entirely non-representational. The Paschal Candle is, in the colourful phrase of Dom Lambert Beauduin, 'no mere accessory to the Vigil, but rather its hero, its principal personality'.[11]

Thirdly, it has to be accepted with realism and honesty that the Easter Vigil will never be able to claim—and probably should not attempt to do so—the same kind of popularity as the Midnight Mass of Christmas. It will always baffle those whose Christian commitment is minimal, and its symbolism, which works so power-fully for those who can open themselves up to its rich and complex background, will remain opaque for those who are indifferent to or ignorant of that background. Preparation and careful teaching is so important because to expect liturgical signs and symbols to speak directly to the newcomer on first sight is to forget that they derive their meaning from the mystery of salvation.

What is more worrying—and must not be accepted with com-placency—is the apparent indifference of many committed Chris-tians, of all liturgically minded denominations, to the Vigil. Those who associate the Resurrection of Christ with sunrise need to understand that the New Testament is silent as to the 'moment' of the Resurrection; what happened very early in the morning ('towards dawn' or 'as the sun was rising' or 'at the first sign of dawn' or 'while it was still dark') was the discovery of the empty tomb. The Easter Vigil is not a celebration that attempts to capture the 'moment' of the Resurrection but one which is concerned with a passing over with Christ from darkness to light, from death to life. It should become once again the normative way of celebrating Easter not just for an elite group of liturgical enthusiasts but for the whole body of committed Christians.

The modern *Roman Missal* presents what it calls the 'Easter Vigil in the Holy Night' in four parts:

- The Solemn Beginning of the Vigil or Lucernarium
- The Liturgy of the Word
- Baptismal Liturgy
- The Liturgy of the Eucharist.

---

[10] For a full discussion of the medieval English practice see Eamon Duffy, *The Stripping of the Altars* (Yale University Press, London, 1992), pp. 29–37.

[11] Dom Lambert Beauduin, 'Le Cierge pascal', *La Maison Dieu* 26 (1951), pp. 23–8.

This traditional order forms Pattern A of the Easter Liturgy in *Common Worship* but, as mentioned earlier, there is also a Pattern B, thus:

- The Vigil—a series of related readings with psalms and prayers
- The Service of Light—a much extended section which includes the presentation of candidates for baptism and leads into the Gloria, Collect, Epistle, Psalm, Gospel and Sermon
- The Liturgy of Initiation
- The Liturgy of the Eucharist.

Although there is a historical element in this second order in the shape of a tenth-century precedent from Jerusalem, pastoral and psychological considerations predominate. It is argued that the movement from darkness to light is more convincing if the Service of Light comes after the Old Testament readings and is made the point of transition from 'waiting' to 'celebrating'. Some, like the compilers of *The Methodist Worship Book*, will see the strength of this argument, but the traditional order has a force and coherence of its own and makes sense not only historically but also liturgically (the Service of Light being a form of entrance rite) and theologically (the traditional opening providing—literally—the light by which the Old Testament is to be read and understood).

Historically, the Service of Light or *Lucernarium* evolved naturally from the domestic custom of the Jews whereby the mother of the household brought in a lamp for the evening meal which ushered in the Sabbaths and Festivals and a blessing for God's gift of light was said over it. It is quite possible that our Lord himself pronounced this blessing at the Last Supper: 'Blessed be thou, Lord our God, King of all eternity, who didst create the lamps of fire.' The ceremony was therefore taken over quite naturally into the Christian Church for use at a vigil service. Indeed, *The Apostolic Tradition* ascribed to Hippolytus in the third century makes provision for a deacon to bring in the lamp for the Lord's Supper and for the bishop to give thanks: 'We give you thanks, O God, through your Son Jesus Christ our Lord, through who you have enlightened us, revealing to us the light that does not perish.'[12] It is from this background and possibly from the same century that

---

[12]   P. F. Bradshaw, *The Apostolic Tradition Reconstructed*, Joint Liturgical Studies 91 (Alcuin Club & Group for Renewal of Worship, Silverton, 2021), section [25] p. 29.

one of the oldest hymns still in current use, the Greek *Phos hilaron* (still in use at Vespers in the Byzantine rite and in a similar context in *Common Worship: Daily Prayer*), has come down to us.

Φῶς ἱλαρὸν ἁγίας δόξης ἀθανάτου Πατρός,
οὐρανίου, ἁγίου, μάκαρος, Ἰησοῦ Χριστέ,
ἐλθόντες ἐπὶ τὴν ἡλίου δύσιν, ἰδόντες φῶς ἑσπερινόν,
ὑμνοῦμεν Πατέρα, Υἱόν, καὶ ἅγιον Πνεῦμα, Θεόν.
Ἄξιόν σε ἐν πᾶσι καιροῖς ὑμνεῖσθαι φωναῖς αἰσίαις,
Υἱὲ Θεοῦ, ζωὴν ὁ διδούς· διὸ ὁ κόσμος σὲ δοξάζει.

Hail gladdening light, of his pure glory poured
Who is the immortal Father, heavenly, blest,
Holiest of holies, Jesus Christ our Lord.

Now we have come to the sun's hour of rest,
The lights of evening round us shine,
We hymn the Father, Son, and Holy Spirit divine.

Worthiest art thou at all times to be sung
With undefiled tongue,
Son of our God, giver of life, alone:
Therefore in all the world thy glories, Lord, they own.[13]

In recent years there has been something of a revival of the *Lucernarium* in both Anglican and Roman Catholic circles. *Common Worship: Daily Prayer* has a Blessing of the Light which may replace the usual opening of Evening Prayer on any occasion,[14] and some monastic communities celebrate a Vigil Office with *Lucernarium* on the eves of Sundays and Solemnities. It is easily understandable how in the unique context of the Easter Vigil the *Lucernarium* developed into the rich and powerful symbolism of the new fire (a pre-Christian ritual, which may have originated in Ireland, baptised by the Church) and the new light and gave the Western liturgy its most eloquent and lyrical piece of prose and one of its most elegant melodies in the Paschal Proclamation or *Exsultet*. First, the text introduces a chain of allusions to ancient antitypes by which, as through a gateway, the hearers are drawn ever deeper into that mystical place where, in the light of paradise regained, even Adam's sin may be regarded as a truly necessary and happy fault.

[13] Translated by John Keble.
[14] *Common Worship: Daily Prayer* (Church House Publishing, London, 2006), p. 110.

Secondly, the great candle itself, the work of bees and hugely costly, is praised as a burnt offering, a type of Christ, marked by grains of incense to represent the five glorious wounds of his Passion. To the existence of the Paschal Candle and of this song of praise (*laus cerei*, literally 'praise of the wax-light') both St Augustine and St Jerome testify in the fourth century, St Jerome indulging in some characteristically caustic comments about deacons showing off![15] It was some time before the text of the *Exsultet* became a fixed one, and even then there was some variation. In particular the *felix culpa* passage ('O truly necessary sin of Adam, destroyed completely by the death of Christ! O happy fault that earned so great, so glorious a Redeemer!') caused great offence. St Hugh of Cluny ordered it to be effaced in his missal and the words have been omitted or crossed out in many medieval texts. It was omitted from the 'Great Vigil of Easter' in the 1977 American *Book of Common Prayer*, and it finds no place in any of the versions provided in *Common Worship* or *The Methodist Worship Book*.

By the sixth century in Rome the singing of the *Exsultet* had become a strikingly dramatic element in the Easter liturgy. For example, both the basilicas of San Clemente and Santa Maria in Cosmedin in that city preserve an elaborate gospel ambo built into the low walls of the *schola cantorum* section of the church. Immediately adjacent in both cases is a fixed Paschal Candlestick of Solomonic pattern in twisted stone, the ambo and the candle-stand providing the stage set, as it were, for the proclamation of the praises of the 'truly blessed night'. Moreover, these Easter praises could frequently be an audio-visual experience for those clustered around the ambo. The deacon would chant this *praeconium paschale* from a long scroll especially designed for visual effect. As he sang, he would unroll the scroll in such a way that it unfurled in front of the ambo, displaying a series of pictorial illustrations of the text to those close enough to see. The British Library has an example of such an illustrated roll, made at the Abbey of Monte Cassino around 1075–80.[16] The images are, of course, upside down as far as the deacon singing is concerned so as to appear the right way

---

[15] *Epistola* 18 *ad Praesidium de Cereo Paschali* (Patrologia Latina 30, cols. 188–94), cf. J. N. D. Kelly, *Jerome* (Duckworth, 1974), p. 111.

[16] British Library, Add. MS 30337. MS Barb.lat 592 in the Vatican Library, also from Monte Casino, has a wonderful illustration of the bees at work preparing the wax for the Paschal Candle.

up to the viewers as the scroll unfurls. Membrane 11 contains a striking illustration of the scroll in use, and it is easy to see how, in the flickering candlelight, this visual aid would have provided an atmospheric way of engaging with the liturgy.

The significance of the Paschal Candle and the ceremonies connected with it have been discussed in Chapter III (p. 49); at this point a further general comment is worth making. The theme of light is one that connects not only with the whole movement of Christ's redemptive work, but also with the activity of Creation; for the Resurrection inaugurates a new creation, and St Paul, quoting Genesis, underlines the unity between the creative and redemptive activity of God: 'For it is the God who said, 'Let light shine out of darkness', who has shone in our hearts to give the light of the knowledge of the glory of God in the face of Jesus Christ' (2 Corinthians 4:6). The theme of light is also intensely eschatological, pointing us to the *parousia*: 'Be dressed for action and have your lamps lit; be like those who are waiting for their master to return from the wedding banquet, so that they may open the door for him as soon as he comes and knocks. Blessed are those slaves whom the master finds alert when he comes' (Luke 12:35–7).

The second part of the Vigil, the Liturgy of the Word, comes immediately after the singing of the *Exsultet*. The high drama of the Service of Light gives way to the sober intensity of meditative reading and, as the faithful extinguish their candles, some may be tempted to feel a sense of anti-climax. Yet this is in fact the core of the Vigil, and it should be presented in such a way that a growing sense of expectant waiting is engendered as the key passages of scripture are read. The 1955 and 1970 reforms of the Roman rite cut down the number of obligatory Old Testament readings (there were Twelve in the Missal of Pius V and four in the *Ordo* of Pius XII) and the latter reform gave greater unity to this part of the rite by placing the Epistle and Gospel in this section. Of the seven Old Testament readings provided in the *Roman Missal* today at least three must be read, one of which must always be Exodus 14. *Common Worship* concurs but suggests that the reading from Genesis 1 is desirable in addition while providing a raft of twenty further possible passages from which to choose at least one more. Those tempted to cut down the readings to a minimum should ponder the reminder in both Roman and Anglican rubrics that this Liturgy of the Word constitutes the oldest feature of and the fundamental element in the Easter Vigil. It is vital therefore that this section of the Easter Liturgy be neither pruned to the bare minimum nor rushed through at great speed. *Paschalis Solemnitatis* explains that:

> the restored order for the Vigil has seven readings from the Old Testament, chosen from the law and the prophets, which are everywhere in use according to the most ancient tradition of East and West; and two readings from the New Testament, namely, from the apostles and from the gospel. Thus, the Church, 'beginning with Moses and all the prophets', explains Christ's paschal mystery. Consequently, wherever this is possible, all the readings should be read in order so that the character of the Easter Vigil, which demands that it be somewhat prolonged, be respected at all costs.[17]

The limited scope of this study prevents the giving of a detailed commentary on each of the readings; it must suffice to make a few remarks of a general character. First of all, it is important to remember that the readings have a dual orientation, not just a preparation of the faithful for the celebration of Easter but a final and immediate preparation of the *electi* for the Sacraments of Initiation. So, for example, the first lesson from Genesis which tells the story of Creation is a preparation not only for the new creation of the Resurrection but also for new creation in baptism, though of course the latter is implicit in the former. Secondly, it is worth reflecting on the particular structure of this Liturgy of the Word which not only enhances its teaching role but gives it the character of a dialogue between God and his people. Each reading is followed by a responsorial psalm, by an invitation to silent prayer and then by a Collect which 'collects' and sums up this time of silent prayer and interprets the message of the Old Testament readings for the present needs of the Christian congregation. A brief introduction to each Old Testament reading, though not expressly ordered, will also be helpful. Thirdly, in the traditional order, Pattern A, the Old Testament readings are read in and by the light of the Paschal Candle, in a darkened church, a powerful symbol of the truth that Scripture only reveals its fill meaning in the presence of the Risen Christ.

A moment of drama comes after the last of the Old Testament readings; as *Gloria in excelsis* is intoned the bells, silent since Maundy

---

[17] *Paschalis Solemnitatis*, para. 85.

Thursday, ring out, the organ, similarly silent, joins in the jubilation, the church is illuminated, and the altar candles are lit. Some clergy encourage the members of their congregation to bring their own bells, gongs and whistles to add to the sounds of triumph. After the Solemn Collect, which in the Roman rite appropriately praises God who makes 'this most sacred night radiant', and the Epistle, which is the great passage from Romans 6 proclaiming the paschal character of baptism, the *Alleluia* (absent from the liturgy since the beginning of Lent) triumphantly returns. In an address given in Harlem in 1979, Pope John-Paul II reminded Christian people, using a phrase traditionally ascribed to St Augustine, that 'we are an Easter people and Alleluia is our song' and in the Easter Liturgy this acclamation should ring out with special conviction. It is used in both Roman and Anglican rites as the refrain in the responsorial psalm — 118 in the Roman Rite and 114 in *Common Worship*. Psalm 118, the last of the *Hallel* psalms so intimately connected with the celebration of the Jewish Passover, seems the more appropriate as it is the Easter psalm *par excellence* and is frequently cited by the Apostles in their Easter preaching (cf. Acts 4:11–12; 1 Corinthians 3:11; Ephesians 2:20; 1 Peter 2:7–8). Psalm 114, on the other hand, looks back to the atmosphere of the Old Testament readings and celebrates the miracles of the Exodus. The Gospel reading is taken from a Synoptic narrative of the Resurrection Matthew in Year A, Mark in Year B and Luke in Year C), with the Johannine account reserved for the Mass of Easter Day.

In the Roman rite, the third part of the Easter Liturgy, the Baptismal Liturgy, can take three forms. The most reduced is for churches — for example churches of religious communities — where there is no font. Here water is blessed in a simpler formula and used to sprinkle the congregation after the Renewal of Baptismal Promises. It is the practice of some religious communities, notably that of Taizé, to have solemn professions at this point: religious profession is nothing other than a particular application of the baptismal covenant. The second form is for use in churches which have a font but where there are no candidates for Initiation; baptismal water is solemnly blessed for use during the Easter season and the faithful renew their baptismal promises. The third, fullest and normative form provides for the solemn blessing of baptismal water, baptism and, if possible, confirmation and then the renewal of baptismal vows by all. *Common Worship* envisages the second and third of these pastoral circumstances and makes provision accordingly, but the *Methodist Worship Book* makes no mention of Initiation in its order for the Easter Vigil, only providing for a Reaffirmation of Baptism, despite its introductory notes making the historical point that in the early Church at this service candidates were presented for baptism. The normative form of the Easter Liturgy is both a joyful proclamation of the Paschal Mystery and an extended service of Christian Initiation and it is important for pastors to try and find candidates for baptism and, if possible, confirmation during the service for their own sake and for the sake of the faithful. Candidates should be adults, or the children of adults, who have been fully and properly prepared for this most solemn form of initiation. Whereas in Roman Catholic parishes confirmation presents no problem as priests with the necessary faculty may administer this sacrament in the absence of the bishop, in the Church of England presbyteral confirmation is not permitted. In these circumstances, particularly when the baptised have been chrismated after emerging from the font, candidates should be admitted to Holy Communion on the grounds that they are 'ready and desirous' to be confirmed — to refuse them Communion on this occasion would be highly inappropriate.

The Litany of the Saints at one time occupied the faithful while the candidates for initiation and the clergy were out of sight in the baptistry; it can now accompany the procession of candidates, sponsors, and clergy, led by the Paschal Candle, to the font. In Anglican parishes where the direct invocation of the prayers of the saints might prove too rich a diet, the words 'pray with us' or 'join in our prayer' can be substituted for 'pray for us' as these words fit the usual chant. While *Common Worship* provides a newly devised litany to accompany the procession which makes no reference to the company of heaven,[18] baptism is an enrolment in the company of the People of God and fellow citizens with the saints, so it is fitting therefore for all to be made aware of their fellowship with the saints and of their continuing intercession.

In the Roman rite, the Prayer of Blessing over the water of baptism is a rich meditation on the theme of water as worked out in the Scriptures and it repays careful study. It begins with Creation and works through Noah's flood and the Exodus narrative to Christ's

18 *Common Worship: Times and Seasons*, pp. 422–3.

baptism in the Jordan, the flow of blood and water from his side upon the cross and his command, 'Go forth, teach all nations, baptising them . . .' (cf. Matthew 28:19). The Prayer over the Water provided in *Common Worship* is briefer and less rich in its typology. It begins with Christ at the Jordan and then moves to the Red Sea before introducing the Pauline teaching from Romans 6 and finally invoking the Holy Spirit as the agent of rebirth in the household of faith. In this rite, the font must be seen as the womb of Mother Church made pregnant by the power of the Holy Spirit through the risen Christ to bring forth children, and the Church is not afraid to make use of frankly sexual imagery when the Paschal Candle is plunged three times into the waters of the font as the Holy Spirit is invoked.

The celebration of baptism and Confirmation during the night of Easter is discussed in some detail in an earlier chapter (pp. 55–6) but it is important at this point to re-emphasise the importance of the Renewal of Baptismal Vows especially when there are no candidates for initiation. For the baptised, this rite is the destination to which the whole directed and guided journey of Lent, begun on Ash Wednesday, has been leading. The people should stand with candles lit from the great glowing pillar of the Paschal Candle and are addressed by the celebrant. He reminds them that through the Paschal Mystery they have been buried with Christ in baptism so that they may rise with him to new life within the family of his Church. Now that the observance of Lent has been completed, he invites them to join him in renewing their baptismal vows, their rejection of evil and their allegiance to Christ. *Common Worship* uses a form of baptismal reaffirmation which was originally drafted for the great ecumenical celebration in Canterbury Cathedral when Pope John Paul II visited in 1982 and is now part of the fuller provision of baptismal material provided in the *Christian Initiation* volume. Anglicans who have forgotten the ecumenical significance of this form will nevertheless rejoice that the Apostles' Creed once again fulfils its original role as a baptismal creed from which it was unaccountably banished by the 1980 *Alternative Service Book*. After the prayer which concludes this renewal, the people are sprinkled with baptismal water while the anthem *Vidi aquam* or a hymn is sung. The *Common Worship* rubric advocates the sprinkling of the people but also suggests as an alternative that individuals might like to approach the font and make the sign of the cross with its waters on their forehead.

The fourth and climactic element in the Easter Vigil is the Liturgy of the Eucharist, introduced by the Universal Prayer (Intercessions) and in the *Common Worship* rite by the Peace. Since *Lent, Holy Week, Easter* first suggested it, many Anglicans have adopted the Easter greeting familiar to Eastern Orthodox Christians, 'Christ is risen! He is risen indeed!' in place of the usual 'Peace be with you'. Every celebration of the Eucharist is a paschal celebration, a celebration of the whole mystery of redemption in its inclusive unity, and a fervent and expectant anticipation of the End. Every Eucharist 'opens up the vision of the divine rule which has been promised as the final renewal of creation, and is a foretaste of it'.[19] These characteristics however, are nowhere expressed and realised with such clarity and force as in the one celebration during the night of Easter, in this Eucharist which sums up the work of the Cross and the Sepulchre and celebrates them in the joy and the light of the Resurrection. This is not an eleventh-hour reversal of the defeat of Good Friday, but a confirmation of a victory already won, a seal of the Father's acceptance and approval of the self-offering of Christ in his Passion. Modern Roman and Anglican Eucharistic Prayers now include acclamations after the Words of Institution (or in the case of Prayers A and E of *Common Worship* after the Anamnesis) derived from the Syrian rites which stress the eschatological character of the eucharistic celebration:

> *Christ has died:*
> *Christ is risen:*
> *Christ will come again.*

Other acclamations provided stress the same note, particularly that one which quotes the Proper Preface of Easter:

> *Dying you destroyed our death,*
> *Rising you restored our life,*
> *Lord Jesus, come in glory.*

At this point it is important to recall the dominant and controlling note of the Jewish Passover, the note of expectation, the eager looking forward to the coming definitive liberation, of which the Exodus experience is the prototype and guarantee. Jeremias has written:

[19]   *Baptism, Eucharist, and Ministry*, Faith and Order Paper no. 111 (World Council of Churches, Geneva, 1982), p. 13, para. 22.

That the Messiah would come on the night of the Passover was both a Jewish and a Christian hope. Each year, therefore, during the Passover night the primitive community waited until midnight, in prayer and fasting, the return of the Lord. They prolonged the waiting into the hours after midnight. If he had not come bodily by cock-crow, then they united themselves with him in the celebration of table fellowship.[20]

Later in the same book, Jeremias quotes St Jerome's *Commentary on Matthew* (chapter 25: the parable of the wise and foolish virgins):

It is a tradition of the Jews that the Messiah will come at midnight according to the manner of the time in Egypt when the Passover was (first) celebrated. Whence I think also the apostolic tradition has persisted that on the day of the paschal vigil it is not permitted to dismiss before midnight the people who are expecting the advent of Christ.[21]

The Paschal Eucharist is 'realised eschatology' *par excellence*; although it is on one level an acknowledgment that the End still lies in the future, it is at another level (the sacramental level) the bringing into the present of the reality and power of that anticipated fulness. 'What we hope for is the fulness of what we already possess in him. What we possess has its meaning only in the hope of his Coming.'[22] The Paschal Eucharist makes real for us the past, present and future dimensions of Christ's paschal mystery, and the Night of Easter is sadly frustrated and unfulfilled if it does not lead into that climax. In the words of Melito of Sardis, which recall the words said over the Paschal Candle at the beginning of the Vigil:

> *He is the Alpha and the Omega;*
> *He is the beginning and end,*
> *Beginning inexpressible and end incomprehensible.*[23]

In trying to summarise the message of this most holy night it is difficult to improve on St Augustine who in one of his sermons at the Easter Vigil said:

Our Lord Jesus Christ, having made this day a day of mourning by his death, changed it into a day of rejoicing by his resurrection.

[20] Jeremias, *The Eucharistic Words of Jesus*, p. 123.
[21] *Ibid.*, p. 206.
[22] G. K. A. Bell, *The Kingship of Christ* (Penguin, London, 1954), p. 174.
[23] Melito of Sardis, *On Pascha*, 105, p. 61.

Now that we are solemnly commemorating both of these events,
let us keep watch in memory of his death, and joyfully welcome
his approaching resurrection. This is our annual festival, our
Paschal feast, not, as prefigured for the people of the Old Law
by the slaughter of a beast, but as fulfilled for the people of the
New Law by the sacrifice of our Saviour. 'For Christ our Pasch
is sacrificed.' ... In watching and praying we pass this night in
which our Lord rose from the dead, the night that brought us
the life where there is neither death nor sleep ... Life began for
us in his risen body.[24]

There is a certain tension in the celebration of the Easter Day
Eucharist which is probably inevitable. On the one hand, there
is the proper desire to emphasise the overwhelmingly greater
importance which should be accorded to the Mass of the Easter
Vigil—to the point perhaps of wondering whether at least in some
communities it is really necessary to have a second celebration.
Can one not emulate the practice of the primitive Church and
the continuing rule of the Orthodox Churches and have only one
Eucharist? On the other hand ,there will be the realisation that
in the hard reality of pastoral practice there will be more people
present in most churches at the eucharistic celebrations of Easter
Day than at the Vigil. While it, is legitimate to see the Easter Vigil
as the one great celebration of the whole Paschal Mystery and the
Easter Day celebration as concentrating principally on the Resurrection, it is of enormous importance that the whole of the Paschal
Mystery should be celebrated at the daytime Eucharists. There will
not only be present those who were not in church for the Vigil but
also those who may not have been at any of the ceremonies of the
Triduum. This consideration will particularly affect the choice of
hymns and readings; preachers too will be well advised to draw
on such material as the Proper Preface for Easter and to explain
the significance of the Paschal Candle.

Already in the fourth century, Egeria describes how at Jerusalem after the Easter Vigil in the Great Church 'they immediately
come with hymns to the Anastasis and there that passage of the
Gospel about the Resurrection is then read, prayer is made, and
then the bishop makes the oblation there'.[25] Following on imme-

[24] *Serm. Guelf.* v (Patrologia Latina 38, col. 1089): cf. Weller, *Selected Easter Sermons
of St Augustine*, pp. 82–6.
[25] Egeria, trans. McGowan and Bradshaw, p. 179.

diately after the Vigil Mass, this seems strange but perhaps there was a desire to celebrate at the very place of the Resurrection. This second Easter Mass was certainly known in North Africa in the time of St Augustine and he himself often preached both at the Vigil and at the second Mass. There is evidence for it from other parts of Christendom, but, typically, it did not take root at Rome until later; the first Roman texts of prayer and readings date from the seventh century.

The principal Eucharist on Easter Day should be celebrated with great joy and solemnity and provision should be made for the best-loved Easter hymns to be sung. The Mass of the Day is one of the two Masses in the *Roman Missal* in which the Sequence before the Alleluia chant remains obligatory (the other is Pentecost). An English translation and the traditional chant for this dramatic hymn, *Victimae paschali* attributed to the eleventh-century Wipo of Burgundy, may be found in the *New English Hymnal* at number 519, and this version has found its way into the Ordinariate Missal. Together with the Easter *Quem quaeritis* trope—another example of the medieval tendency to amplify the proper of the Mass with free poetic compositions—this beautiful sequence, with its few sentences of dialogue, has been seen by some scholars as the origin of liturgical drama and the beginning of Western theatre.

> *Speak Mary, declaring what thou sawest wayfaring:*
> *'The tomb of Christ who is living, the glory of Jesu's resurrection:*
> *Bright angels attesting, the shroud and napkin resting.*
> *Yea, Christ my hope is arisen: to Galilee he goes before you.'*

Other particular features of the Roman rite include the possibility of using water blessed at the Vigil for the Sprinkling with Holy Water which can replace the Penitential Rite at the beginning of the Mass and during which the antiphon *Vidi aquam* (among other possible antiphons) is sung: 'I saw water flowing from the Temple, from its right-hand side, alleluia: and all to whom this water came were saved and shall say: alleluia, alleluia.' *Common Worship: Times and Seasons*, includes an Act of Penitence which 'may appropriately be used at the Sunday Eucharist in Eastertide', based on the *Vidi aquam* model; the antiphon is not given but 'suitable hymns, songs or anthems may be sung'.[26] The Renewal of Baptismal Promises

---

[26] *Common Worship: Times and Seasons*, p. 430.

may replace the Nicene Creed and, if this has not already happened at the beginning of Mass, the people may be sprinkled. A Solemn Blessing formula is also provided which may be used at the Vigil and on Easter Day and *Common Worship* offers one also with a more strongly Trinitarian emphasis.

The inevitable tension felt by those planning the worship of Easter Day is particularly apparent when it comes to deciding whether to repeat the Renewal of Baptismal Promises which is so integral a part of the Liturgy of Baptism at the Vigil: liturgical and pastoral considerations may pull in opposite directions. *Common Worship* attempts to help Anglicans in this dilemma by providing an outline order for a 'Mid-morning Eucharist on Easter Day using Elements from the Easter Liturgy'[27] primarily for use when there has been no Vigil service. It suggests a rudimentary Service of Light, a procession with the Easter Candle making the traditional three stations, and the singing or saying of the *Exsultet*, but draws attention to the danger of presenting the worship in such a way that it seems to be a nocturnal service that is accidentally being celebrated during the day. A rubric declares it 'particularly appropriate for the congregation to re-affirm their baptismal vows using a form which includes the Prayer over the Water'. For those churches where the daytime Eucharist will be the principal act of Easter worship, this order provides a distinctive beginning in the way that the Commemoration of the Lord's Entry into Jerusalem is distinctive to Palm Sunday.[28]

After a period of neglect, apocryphally owing to the lure of Sunday evening television, Anglican Evensong has once again become popular. Evening Prayer on Easter Sunday brings the Paschal *Triduum* to a close and every effort should be made to give it a particular and festive character. Evidence from the seventh century suggests that at least by that time Vespers on Easter Day had acquired a very particular character in Rome. The eighth-century *Ordo Romanus XXVII* provides some detail as to what was distinctive: the newly baptised were invited together with the faithful to the Lateran basilica (at that time as a general rule only cathedrals had baptisteries), and the whole congregation went in procession first to the Baptistry and then to the Chapel of the Cross where

---

27 *Ibid.*, pp. 401–3.
28 Kennedy, *Using Common Worship*, p. 88.

confirmation had been conferred. This 'glorious office' (*gloriosum officium*) later spread to the rest of Western Christendom and seems to have had a more tenacious hold in parts of France and Germany than in Rome itself. A procession to the font seems to have been a particular feature of the liturgical life of the greater French churches in the seventeenth and eighteenth centuries. In his *Voyages liturgiques de France* of 1718, the Sieur de Moléon writes with particular enthusiasm of the procession *ad Fontes* in Rouen Cathedral, during which the holy oils and the Paschal Candle were carried to the font. 'Cette procession,' he comments, 'est fort propre a faire souvenir les Chrétiens des voeux de leur baptême' ('This procession is very appropriate to remind Christians of their baptismal vows').[29] Earlier in the same work he writes of a similar procession at Vespers (but this time on Easter Monday and directly after the Magnificat) in the church attached to the Hôpital de la Salpêtrière in Paris. The little girls of the institution are led in procession to the font and there one of them pronounces in a loud voice the renewal of baptismal promises. De Moléon expresses the wish that such a ceremony could take place in parish churches; it might be that this is one of the sources from which those who revised the Easter Vigil liturgy under Pius XII drew their inspiration. In a later phase of the Tractarian Movement in the Church of England there was an attempt to revive this tradition and from its first edition in 1906 *The English Hymnal* provided for a procession at the end of Evensong with the singing of *O filii et filiae*, followed by a versicle and response and the Collect for Easter Even to be recited at the font.[30] *Common Worship: Daily Prayer* makes provision for a Thanksgiving for Holy Baptism which is to be celebrated at the font and should include the Apostles Creed or an authorised Affirmation of Faith.[31] Prefaced by a suitable processional hymn, this would make an admirable conclusion to a Festal Evensong, ensuring it does not become an anticlimax; the joy which characterises the celebration of Easter should be maintained.

[29] Jean Baptiste le Brun des Marettes, *Voyages liturgiques de France, recherches faites en diverses villes du royaume* (Delaune, Paris, 1718; Gregg Publishing, Farnborough, 1969), pp. 261, 325–7.

[30] Now in *New English Hymnal* as no. 527, with an alternative Collect.

[31] *Common Worship: Daily Prayer*, pp. 306–7.

The Great Fifty Days

Easter Day is a climax; it is not a conclusion. As will have become clear from earlier chapters, by the middle of the fourth century the *Pascha* was basically an all-night vigil from Saturday to Sunday, prepared for originally by one or two days of strict fasting but now by the preceding forty days of Lent. But the *Pascha* also had its prolongation—the subsequent Great Fifty Days. These fifty days were regarded liturgically as a single and undivided whole, what Tertullian called in his treatise on baptism 'the most joyful period', *laetissimum spatium*; even as a single day, what St Athanasius called 'the great Sunday'.[1] During this time *alleluia*, forbidden in Lent, was sung repeatedly and both kneeling for prayer and fasting were strictly prohibited; a prohibition already recorded at the end of the second century and reiterated in the 20th canon of Nicaea in 325. On the Day of Pentecost at Vespers in the Byzantine Rite, there is a 'kneeling office' which is both a solemn invocation of the Holy Spirit and a reminder that at the conclusion of the Great Fifty Days the ban on kneeling comes to an end. Egeria's account of the celebration of Pentecost is almost as exhausting to read as it must have been to participate in 'when there is very great labour for the people'.[2] The Descent of the Spirit was commemorated with the reading of Acts 2 at the third hour on Sion, where the event was held to have happened and at that hour of the day, and the Eucharist was celebrated. The Ascension was celebrated at the sixth hour on the Mount of Olives at the place known as the Imbomon, where the event was supposed to have happened. The Armenian Lectionary has a note recording that everyone knelt after the Gos-

---

[1]   Tertullian, *De Baptismo* 19 (Patrologia Latina 1, col. 1222); Athanasius, *Epistula festalis* 1. See Cantalamessa, *Easter*, for texts.
[2]   Egeria, trans. McGowan and Bradshaw, p. 183.

pel reading, a symbolic act which might mark the closing of the Easter season and the resumption of kneeling for prayer.[3] Finally, the procession entered the city by candlelight for further services in the Martyrium and Anastasis.

> Thus, they endure very great labour that day, because they kept vigil from first cockcrow at the Anastasis and from there never stopped for the whole day; every celebration lasts so long that all return to their homes in the middle of the night after the dismissal that was done on Sion.[4]

The only primitive distinction within the fifty days was the special character given to the Easter Octave itself, a feature taken over from the Jewish Passover (Exodus 12:15–20 and Deuteronomy 16:1–8) but also possibly influenced by the Fourth Gospel's account of the disciples coming together seven days after the Resurrection (John 20:26–9). In the Jerusalem of Egeria's time there was a daily Eucharist during this week largely because for those who had been baptised at Easter the week was a time for mystagogic catechesis — instruction on the meaning of the Sacraments which, according to the *disciplina arcani* of the early Church, had to be kept secret even from the catechumens.[5] The newly baptised continued to wear their white garments until the following Sunday — known mysteriously until recent times as *dominica in albis (depositis)*, signifying the Sunday on which white robes were laid aside. Moreover, not only was there no Ascension Day (which only appeared towards the end of the fourth century); there was not even a clear distinction between the *Pascha* as the celebration of the Cross and Resurrection and Pentecost as the celebration of the Descent of the Spirit. The whole period was described either as the *Pascha* or more commonly as Pentecost. For if Pentecost means literally 'the fiftieth' and therefore describes the fiftieth day, it came to mean for the early Church more often the whole period of fifty days — as in the 20th canon of Nicaea forbidding kneeling for prayer 'in the days of the Pentecost'.

---

[3]   *Ibid.*, p. 186, note 8, and A. Renoux, 'Le Codex armenien Jerusalem 121' (Patrologia Orientalis 35/1, 36/2, 1969–71), 43.5.

[4]   Egeria, trans. McGowan and Bradshaw, p. 187.

[5]   Talley, *Origins of the Liturgical Year*, p. 55; Egeria, trans. McGowan and Bradshaw, p. 181; Maxwell Johnson, ed., *Lectures on the Christian Sacraments: The Procatechesis and the Five Mystagogical Catecheses Ascribed to St Cyril of Jerusalem*, Popular Patristics 57 (St Vladimir's Seminary Press, New York, 2017).

There is a vestigial reminder of this in the Old Vulgate translation of Acts 2:1, 'Cum complerentur dies Pentecostes', that is to say in a plural form, 'when the days of the Pentecost were completed', rather than the singular form of the Greek.

The introduction of a chronological sequence working *backwards* from the night of Easter into the days of Holy Week brought both loss and gain; the loss being a weakening of the unity of the Paschal Mystery, a weakening of the unity between Cross and Resurrection. In the same way, the introduction of a chronological sequence working *forwards* from the Night of Easter also brought both loss and gain; the loss being again a weakening of the unity between Resurrection, Ascension and the Descent of the Spirit. This unity was broken in the latter part of the fourth century with the introduction of the Feast of the Ascension on the fortieth day after Easter. Following the accounts in Luke's Gospel and that of John, the Ascension had originally been commemorated either on Easter Day itself—stressing the continuity with the Resurrection, or at Pentecost, the fiftieth day—perhaps stressing the link with the gift of the Spirit. Egeria's Jerusalem diary records an extra Eucharist celebrated that day on Sion, the traditional site of the Descent of the Spirit, and a non-eucharistic service in the afternoon at the Imbomon, revered as the site of the Ascension.[6] Under the influence of the chronology of Acts 1:3 and, perhaps, the historicisation brought about by increased devotion to the Holy Places, the commemoration was transferred to the fortieth day and treated as a feast in its own right.[7] This in turn let to the introduction of the customary preparatory fast and the integrity of the *laetissimum spatium* was sundered. The integrity of the fifty days was further compromised with the introduction of an octave of Pentecost, as if this feast were a quasi-autonomous celebration of the Holy Spirit.

For all these reasons, the liturgical reform which had been concentrated first of all on Lent and Holy Week, was focused after Vatican II on the Great Fifty Days also. It was re-affirmed that 'the fifty days from the Sunday of the Resurrection to Pentecost Sunday are (to be) celebrated in joy and exultation as one feast day, indeed as one 'great Sunday'.[8] As a result the unity of the whole period is

[6] Egeria, trans. McGowan and Bradshaw, pp. 183–4.
[7] Talley, *Origins of the Liturgical Year*, pp. 63–5.
[8] Sacred Congregation of Rites, *General Norms for the Liturgical Year and Calendar*

now more clearly emphasised: Ascension Day is no longer allowed to be seen as if it were the end of Eastertide, for the Paschal Candle (formerly extinguished after the Gospel on Ascension Day) remains in the sanctuary until after Evening Prayer on the Day of Pentecost and the Sunday after Ascension Day is now called the 7th Sunday of Easter. This designation is used also in the *Common Worship* Calendar but with the former name as a subtitle. A subtle change in the naming of post-Easter Sundays also stresses that the season as a liturgical unity: they are designated Sundays *in* Eastertide or Sundays *of* Easter and no longer Sundays after Easter. The *Common Worship* 'Rules to Order the Christian Year' is explicit:

> The paschal character of the Great Fifty Days of Easter, from Easter Day to Pentecost, should be celebrated throughout the season, and should not be displaced by other celebrations. Except for a Patronal or Dedication Festival, no Festival may displace the celebration of Sunday as a memorial of the resurrection, and no saint's day may be celebrated in Easter Week. The paschal character of the season should be retained on those weekdays when saints' days are celebrated.[9]

The modern Roman Sunday Lectionary, now also used in a modified form by the Church of England, also emphasises the unity of the Easter season. The Gospel selections for the Sundays of Easter recount the appearances of the risen Christ until the third Sunday and, to avoid interrupting the narrative, the old observance of 'Good Shepherd Sunday', previously kept on that day, is transferred to the following Sunday. The Gospels for the remaining Sundays of Easter are excerpts from the discourse and prayer of Christ after the Last Supper.

The days of fasting and prayer called Rogation Days (from the Latin *rogare* to ask), on the Monday, Tuesday, and Wednesday before Ascension Day, used to strike an alien note, having been first marked by penitential litanies in Vienne in Gaul in the fifth century under circumstances of natural and other disaster. Over the years they had become days on which the Church asked for God's blessing on the fruits of the earth and on human labour; days which, freed from their previous penitential character, should not intrude upon the joyful celebration of Eastertide. In the Roman

(Preliminary matter in the *Roman Missal*), ch. 1, para. 22.
[9]   *Common Worship*, Core Volume, p. 527.

rite it is left to the local episcopal conference to decide on what day or days around this time for Masses for 'the sanctification of human labour' or at 'seed time' to be celebrated and propers are provided in the *Missal*. *Common Worship* retains the traditional three days before Ascension Day as the time 'when prayer is offered for God's blessing on the fruits of the earth and on human labour' and liturgical resources are provided in a section of *Times and Seasons* designated 'Rogationtide'[10] which sits among other sections called 'Seasons and Festivals of the Agricultural Year'. What was once known as Rogation Sunday (and, interestingly, still is in the Ordinariate Missal and Office Book) is now the Sixth Sunday of Easter and its collect, unlike that in the *Alternative Service Book*, has no hint of rogation.

Roman and Anglican reforms have abolished the observance of the Vigil of Pentecost (understood as the day preceding the feast) as a day of fasting. More importantly, perhaps, both Roman and Anglican rites no longer keep an Octave of Pentecost. Some have chosen to interpret this reform as a downgrading of Pentecost; it is important to realise that it is nothing of the kind. In the Old Testament, as Thomas Talley has noted, 'in contrast to Passover and the Feast of Tabernacles, both of which were observed over a week, Pentecost was kept on a single day, although pilgrims assembled for it not only from Judaea but from Galilee and other parts'.[11] For the Jewish Feast of Weeks was itself seen not as a new beginning but as a completion, the solemn conclusion of a period of fifty days or seven weeks (a 'week of weeks') whose beginning was defined by Passover. So too for the Christian Church Pentecost is both the fiftieth day and the solemn conclusion of a period of fifty days. It both sums up the mystery celebrated throughout those fifty days and links the particular event which it commemorates with all that has gone before it. It casts its shadow not so much before as behind it, and, in particular, if it has lost an octave (which it should never have had) it has gained a novena, for, as the *Common Worship* 'Rules to Order the Christian Year' make clear, 'the nine days after Ascension Day until Pentecost are days of prayer and preparation to celebrate the outpouring of the Spirit'.[12]

[10] *Common Worship: Times and Seasons*, pp. 608–18.
[11] Talley, *Origins of the Liturgical Year*, p. 59. cf. Deuteronomy 16:1–15.
[12] *Common Worship*, Core Volume, p. 527.

The union of joyful exultation in the glorification Christ and eager yearning for the promised outpouring of the Holy Spirit has been admirably captured in the Magnificat antiphon for Vespers on Ascension Day in the Roman Office, *O Rex gloriae*:

> O King of glory, Lord of Sabaoth, who in this day ascendest with exceeding triumph far above all heavens: we pray thee, leave us not comfortless, but send the promise of the Father on us, even the spirit of truth, alleluia.[13]

It is recorded of the Venerable Bede that during the days leading up to his death on the eve of Ascension Day, 735, this was one of the antiphons he found strength to sing, though, when he reached the words 'leave us not comfortless', he broke into tears and wept.[14] Cranmer adapted this antiphon to form the Collect for the Sunday after Ascension Day in the Book of Common Prayer and, in contemporary and traditional language versions, it is retained for this Sunday and the days of the following week in *Common Worship*. The *Roman Missal* provides a collect for each of the weekdays after the Seventh Sunday of Easter: they all have a clear pneumatological reference.

This understanding of the Great Fifty Days is given fine liturgical expression in the Preface 'The Mystery of Pentecost' provided for the Sunday in the *Roman Missal*:

> For bringing your Paschal Mystery to completion,
> you bestowed the Holy Spirit today
> on those you have made your adopted children
> by uniting them to your Only Begotten Son.
> This same Spirit, as the Church came to birth,
> opened to all peoples the knowledge of God
> and brought together the many languages of the earth
> in profession of the one faith.
> Therefore, overcome with paschal joy,
> every land, every people exults in your praise ...[15]

This echoes a passage from a sermon for the feast of Pentecost attributed to St Augustine: 'See how the solemnity of the Pasch

[13] As given in the Ordinariate Office, *Divine Worship, Daily Office* (CTS, London, 2021), p. 237.
[14] Cuthbert's Letter to Cuthwin, in Bede, *Ecclesiastical History of the English People*, ed. D. H. Farmer (Penguin, London, 1990), p. 357.
[15] *Roman Missal*, p. 495

has reached its conclusion without losing any of its splendour. The Pasch is the beginning of grace, Pentecost is the crown.'[16] Sadly, the extended preface provided in *Common Worship* lacks any paschal reference and celebrates only the outpouring of the Spirit 'filling us with your gifts, leading us into all truth, and uniting peoples of many tongues in the confession of one faith'.

For a renewed understanding of Pentecost, it has been necessary to go back to the pre-Nicene and Nicene Church. But it is necessary to go back further still, for just as the Christian *Pascha* cannot be understood unless its Old Testament and Jewish background is given the most serious attention, so the same is true of the Christian Pentecost and the Feast of Weeks. For although the content of the Christian Pentecost is in one sense completely new — the Descent of the Holy Spirit, there yet remains an important relationship with the Jewish Feast of Weeks which needs to be explored and understood.

One element in Passover was the agricultural feast of *Azymes*, Unleavened Bread, which took place on the following day. It marked the beginning of the barley harvest and comprised an initial offering of the first fruits, a sheaf of barley, to Yahweh. The harvest itself lasted seven weeks and the real harvest festival, when the. cereal offerings were solemnly presented to the Lord, took place at the end of that period, at Pentecost — the Feast of Weeks — one of the three great pilgrimage feasts of the people of Israel. It is not altogether implausible to find a connection here with the Christian celebration. According to St Paul, the risen Lord is 'the first fruits of those who have died' (1 Corinthians 15:20) and the idea of a Pentecostal harvest is familiar to many of the Fathers. A passage from St Irenaeus which is one of the readings for Pentecost Sunday in the Roman Office reads: 'For the Spirit brought the scattered races together into a unity, and offered to the Father the first fruits of all the nations.'[17]

For just as the Passover of the Jews was the union of a pastoral and an agricultural festival which had come to be identified with an event in the salvation history of Israel, so it was with Pentecost — although this identification came much later and is not made in the

[16] This attribution is made in John Gunstone, *The Feast of Pentecost* (Faith Press, London, 1967), p. 49, following Dom E. Flicoteaux, *Le Rayonnement de la Pentecôte* (Cerf, Paris, 1957).
[17] *Adversus Haereses*, III, 17:2 (Patrologia Graeca 7, col. 929–30).

Old Testament. In later Judaism it came to be the memorial day of the giving of the Law on Mount Sinai and the establishment of the Mosaic Covenant. In his homily on Pentecost, the Venerable Bede called upon this tradition:

> The Jewish feast of the Law is a foreshadowing of our feast today. When the children of Israel had been freed from slavery in Egypt by the offering of the paschal lamb, they journeyed through the desert toward the Promised Land, and they reached Mount Sinai. On the fiftieth day after the Passover, the Lord descended upon the mountain in fire, and with the sound of a trumpet and with thunder and lightning, he gave them the ten commandments of the Law. As a memorial ... he decreed an annual feast on that day, and offering of the first-fruits, in the form of two loaves of bread, made from the first grain of the new harvest, which were to be brought to the altar. Just as the Law was given on the fiftieth day after the slaying of the lamb, when the Lord descended on the mountain in fire; likewise on the fiftieth day after the resurrection of our Redeemer ... the grace of the Holy Spirit, descending in the outward appearance of fire, was given to the disciples as they were assembled in the upper room.[18]

Not much attention has been paid to this in the later Christian liturgical tradition; and honourable exception is Keble's hymn from the *Christian Year*:

> *When God of old came down from heaven,*
> *In power and wrath he came;*
> *Before his feet the clouds were riven,*
> *Half darkness and half flame.*
>
> *But when he came the second time,*
> *He came in power and love;*
> *Softer than gale at morning prime*
> *Hovered his holy Dove.*
>
> *The fires that rushed on Sinai down*
> *In sudden torrents dread,*
> *Now gently light a glorious crown*
> *On every sainted head.*[19]

---

[18] Quoted in Kennedy, *Using Common Worship*, p. 118. See Bede the Venerable, Homilies on the Gospels: Book Two, Lent to the Dedication of a Church, trans. Martin and David Hurst (Cistercian Publications, Kalamazoo, 1991).

[19] Unaccountably, this hymn is not included in *New English Hymnal* but it is in *Common Praise* as no. 199.

The link between the exodus from Egypt and the Law-giving on Mount Sinai was important for the Jews, for, as the twelfth-century Jewish philosopher Moses Maimonides was later to explain, 'the latter was the aim, an object of the exodus from Egypt'.[20] The link was important too for the Fathers, who point out that in the Old Testament was given to Israel written 'with the finger of God' and in the New Testament 'the finger of God' is declared to be none other than the Holy Spirit himself. With the Christian Pentecost the guidance of the Spirit replaces the guidance of the Law. It cannot be said with certainty that St Paul's own contrast between the written code of the Mosaic Law and the Spirit, 'the letter kills, but the Spirit gives life' (2 Corinthians 3:6) is made consciously in the light of this understanding of Pentecost, but this link was certainly made in Patristic preaching.

Two conclusions can be drawn from this evidence. The first must be that just as for the Jews Passover leads to Pentecost—the first fruits leading to the harvest, the giving of the Law being seen as the object and aim of the exodus—so it is for us. *Pascha* leads to Pentecost: Christ rose from the dead to be the first fruits of a new humanity, and that humanity first found its identity, its unity, its inner-dynamism, and its mission in the Descent of the Spirit at Pentecost. Jesus is the second Moses, but whereas Moses liberated the Israelites from Egypt in order to seal a covenant with God on Mount Sinai by means of the Law, Jesus liberates his people from the tyranny of sin and death in order to seal the new covenant in the gift of his Spirit. The Paschal Mystery is indeed brought to completion on the Day of Pentecost.

The second conclusion is that Easter and Pentecost belong to each other inseparably and indivisibly. This, paradoxically, leads to the discovery that Easter is a feast of the Spirit and Pentecost is a feast of Christ. The Resurrection is itself an outpouring of the Holy Spirit by the Father upon the Son: Christ is raised by the Spirit, transformed by the Spirit and in resurrection has become 'a life-giving spirit' (1 Corinthians 15:45). The action of the Father in raising Jesus in the Spirit is inseparably one with his action of conveying the Spirit through Jesus to all believers. Pentecost cele-

---

[20] *Doctor Perplexorum*, III, 43, *Guide to the Perplexed: A New Translation*, trans. L. E. Goodman and P. I. Lieberman (Stanford University Press, Redwood City, 2024).

brates the new means of Christ's presence with and to and for his people, and the Church is celebrated as the Body of Christ, but only and precisely because it is filled and vivified by his Spirit. Thanks to Easter there is something to celebrate, thanks to Pentecost there is the possibility of celebrating; for it is by the power of the Spirit that the gifts of bread and wine brought to the altar become the Body and Blood of the crucified and risen Christ.

The liturgy of the Feast of Pentecost was reformed in the light of this understanding. In *The Book of Common Prayer* it was called Whit-Sunday (though 'Pentecost' appears among the tables and rules), a name which refers to the custom of baptising on that day and, more particularly, to the white robes of the newly initiated. The opening rubric of the baptismal liturgy in the *First English Prayer Book* of 1549 recalls this tradition:

> It appeareth by ancient writers that the Sacrament of Baptism in the old time was not commonly ministered but at two times in the year, at Easter and Whitsuntide, at which times it was only ministered in presence of all the congregation: which custom now being grown out of use, although it cannot for many considerations be well restored again, yet it is thought good to follow the same as near as conveniently may be.

In *Common Worship* it is called the Feast of Pentecost and *Times and Seasons* offers a fully worked out eucharistic liturgy with an extended Gathering which takes the place of the Penitential Rite. It invokes the Holy Spirit, rehearses the account of the Descent of the Spirit (Acts 2:1–13), and provides a 'Prayer for Personal Renewal which can include anointing. As found here, this prologue is a poor substitute for a Pentecost Vigil which the *Roman Missal* provides, as does the 1979 American *Book of Common Prayer* (even though you have to look very hard to find it in the latter).[21] Nevertheless, *Common Worship: Christian Initiation* provides a 'Celebration of Baptism and Confirmation within a Vigil Service on the Eve of Pentecost' which appears to be very much designed for a cathedral setting but could be held in a minster church where there is room for processional movement.[22] It is a non-eucharistic service beginning with a Service of Light, with readings placed at various points as the rites of Initiation unfold. The implication is that the

---

[21] Outline rubrics only on pp. 175 and 227.
[22] *Common Worship: Christian Initiation*, pp. 134–49.

newly baptised and confirmed present themselves the following day at the Pentecost Eucharist to receive Holy Communion for the first time. The Roman Rite replaces the old vigil Mass of Saturday morning with its six Old Testament prophecies and blessing of the font with an evening vigil Mass which is not explicitly baptismal but provides readings with some baptismal allusions (Genesis 11:1–9; Exodus 19:3–8, 16–29; Ezekiel 37:1–14 and Joel 3:1–5). The American Prayer Book vigil outline suggests beginning with a Service of Light and the inclusion of a baptismal liturgy on the model of the Easter Vigil.

The reform of the Roman Lectionary, as has been mentioned above, emphasises the unity of the Easter season and, at its conclusion gives prominence at the Mass of the day to a Gospel reading which, despite the provision of alternatives in years B and C, may be used every year. The reading in question is the account from the Fourth Gospel (John 20:19–23) of the appearance of the Risen Christ to his disciples on the evening of the first Easter Day.

> When it was evening on that day, the first day of the week, and the doors of the house where the disciples had met were locked for fear of the Jews, Jesus came and stood among them and said, 'Peace be with you.' After he said this, he showed them his hands and his side. Then the disciples rejoiced when they saw the Lord. Jesus said to them again, 'Peace be with you. As the Father has sent me, so I send you.' When he had said this, he breathed on them and said to them, 'Receive the Holy Spirit. If you forgive the sins of any, they are forgiven them; if you retain the sins of any, they are retained.'

This account of the gift of the Spirit on the first Easter Day is crucial for any understanding of the profoundly theological basis of the unity between Easter and Pentecost. This unity is already anticipated in the 7th chapter of John in the passage appointed as the Gospel for the vigil Mass of Pentecost and as the second lesson for Evening Prayer in years B and C in *Common Worship* (John 7:37–9).

> On the last day of the festival, the great day, while Jesus was standing there, he cried out, 'Let anyone who is thirsty come to me, and let the one who believes in me drink. As the scripture has said, 'Out of the believer's heart shall flow rivers of living water.' Now he said this about the Spirit, which believers in him were to receive; for as yet there was no Spirit, because Jesus was not yet glorified.

The hour of Christ's glorification is the hour of the Cross and Resurrection. In the hour of his death he cries, 'It is finished', and he gives up — or rather, hands over — his Spirit, while blood and water gush from his side. And so it is on the first Easter day, which is for the Fourth Gospel both *Pascha* and Pentecost, that the risen and glorified Christ, filled with the Spirit, and utterly transparent to the Spirit, breathes on his disciples and says to them, 'Receive the Holy Spirit'.

The extended celebration of the Pasch may reach its conclusion 'without losing any of its splendour' (see above, p. 186) but while this is indeed true from a liturgical/theological point of view, the Great Fifty Days nevertheless present a pastoral problem if church attendance figures are anything to go by. Yes, many people may go on holiday after the Easter weekend — the clergy, exhausted by the Holy Week and Easter ceremonies, frequently do — but the fall off in attendance may indicate that compared with Lent and the *Triduum*, Eastertide and its liturgical readings, are curiously far less compelling. As Anne McGowan has observed:

> This is ironic because New Testament texts proclaiming the early church's understanding of Christ as the crucified and risen One provide a foundation for the central activities Christians have been doing ever since: baptising and teaching (Matthew 28:19), breaking open the Scriptures in the context of meals (e.g. Luke 24:30–2), calling on Christ in prayer with faith and confidence, and preaching Christ crucified and risen. For those still regularly engaged in the church's liturgy, Easter is the season to incorporate the newly baptised and the time when the whole church can aspire to live into the fullness of their Christian initiation. Having completed forty days of preparation, they are primed for fifty days of participation.[23]

The Eastertide lectionary is not lacking in engaging stories and encouraging appeals to enter with ever more commitment into life in the Paschal Mystery, but the season can often fall flat. Bruce Morrill suggests that 'the fifty days of Easter flags in its long run because, unlike its shorter partner, the forty days of Lent, its terminus, its ending, is actually, paradoxically, an eschatological open-

---

[23] A. McGowan, 'Living Lent and Engaging Easter: Scriptures' Potential and Liturgy's Limits', in G. Jeanes and B. Nichols, ed., *Lively Oracles of God*, Alcuin Club Collections 97 (Liturgical Press, Collegeville, 2022), pp. 70–1.

ing'.[24] The Church may acclaim, 'Alleluia! Christ is risen. He is risen indeed!' and be assured that the Holy Spirit has been poured out upon her, but, in the sense that something cosmic has happened but has yet to be realised, all of creation is not yet redeemed. Christians are called to mission. Jeremy Driscoll observes that if Easter Day marks a climax so does Pentecost. It is a 'lavish outpouring, a reaching of the point at which God cannot have given more, a point of arrival. And yet it is also a point of departure, the beginning of the "last days" and the birth of the church, that is, a whole new way of being in the world'.[25] The Church is called continually to proclaim Christ's death and resurrection as the foundation of her faith and the basis of her hope in God's will to redeem all that is. So, perhaps the last words of this study should be those of the President at the concluding part of the *Common Worship* Pentecost liturgy:

> For fifty days we have celebrated the victory of our Lord Jesus Christ over the powers of sin and death. We have proclaimed God's mighty acts and we have prayed that the power that was at work when God raised Jesus from the dead might be at work in us. As part of God's Church, I call upon you to live out what you proclaim.[26]

[24] B. T. Morrill, 'Faith's Unfinished Business: Can the Easter season's mysticism empower ethical praxis?', *Proceedings of the North American Academy of Liturgy* (2019), p. 10. Quoted in McGowan, 'Living Lent'.

[25] J. Driscoll, OSB, *Awesome Glory. Resurrection in Scripture, Liturgy and Theology* (Collegeville, Liturgical Press, 2019), p. 34.

[26] *Common Worship: Times and Seasons*, p. 501.

BIBLIOGRAPHY

LITURGICAL BOOKS

ANGLICAN LITURGICAL TEXTS AND HYMN BOOKS

The Alternative Service Book 1980 (1980).
The Book of Common Prayer (1549, 1552, 1662, 1928).
The Book of Common Prayer according to the use of The Episcopal Church (Church Hymnal Corporation and The Seabury Press, New York, 1979).
Common Praise (Hymns Ancient and Modern Ltd, London, 2001).
Common Worship (Church House Publishing, London):
—*Services and Prayers for the Church of England*, Core Volume (2000).
—*Christian Initiation* (2006).
—*Daily Prayer* (2006).
—*Ordination Services* (2007).
—*Pastoral Services* (2000).
—*Times and Seasons* (2006).
Lent, Holy Week, Easter—Services and Prayers (SPCK and others, London, 1986).
Missale Anglicanum, The English Missal (Knott, London, 1912).
The New English Hymnal (Canterbury Press, Norwich, 1986).

ROMAN CATHOLIC LITURGICAL TEXTS

The Divine Office, 3 vols (William Collins, London, 1974).
Divine Worship, The Missal (Catholic Truth Society, London, 2015).
Divine Worship, Daily Office (Catholic Truth Society, London, 2021).
Rite of Christian Initiation of Adults (Geoffrey Chapman, 1987; Continuum, London, 2004).
The Roman Missal (Catholic Truth Society, London, 2011).
The Roman Pontifical (Congregation for Divine Worship and the Discipline of the Sacraments, Vox Clara Committee, 2012).
Walpole, A. S., *Early Latin Hymns* (Cambridge University Press, Cambridge, 1922).

ORTHODOX LITURGICAL TEXTS

The Lenten Triodion, ed. Kallistos Ware and Mother Mary (Faber & Faber, London, 1978).

MISCELLANEOUS LITURGICAL TEXTS

From Ashes to Fire, Supplemental Worship Resources 8 (United Methodist Church of America, Abingdon, Nashville, 1979).
Holy Week Services, Joint Liturgical Group (SPCK/Epworth Press, London, 1968 and 1983).

The Methodist Worship Book (Methodist Publishing, London, 1999).
A Passover Haggadah, ed. Herbert Bronstein (Penguin Books, London, 1978).

PATRISTIC TEXTS

Ambrose, *Epistolae* (Patrologia Latina 16, col. 1030).
The Apostolic Fathers, trans. K. Lake, Loeb Classical Library (Heinemann, London, 1913).
Athanasius, *Epistolae Festales I* (Parker, Oxford, 1854).
Augustine, *De Civitate Dei* (Patrologia Latina 41).
— *Enarrationes in Psalmos* (Patrologia Latina 36).
— *Epistolae* (Patrologia Latina 33).
— *Sermones* (Patrologia Latina 38).
— *Selected Easter Sermons of St Augustine* , trans. P. T. Weller (Herder, St Louis, Missouri, 1959).
Bede, *De Temporum Ratione* (Patrologia Latina 90).
— *Historia Ecclesiastica Gentis Anglorum* (Patrologia Latina 95).
— *In Libros Regum* (Patrologia Latina 91).
— *De Templo Salomonis* (Patrologia Latina 91).
Cyril of Jerusalem, *Lectures on the Christian Sacraments: The Procatechesis and the Five Mystagogical Catecheses Ascribed to St Cyril of Jerusalem*, ed. M. E. Johnson, Popular Patristics 57 (St Vladimir's Seminary Press, New York, 2017).
The Didache, trans. and commentary by K. Niederwimmer (Fortress Press, Minneapolis, 1998).
Egeria, *Itinerarium: The Pilgrimage of Egeria, A New Translation of the Itinerarium Egeriae*, trans. A. McGowan and P. F. Bradshaw, Alcuin Club Collections 93 (Liturgical Press, Collegeville, Minnesota, 2018).
Eusebius, *Vita Constantini* (Patrologia Latina 8).
Hippolytus, *The Treatise on the Apostolic Tradition of St Hippolytus of Rome*, ed. G. Dix (London, 1937, repr. with corrections by Alban Press, 1995).
Irenaeus, *Adversus Haereses* (Patrologia Graeca 7).
Jerome, *Epistola XXVIII, Ad Praesidium, de Cereo paschali*.
John Chrysostom, *Homilies on St John LXXXV*, Library of the Fathers, vol. 36 (Parker, Oxford, 1852).
John Chrysostom, *Hieratikon* or *Paschal Homily* (Patrologia Graeca 59).
Leo the Great, *Sermones* (Patrologia Latina 54).
Maimonides, *Doctor Perplexorum*: Guide to the Perplexed. A New Translation, trans. L. E. Goodman and P. I. Lieberman (Stanford University Press, Redwood City, 2024).
Melito of Sardis: *De Pascha*, ed. S. G. Hall (Oxford University Press, Oxford, 1979).
Origen, *De Pascha*, in *Ancient Christian Writers*, vol. 54, ed. W. J. Burhardt, T. Comerford Lawler and John J. Dillon (Paulist Press, Mahwah).
Origen, *Homilia in Exodum* (Patrologia Graeca 12).

Bibliography

Renoux, A., 'Le Codex armenien Jerusalem 121', Patrologia Orientalis 35/1 36/2 (1969–71).

Tertullian, *De Anima* (Patrologia Latina 2).

—*De Baptismo* (Patrologia Latina 1); *Tertullian's Homily on Baptism*, ed. and trans. E. Evans (SPCK, London,1964).

GENERAL WORKS

Akehurst, P., *Keeping Holy Week* (Grove Books, Bramcote, Nottingham, 1976).

Anglican-Roman Catholic International Commission, *The Final Report* (CTS, SPCK, London, 1982).

Aulén, G., *Christus Victor*, trans. A. G. Hebert (SSM, SPCK, London, 1931).

—*The Faith of the Christian Church* (Fortress Press, Philadelphia, 1960).

Austerberry, D., *Celebrating Holy Week* (Mowbray, London, 1982).

Baldovin, J., *The Urban Character of Christian Worship*, OCA 228 (Pontifical Oriental Institute, Rome, 1987).

Barker, M., *Temple Theology: An Introduction* (SPCK, London, 2004).

Barrett, C. K., *The Gospel according to John* (SPCK, London, 2nd edn, 1978).

Beauduin, Dom L., 'Le Cierge pascal', *La Maison Dieu* 26 (1951), pp. 23–8.

Becon, T., *The Early Works of Thomas Becon*, ed. J. Ayre (Parker Society, Cambridge, 1843).

Bell, G. K. A, *The Kingship of Christ* (Penguin, London, 1954).

Bishop, J. G., 'The Anglican Tradition' in *A Manual for Holy Week*, ed. C. P. M. Jones (SPCK, London, 1967).

Bonner, C., 'The Homily on the Passion by Melito, Bishop of Sardis', in *Mélanges Franz Cumont*, Annuaire de l'Institut de philologie et d'histoire orientales et slaves 4 (Brussels, 1936).

Boulding, M., *Marked for Life: Prayer in the Easter Christ* (SPCK, London, 1979)

Bouyer, L., *Eucharist (Theology and Spirituality of the Eucharistic Prayer)*, trans. C. H. Quinn (University of Notre Dame Press, Indiana, 1968).

Bouyer, L., *The Paschal Mystery*, English translation of the 2nd edition of 1947 of *Le Mystère paschal* (Allen & Unwin, London, 1951).

Bradshaw, P. F., *The Apostolic Tradition Reconstructed*, Joint Liturgical Studies 91 (Alcuin Club & Group for Renewal of Worship, Silverton, 2021).

—*Eucharistic Origins* (SPCK, London, 2004).

—ed., *The New SCM Dictionary of Liturgy and Worship* (SCM-Canterbury Press, London 2002).

—*The Search for the Origin of Christian Worship* (SPCK, London, New York, Oxford University Press, 2nd edn, 2002).

—and L. Hoffman, ed., *Passover and Easter: Origin and History to Modern Times* (University of Notre Dame Press, Notre Dame, 1999).

—and M. E. Johnson, *The Origins of Feasts, Fasts and Seasons in Early Christianity*, Alcuin Club Collections 86 (Liturgical Press, Collegeville, Minnesota, 2011).

Bronstein, H., ed., *A Passover Haggadah* (Penguin Books, London, 1978).

Brown, R. E., *The Gospel according to John XIII–XXI*, Anchor Bible (Yale University Press, New Haven, 1966).

le Brun des Marettes, J. B., *Voyages liturgiques de France, recherches faites en diverses Villes du Royaume* (Delaune, Paris, 1718; Gregg Publishing, Farnborough, 1969).

Buchinger, H., 'Was there ever a liturgical Triduum in antiquity? Theological idea and liturgical reality', *Ecclesia Orans* 27/3 (2010), pp. 257–70.

Bugnini, A., *The Reform of the Liturgy, 1948–1975* (Liturgical Press, Collegeville, Minnesota, 1990).

—and C. Braga, 'Ordo Hebdomadae Sanctae Instauratus', *Ephemerides Liturgicae* 70 (1956).

Cantalamessa, R., *Easter in the Early Church* (The Liturgical Press, Collegeville, Minnesota, 1993).

Casel, O., OSB, 'Art und Sinn der ältesten christlichen Osterfeier', *Jahrbuch für Liturgiewissenschaft* 14 (1934), 197–223.

— *The Mystery of Christian Worship* (Crossroad Publishing, Chestnut Ridge, New York, 1999).

Crichton, J. D., *Christian Celebration* (Chapman, London, 1981).

— *The Liturgy of Holy Week* (Goodliffe-Neale, London, 1971).

Cross, F. L., *1-Peter, A Paschal Liturgy* (Mowbray, London, 1954).

Cullmann, O., *Early Christian Worship* (SCM, London, 1978).

Davis, C., *Liturgy and Doctrine* (Sheed & Ward, London, 1960).

Dix, G., OSB, *The Shape of the Liturgy* (Dacre Press, London, 1945).

Dodd, C. H., *Historical Tradition in the Fourth Gospel* (Cambridge University Press, Cambridge, 1963).

Donne, J., *The Complete English Poems* (David Campbell Publishers, London, 1991).

Driscoll, J., OSB, *Awesome Glory. Resurrection in Scripture, Liturgy and Theology* (Liturgical Press, Collegeville, Minnesota, 2019).

Drury, J., *Music at Midnight, The Life and Poetry of George Herbert* (Allen Lane, London, 2013).

Duffy, E., *The Stripping of the Altars* (Yale University Press, London, 1992).

Duncan-Jones, A. S., *The Chichester Customary* (SPCK, London, 1948).

Durrwell, F.-X., CSsR, *The Resurrection* (Sheed & Ward, London, 1960).

Eliot, T. S., *Murder in the Cathedral* (Faber & Faber, London, 3rd edn, 1935).

Elliott, P. J, *Ceremonies of the Liturgical Year according to the Modern Roman Rite* (Ignatius Press, San Francisco, 2002).

Flicoteaux, Dom E., *Le Rayonnement de la Pentecôte* (Cerf, Paris, 1957).

van Gennep, A., *The Rites of Passage* (Routledge & Kegan Paul, London, 1960).

Golinkin, D., *The Origins of the Seder* (The Schechter Institute of Jewish Studies, Jerusalem, 2006).

Gunstone, J., *The Feast of Pentecost* (Faith Press, London, 1967).

Härdelin, A., in *Pâques et rédemption*, Collectanea Cisterciensia, fasc. I (Cisterciens de la stricte observance, Westmalle, Belgium, 1981).

Bibliography

Harries, R., *The Image of Christ in Modern Art* (Ashgate Publishing, Farnham, 2013).

Heid, S., *Altar and Church: Principles of Liturgy from Early Christianity* (Schnell & Steiner, Washington, DC, 2023).

Herrman, S., *Israel in Egypt*, Studies in Biblical Theology, Second Series 27 (SCM, London, 1973).

Hopko, T., *The Lenten Spring* (St Vladimir's Seminary Press, New York, 1983).

Hoskyns, E., and N. Davey, *Crucifixion–Resurrection: The Pattern of the Theology and Ethics of the New Testament*, ed. Gordon Wakefield (SPCK, London, 1981).

Hugh, S. S. F., *No Escape from Love* (Faith Press, London, 1959).

Hunter, A. M., *According to John* (SCM, Londong, 1968).

Irvine, C., *The Cross and Creation in Christian Liturgy and Art* (SPCK, London, 2013, Alcuin Club Collections 88).

Jacobus de Voragine, *The Golden Legend*, trans. W. Caxton, 7 vols. (J. M. Dent, London, 1900).

Jeanes, G., and B. Nichols, *Lively Oracles of God*, Alcuin Club Collections 97 (Liturgical Press, Collegeville, 2022).

Jeremias, J, SJ, *The Eucharistic Words of Jesus*, trans. Norman Perrin (SCM, London, 1966).

Johnson, M. E., 'The Paschal Mystery: Reflections from a Lutheran Viewpoint', *Worship* 57/2 (March 1983), pp. 131–50.

Jungmann, J. A., SJ, *The Early Liturgy*, trans. F. A. Brunner (DLT, London, 1960).

Kelly, J. N. D., *Jerome: His Life, Writings and Controversies* (Harper & Row, New York, 1975).

Ken, T., *The Prose Works of the Right Reverend Thomas Ken, D.D.*, ed. W. Benham. Ancient and Modern Library of Theological Literature (Griffith, Farran, Okeden & Welsh, London, 1889).

Kennedy, D., *Using Common Worship: Times and Seasons—Lent to Embertide* (Church House Publishing, London, 2008).

Klauser, T., *A Short History of the Western Liturgy*, trans. John Halliburton (Oxford, 2nd edn, 1979).

Lewis, A. E., *Between Cross and Resurrection, A Theology of Holy Saturday* (Eerdmans, Grand Rapids, 2003).

Lewis, C. S., 'The Weight of Glory', in *They Asked for a Paper* (Bles, London, 1962).

Lloyd, T., *Celebrating Lent, Holy Week and Easter* (Grove Books, Bramcote, Nottingham, 1985).

McArthur, A. A., *The Evolution of the Christian Year* (SCM, London, 1953).

MacCarron, M., *Bede and Time. Computus, Theology and History in the Early Medieval World* (Routledge, London, 2021).

Malloy, P., *How Firm a Foundation: Leaders of the Liturgical Movement* (Liturgical Training Publications, Chicago, 1990).

Marsh, J., *The Gospel of St John*, Pelican New Testament Commentaries (Penguin, London, 1968).

Martin, J. T., *Christ our Passover* (SCM, London, 1958).

Milner, White E., *A Procession of Passion Prayers* (SPCK, London, 1962).

Mohlberg, L. C., *Liber Sacramentorum Romanae Aeclesiae Ordinis Anni Circuli*, Rerum Ecclesiasticarum Documenta, Series Maior, Fontes IV (Herder, Rome, 1960).

Monti, J., *The Week of Salvation: History and Traditions of Holy Week* (Our Sunday Visitor, Huntingdon, Indiana, 1993).

Morrill, B. T., 'Faith's Unfinished Business: Can the Easter Season's Mysticism Empower Ethical Praxis?', *Proceedings of the North American Academy of Liturgy* (2019), pp. 5–18.

Mosshammer, A. A., *The Easter Computus and the Origins of the Christian Era* (Oxford University Press, Oxford, 2009).

Nocent, A., OSB, *The Liturgical Year*, trans. M. J. O'Connell, 4 vols (Liturgical Press, Collegeville Minnesota, 1977).

O'Collins, G., SJ, *Jesus Risen* (DLT, London, 1987).

Papageorgiou, P., 'The Paschal Catechetical Homily of St. John Chrysostom: A Rhetorical and Contextual Study', *The Greek Orthodox Theological Review* 43 (1998), pp. 93–104.

Parry, Dom David, OSB, *Households of God* (DLT, London, 1980).

Perham, M., and K. Stevenson, *Waiting for the Risen Christ, A Commentary on 'Lent, Holy Week, Easter'* (SPCK, London, 1986).

Pitre, B., *Jesus and the Last Supper* (Eerdmans, Grand Rapids, 2015).

Prestige, G. L., *Fathers and Heretics*, Bampton Lectures for 1940 (SPCK, London, 1940).

Ramsey, A. M., *The Resurrection of Christ* (Fontana, Glasgow, rev. edn, 1961).

Raphael, C., *A Feast of History* (Weidenfeld & Nicolson, London, 1972).

Rowell, G., *The Liturgy of Christian Burial*, Alcuin Club Collections 59 (SPCK, London, 1977).

Rutledge, F., *The Crucifixion. Understanding the Death of Jesus Christ* (Eerdmans, Grand Rapids, 2015).

Schmemann, A., *Great Lent* (St Vladimir's Seminary Press, New York, 1974).

Schmidt, H. A. P., *Hebdomada Sancta* (Herder, Rome, 1957).

Shepherd, M. H., *The Paschal Liturgy and the Apocalypse* (Lutterworth, London, 1960).

Stookey, L. H., *Calendar: Christ's Time for the Church* (Abingdon Press, Nashville, 1996).

Taft, R., 'Historicism Revisited', in *Beyond East and West: Problems in Liturgical Understanding* (Edizioni Orientalia Christiana, Rome, 2nd edn, 1977).

Talley, T. J., *The Origins of the Liturgical Year* (Pueblo Publishing, New York, 1986).

Thurston, H., SJ, *Lent and Holy Week* (Longmans, London, 1904).

Treharne, E., trans., *Old and Middle English: An Anthology* (Blackwell Publishers, Oxford, 2000).

Bibliography

Tyrer, J. W., *Historical Survey of Holy Week*, Alcuin Club Collections 29 (Oxford University Press, Oxford, 1932).

Vanstone, W. H., *The Stature of Waiting* (DLT, London, 1982).

Weston, F., 'Our Present Duty', *Report of the Anglo-Catholic Congress, London, July 1923* (SSPP, London, 1923).

Wickham, Legg J., *English Church Life from the Restoration to the Tractarian Movement* (Longmans Green, London, 1914).

Williams, C., 'The Index of the Body', *The Dublin Review* 211 (July 1942), pp. 39–51.

Willis, G. G., *A History of Early Roman Liturgy* (Henry Bradshaw Society, London, 1994).

Wright, W. M., *The Rising. Living the Mysteries of Lent, Easter, and Pentecost* (Upper Room Books, Nashville, 1994).

Yarnold, E. J., SJ, *Cyril of Jerusalem* (Routledge, Abingdon, 2000).

Index of Scriptural References

NEW TESTAMENT

INDEX

Capelle, Bernard 148
Casel, Odo 76, 77, 87, 99
Catechumenate, Adult 12, 58, 89, 90
Caxton, William 69
Chavasse, Antoine 80
Chrism, Mass of 121, 123–7, 132
Christmas 79, 83, 162, 165
Chrysostom, John, St 59, 113
Cistercians 84
Commination Service 14, 18
Common Worship (Church of England) viii, 7, 17–18, 24, 26, 36, 50, 55, 58, 64, 68, 95, 97, 117–18, 119, 121, 122, 124, 125, 126, 130, 135, 137, 139, 140, 141, 143, 146, 147, 148, 150, 152, 154–5, 160, 162, 163, 167, 168, 171, 172–4, 177–8, 179, 184, 185, 186–7, 190, 191, 193
confession (sacrament of reconciliation) 18, 111, 122–3
confirmation 58, 172–3
Constantine, Emperor 7, 102, 108
Constantinian Peace of the Church 107
Constantinople 110, 147 n.5
cosmology, Hebrew 41
covenant 9, 19, 28, 29–30, 31, 32, 44, 61, 122, 123, 124, 126, 137, 152, 154, 171, 188, 189
Cranmer, Thomas 153, 186
Crichton, J. D. 91
Cross, F. L. 25
Cross, mystery of the 67–81
Cross, Veneration of the 146–7, 152–4
Cyril of Jerusalem, St 104, 107

Davey, Noel 86
Davis, Charles 78
deacons, role of 48, 87, 96, 106, 118, 125, 126, 137, 148, 166, 168
Devil, renunciation of 18, 20, 56
Distomo, Greece 160
Divine Worship (Ordinariate missal) 5, 50, 177, 185

Divine Worship, Congregation for 90, 95
Dix, Gregory 101, 107
Donne, John 69
The Dream of the Rood (poem) 155–6
Driscoll, Jeremy 193
Durrwell, François-Xavier 63, 85–6
Duruflé, Maurice 139

Easter Day 58, 64, 65, 91, 97, 109, 114, 159, 163, 171, 176, 177, 178–9, 181, 183, 191, 192, 193; Dawn Service 163, 165
Easter Sepulchre 141, 164
Easter Vigil 10–11, 12, 13, 14, 23, 24, 27, 48–9, 67, 79, 80, 88, 90, 91, 96–9, 104, 113–14, 123, 129, 131, 133, 147, 148, 150, 162–78; baptismal liturgy, *see* baptism; Eucharist in 174–7; *Exsultet*, *see* Exsultet; Light, Service of (*Lucernarium*) 165, 166–7; Liturgy of the Word 169–71; New Fire 162, 167; Paschal Candle, *see* Paschal Candle
ecumenism vii, viii, 87, 95, 98, 145, 149, 173
Egeria 13, 104–7, 109, 140, 146, 150, 176, 151, 182, 183
Egypt 4
Eliot, T. S. 79
English Missal ix
Eostre (goddess) 23
Epiphany, Feast of 4
eschatology 8, 36, 45, 48, 101, 114, 118, 169, 174, 175, 192
Eucharist 8, 9, 15, 17, 21, 36, 43–4, 45, 47, 56, 58–9, 60–3, 66, 74, 77, 105, 110, 111, 112, 113–14, 116, 118, 119, 121, 122, 123–4, 125, 129, 132–8, 139, 140, 141, 143–4, 147, 148–50, 159, 160, 162, 163, 165–6, 174–8, 181, 182, 183, 190–1
Eusebius of Caesarea 102